WOMEN COMPOSERS:

A Handbook

by

SUSAN STERN

The Scarecrow Press, Inc.
Metuchen, N.J. & London
1978

Library of Congress Cataloging in Publication Data

Stern, Susan, 1953–
    Women composers.

    CONTENTS: Introduction.—List of sources.—The
handbook.—Supplementary list of composers. [etc.]
    1. Women composers—Biography. 2. Music—Bio-
bibliography—Indexes. I. Title.
ML105.S7   780'.92'2 [B]   78-5505
ISBN 0-8108-1138-3

CONTENTS

INTRODUCTION

In music (as in too many other fields), for some reason it has been assumed that women do not put as many long, self-sacrificing hours into their art as men do. The woman stepping outside her traditional bounds by composing music risks ridicule and rejection. It seems odd that an area such as music which is supposed to be universally loved should be held in check by the antique rejection of women as composers of worthy music. My purpose in the present handbook is to try and clear away over-used stereotypes and direct the ears of some to the "other side"--to choose from any of the women I name, listen to what they've written and see if perhaps they might admit they were wrong about women composers.

I have chosen to represent women from the United States, Canada, England (not all of Great Britain), Belgium, France, West Germany, Austria, the Netherlands, Switzerland and Italy. West Germany and Austria I have "defined" by present-day European boundaries. Thus, a composer born in Budapest in 1890 would not be included whereas one born in Vienna at the same time would. The time period represented is generally from the 16th century on, although one or two earlier composers who had an ample bibliography have been included.

The women listed have either had a composition published or performed in public, or have won an award for one. The listing does not include composition students or women who wrote strictly teaching material. Also women who wrote only popular songs or jazz have been omitted. Only "classical" composers are included.

The book is divided into four parts: List of Sources, which is a largely annotated bibliography of the indexed works; the Handbook proper; a Supplementary List of Composers and a Supplementary Bibliography. The List of

Sources is in alphabetical order under the double-letter codes referred to in the main section.   The sources are those that make direct reference to a composer, giving biographical information.   A few of these sources give discographies, complete lists of works, and/or indications where the works can be found.   In general, sources that give only titles of a few works by a composer, without further information on the works, are not included.   Reviews are not included.

Very brief descriptions are included for most of the coded sources; when the title sufficiently describes the source, I let that title speak for itself.   I used some state composers sources but found them too overwhelming to continue.   Hopefully this will lead not to disappointment but, for the interested reader, to the pursuit of research on women composers by state.

The Handbook proper lists the names of women composers in alphabetical order, identifying them by the name they are known under, be it married or single.   Cross references are provided for those women found under more than one name; all variations will be listed under the main entry name.   Pseudonyms are given when appropriate and husband's first name is provided when known.   Following the name information are birth/death dates and places; "flourished" dates and places are used only when necessary.   The only variation to the order this information appears in, is (for example) b. Philadelphia, 20th cent.   This means the person was born in Philadelphia and flourished in the 20th century. When the city of birth is not known, it will read (for example) fl. 20th cent., America.   Other fields of musical/job activity follow (pianist, poet ...).   Major types of music the woman composed are given next; when there is no major type, the number of works within each genre is given (1 piano, 1 chamber ...).   If hymns, anthems, partsongs and psalms are part of the composer's oeuvre, but other choral music and songs are not, then those designations will be given; otherwise, those types will be under the general heading "choral" or "songs."   Madrigals and motets are indicated as such.   Operettas are part of the "opera" designation.   Incidental music consists of music to plays, films and television.   Orchestral music includes symphonies, ballets and concertos.   Items in the List of Sources are then referred to by the two-letter codes.   If a source work is arranged alphabetically no page number will be indicated; otherwise page numbers will immediately follow the source code.   When titles of compositions are given in a source, an asterisk will

mark that code.   If a portrait is printed, then the designation "+pict" will be written.   The note "+biblio" indicates a
bibliography is included in the source.   (This note will not
be present for those sources which are themselves bibliogra-
phies.)   Variations of dates, spelling of name, etc., will be
noted by source.

Following the main section of the book is a Supplementary List of Composers for whom I could locate no other
information.   They are in alphabetical order.

Names beginning with "van," "la," "de" and the like
are alphabetized according to what I could determine was the
most common usage, and are cross-referenced from alternate
forms.   "Mc" surnames are found in alphabetical order as
if spelled "Mac."

The Supplementary Bibliography consists of those
sources which speak about women composers in general,
with no reference to a specific composer; sources studying
attitudes; and general histories.   As in the List of Sources,
works including lists of names with no further information
and/or lists of titles of works only are not included.   These
works of secondary interest are not coded and are not referred to anyplace else in the book.

To avoid making my work a bibliography of bibliogra-
phies, I placed the Historical Records Survey's Bio-biblio-
graphical Index of Musicians... (1972) in the supplementary
list.   Ireland's and Hixon/Hennessee's bibliography/index
works do however include a few sources I had not checked,
so they remain in the coded sources list.

Stylistically, Women Composers is reminiscent of the
Hixon and Hennessee Women in Music: A Biobibliography
(Scarecrow Press, 1975).   The content and goals, however,
differ quite a bit.   I concentrate entirely on women as composers, and do not limit my sources to only those found in
Duckles.   Consequently, the number of women composers
represented here far exceeds that of the other book.   Cover-
ing women of all time periods and countries, as Hixon and
Hennessee set out to do, was for me too overwhelming a
job.   I found it necessary to set up geographical (and time)
restrictions to cover each composer more thoroughly.   I
have included genre as part of the "biographical" data for
each composer.   There are several errors in the other book
which have been corrected here (and noted when the source
is cited).

Immeasurable gratitude goes to Dr. Dominique-René de Lerma for his in-town and long distance support--I am proud to have worked with a teacher who extends devotion towards his students so unselfishly. Much appreciation goes to the countless librarians consulted, to my family, to all the roommates who have had to endure my persistent typing, scattered papers and odd hours. And just as important, to all those wonderful people who discouraged me every step of the way: your frame of mind gave me all the fuel I needed to make this project come to life.

LIST OF SOURCES

AA   Adams, Mrs. Crosby. "An American Genius of World
      Renown: Mrs. H. H. A. Beach," Etude, January
      1928, p34. Biographical sketch.

AB   _____. Chapters from a Musical Life. Chicago:
      C. Adams, 1903. Autobiography.

AC   Allen, Frank. Modern British Composers. London:
      Dennis Dobson, 1953. 112p. Biographical sketches;
      alphabetical order.

AD   Alley, Marguerite, and Alley, Jean. Une Amitié pas-
      sionée: Clara Schumann, Johannes Brahms.
      Paris: Laffont, 1955. 246p. Letters.

AE   Altmann, Wilhelm. "Nochmals: musikalisch-schop-
      ferische Frauen." Neue Musikzeitschrift, Decem-
      ber 1948, p362-7.

AF   "An American Composer-Pianist with World-Wide
      Recognition." Etude, November 1922, p746. On
      Mrs. H. H. A. Beach.

AG   American Composers Alliance Bulletin 10, no. 2 (May
      1962), p2-3. Reviews opera by Peggy Glanville-
      Hicks with a biographical sketch included.

AH   "American Women Composers Radio Series." Symphony
      News 24, no. 6 (December 1973-January 1974),
      p13. Thirteen radio programs of music by Amer-
      ican women composers of the 20th century.

AI   "Among the Composers." Etude, January 1944, p11-
      2. Biographies on Mrs. H. H. A. Beach and
      Ada Richter.

AJ   Anderson, E. Ruth, comp. Contemporary American

Composers: A Biographical Dictionary. Boston:
G. K. Hall, 1976. 513p. Biographical articles on
American composers born no earlier than 1870,
who have had at least one original composition published, performed, recorded or awarded a prize
(being in the classical genre); index of American
women composers included. Alphabetical order,
plus addendum requiring page numbers for those
composers.

AK   Antheil, G. "Peggy Glanville-Hicks." American Composers Alliance Bulletin 4, no. 1 (1954), p2-9.
Biographical sketch.

AL   Apel, Paul H. Music of the Americas North and South.
New York: Vantage Press, 1958. 252p. Dictionary of musicians of North America, Mexico and
Central America, and South America, including
brief introductions to each country's musical trends
and spotted information about the musicians; sub-
divided by country; no index.

AM   Apthorp, W. [Sketch of Mrs. H. H. A. Beach's life,
and analysis of the Gaelic symphony] in Boston
Symphony Orchestra Programmes 16 (1896/1897),
p77.

AN   The ASCAP Biographical Dictionary of Composers, Authors and Publishers. New York: Thomas Y.
Crowell, 1966. 845p. This source has been indexed only for those composers with other bibliographic support; the distinction between "author"
and "composer" was not presented clearly enough
to draw any conclusions without other evidence.

AO   Ashley, Patricia. "Here They Are on a Plastic Plat-
ter; A Complete Discography of Women Composers."
Ms, November 1975, p111-4. Reviews recent recordings of several women composers, with a
discography of recordings found in the U.S.A.

BA   Baker, Theodore. Baker's Biographical Dictionary of
Musicians, 5th ed. New York: G. Schirmer,
1958. 1855p. Used only when Hixon/Hennessee
(HL) omitted.

BB   _____. Baker's Biographical Dictionary of Musi-
      cians. Supplement. New York: G. Schirmer,
      1965. 143p.

BC   Baltzell, W. J. Noted Names in Music. Boston: O.
      Ditson, 1927. 108p. Selected composers up to
      1927; alphabetical order.

BD   Barillon-Banche, Paula. Augusta Holmes et la femme
      compositeur. Paris: Fischbacher, 1912. 118p.

BE   Barnes, Edwin Ninyon Chaloner. American Women in
      Creative Music; Tuning in on American Music.
      Washington, D. C. : Music Educational Publications,
      1936. 44p. Biographical sketches, with list of
      names at end.

BF   Barrell, Edgar. "Notable Musical Women." Etude,
      November 1929, p805-6; December 1929, p827;
      January 1930, p12; February 1930, p92. Brief
      biographical notes of women in music.

BG   Barth, Prudentiana; Ritscher, M. Immaculata; and Jo-
      seph Schmidt-Görg, eds. Hildegard von Bingen:
      Lieder. Salzburg: Otto Müller, 1969. 328p.

BH   Bean, H. J. "Woman in Musichouse." American Mu-
      sic Teacher, March-April 1957, p5. On Mrs. H.
      H. A. Beach.

BI   Bender, William. "Sarah's Women." Time, Novem-
      ber 24, 1975, p88. Review of Sarah Caldwell di-
      recting "A Celebration of Women Composers" in
      New York; names three composers and gives infor-
      mation about them.

BJ   Boroff, Edith. An Introduction to Elisabeth-Claude
      Jacquet de la Guerre. Brooklyn: Institute of
      Mediaeval Music, 1966. History and study of her
      works; plates of her compositions, her will; bibli-
      ography and list of publications included.

BK   _____. "Women Composers: Reminiscence
      and History." College Music Symposium 15 (fall
      1975), p26-33.

BL   Bourges, Maurice. "Des femmes-compositeurs."

Revue et Gazette Musicale de Paris 38, (September 19, 1847), p305-7; v. 39, p313-5.

BM   Bradshaw, Susan. "The Music of Elisabeth Lutyens." Musical Times, July 1971, p653-6. Study of Lutyens and her style of composition; illustrated.

BN   "Breaks." Etude, November 1933, p729-30. Talks about Evangeline Lehman's having attained recognition so quickly following publication of her pieces; discusses some of those compositions.

BO   Brooks, B. "How of Creative Composition." Etude, March 1943, p151+. Mrs. H. H. A. Beach talks about the process of musical composition (and its relation to herself).

BP   Brown, James D., and Stratton, Stephen S. British Musical Biography. Derby, England: Chadfield & Son, 1897. 462p. Emphasis on composers living in the late 19th century; this citation is only used when Hixon/Hennessee (HL) left it out.

BQ   Brown, Royal S. "French Music Since Debussy and Ravel." High Fidelity/Musical America 23 (September 1973), p50-65. Discusses "Les Six" and selected composers after them, G. Tailleferre and B. Jolas among those.

BR   Browne, C. A. "Girlhood of Famous Women in Music." Etude, July 1909, p488-9. On Mrs. H. H. A. Beach.

BS   Burk, John Naglee. Clara Schumann; A Romantic Biography. New York: Random House, 1940. 438p.

BT   Burns, Don. "The Distaff'd Composers." Music Journal, March 1974, p16+. Traces the development of women as composers of music in various forms from the days of the Muses to the present with thoughts on their acceptance nowadays; many names included.

CA   Campbell, Mary. "Women's Evening Highly Successful." Columbus [Ohio] Dispatch, November 12, 1975. pB-6. Mentions those women composers represented in a woman's concert.

CB   Canadian Broadcasting Corporation.   Thirty-Four Biog-
       raphies of Canadian Composers.   Prepared and dis-
       tributed by the International Service of the Canadi-
       an Broadcasting Corp. , English and French texts.
       Montreal: Canadian Broadcasting Corp. , 1964.
       110p.

CC   Cardosa, Sylvio Tullio.   Dictionario biografico de mu-
       sica popular.   Rio de Janeiro: n.p. , 1965.   351p.
       Brief biographical sketches in two parts: national
       and international; gives titles of works, not genre,
       and LP representatives.

CD   Centre belge de documentation musicale.   Music in
       Belgium--Contemporary Belgian Composers.   Bel-
       gium: A. Manteau, 1964.   158p. Survey (incom-
       plete) of contemporary Belgian music in alphabeti-
       cal order by composer; includes articles written
       on the composer and a list of major works.

CE   Chamfory, Claude.   "Hommage à Germaine Tailleferre."
       Le Courrier Musical de France 37 (1972), p119.

CF   Chase, Gilbert.   America's Music.   New York:
       McGraw-Hill, 1955.   733p. Study of the rise of
       American music in relation to its European back-
       ground from Puritan times to 12-tone; bibliography,
       index included.

CG   Chauvin, Marie-Jose.   "Entretien avec Betsy Jolas. "
       Le Courrier Musical de France 27 (1969), p162-73.

CH   Clepper, P. M.   "After God Comes Papa. " Stereo 5
       (spring 1972), p38-44.   Discusses women compos-
       ers and society problems.

CI   Cole, Rossetter G.   "Fanny Bloomfield-Zeisler. "
       Proceedings, Music Teachers National Association,
       series 22, 1927, p76-83.   Biographical article on
       her career.

CJ   Complete Catalog of Works by Mana-Zucca.   Miami,
       Fla. :   Congress Music Publications, n. d.   12p.
       Partially complete list of works; price, grade,
       range included; copies of first four bars of some

pieces.

CK   Composium: Directory of New Music, 1974-1975 ed.
      Los Angeles: Crystal Record Co., 1974. Lists
      composers with recent publications; some with ad-
      dresses; information in abbreviations; alphabetical
      listing.

CL   Contemporary Music Catalogue. New York: C. F.
      Peters, 1975. 110p. Lists contemporary compo-
      sitions in alphabetical order by composer with bio-
      graphical sketches on selected composers.

CM   Cooke, James Francis. "A Short Sketch of Music in
      America." Etude, July 1910, p443-4. Includes
      biographical sketch of Mrs. H. H. A. Beach.

CN   Craig, M. "Composer and Ambassadress of U.S. Mu-
      sic." Musical Courier, July, 1959, p7. On Julia
      Smith.

CO   Cuney-Hare, Maud. Negro Musicians and Their Music.
      Washington, D.C.: Associated Publishers, 1936.
      439p. Study of the development of black music
      from its origins in Africa to the present.

DA   Davenport, M. Marguerita. Azalia; The Life of Mad-
      ame E. Azalia Hackley. Boston: Chapman &
      Grimes, 1949. 196p.

DB   Davies, Laurence. César Franck and His Circle.
      London: Barrie & Jenkins, 1970. 380p. Chapter
      on Augusta Holmès.

DC   "Le donne compositrici." Musica d'oggi 4 (1922),
      p174. On Ethel M. Smyth.

DD   Drewes, Heinz. Maria Antonia Walpurgis als Kompo-
      siten. Ph.D. diss. University of Köln, 1934.
      122p.

DE   Dumesnil, Rene. Portraits de musiciens français.
      Paris: Librairie Plon, 1938. 248p. Includes
      some women composers; no index or contents list;
      in alphabetical order.

EA   Ebel, Otto. Women Composers: A Biographical Hand-
       book of Woman's Work in Music. Brooklyn: F. H.
       Chandler, 1902. 151p. Composers of several
       centuries represented; alphabetical order.

EB   Edmunds, John, and Boelzner, Gordon. Some Twenti-
       eth Century American Composers. New York:
       New York Public Library, 1959. 2 vols. Lists
       writings (alphabetically) by the composer, and
       about the works by the composer.

EC   "Eleanor Everest Freer's Songs. " Musical Courier,
       January 3, 1906, p25.

ED   Elson, Arthur. "Famous Musical Women of the Past."
       Etude, November 1918, p691-2. History of women
       as composers from Greek times to the 19th cen-
       tury.

EE   . "Famous Women in Musical History. "
       Musical Standard 32 (1909), p89-91; Etude, July
       1909, p441. Several women composers named.

EF   . "Women Composers in Europe. " Musician
       10 (1905), p136-8.

EG   Elson, Arthur, and Truette, E. Woman's Work in
       Music. Boston: L. C. Page, 1931. 301p. List
       of women composers at end; deals with the subject
       by country.

EH   Elson, Louis. The History of American Music, rev.
       ed. New York: Macmillan, 1925. 423p. Chap-
       ter on American women in music, p293-310.

EI   Elvers, Rudolf, ed. Fanny Hensel, geboren Mendel-
       ssohn Bartholdy. Dokumente ihres Lebens. Ber-
       lin: n.p. , 1972.

EJ   "The Etude Gallery of Musical Celebrities (EGMC). "
       Etude, February 1910, p87-8; June 1910, p375-6;
       September 1910, p583-4; October 1910, p449-50;
       December 1910, p801-2; July 1929, p511-2.

EK   "Etude Historical Musical Portrait Series. " Etude,
       January 1932-October 1940 issues. Alphabetical
       listing of composers and musicians, with pictures

and brief summary of their accomplishments.

EL   Ewen, David, ed. <u>Composers Since 1900.</u> New York:
        H. W. Wilson, 1969. 639p. Selected composers'
        biographies; includes portraits, list of major works,
        and short bibliographies.

EM   _____. <u>European Composers Today.</u> New York:
        H. W. Wilson, 1954. 200p. Biographical and
        critical articles on the more influential composers
        writing since 1900; list of works and bibliography
        included; illustrated.

EN   _____. <u>Living Musicians.</u> New York: H. W. Wil-
        son, 1940. 390p. A dictionary of performers,
        especially American or those active in America;
        portraits given.

FA   "Famous Women Composers." <u>Etude,</u> April 1917,
        p237-8. Paragraphs on Beach, Chaminade, Leh-
        man, Smyth; other names given in list.

FB   Farga, Franz. <u>Die goldene Kehle: Meistergesang aus</u>
        <u>drei Jahrhunderten.</u> Vienna: A. Franz Goth,
        1948. 315p. Singers' biographies; index includes
        name and area singer is active in (e.g. as com-
        poser, soprano, writer ...).

FC   Farwell, Arthur, and Darby, W. Dermot, ed. <u>Music</u>
        <u>in America.</u> Vol. 4 of <u>Art of Music.</u> D. G. Ma-
        son, ed. New York: National Society of Music,
        1915. 478p.

FD   "A Favorite Composer." Issues of <u>Etude.</u> Articles
        on selected composers (one per month citation) in-
        cluding a brief biography, a list of works and a
        portrait. Each composer in the Handbook citing
        FD gives the issue in which she is found.

FE   Fay, Amy. "Women and Music." <u>Music</u> 18 (1900),
        p505-7. Discusses the change in attitudes towards
        women and the imminent upsurge of women com-
        posers.

FF   Fellerer, Karl Gustav. <u>Die Musikerin Annette von</u>
        <u>Droste-Hulshoff.</u> Munster: n.p., 1954.

FG   Fetis, François J. <u>Biographie universelle des musi-</u>
<u>ciens et bibliographie générale de la musique.</u>
<u>Paris: Firmin Didot Frères, 1866-70.</u> 8 vols.
A particularly good source for earlier composers
(as well as musicians), including generous biographies and bibliographic information, and list of
works.

FH   Finck, Henry T. "The Most Beautiful Romance in Musical History." <u>Etude,</u> June 1910, p443-4. On
Clara and Robert Schumann.

FI   Fitzlyon, April. <u>The Price of Genius; A Life of Paul-</u>
<u>ine Viardot.</u> <u>New York: Appleton-Century, 1964.</u>
<u>520p.</u>

FJ   Flothuis, Marius. <u>Modern British Composers.</u> London: <u>Continental Book Co.,</u> [ca. 1949]. 60p.
History by generations of composers with appendix
of composers.

FK   Foster, Agnes Greene. <u>Eleanor Everest Freer--Patri-</u>
<u>ot and Her Colleagues.</u> Chicago: <u>Musical Art</u>
<u>Publ. Co., 1927.</u> 186p.

FL   "Frauen als Komponisten." In <u>Ullstein Lexikon der</u>
<u>Musik,</u> Frederick von Herzfeld, ed. Frankfurt:
<u>Verlag Ullstein, 1973.</u> p472.

FM   Freed, Richard. "The Piano Works of Mrs. H. H. A.
Beach: Demonstrating the Irrelevance of Gender."
<u>Stereo Review</u> 35 (December 1975), p82-3. Re-
view of album of 16 of Beach's piano pieces as
performed by Virginia Eskin, and a look at Beach's
piano style in light of the early 20th century.

FN   Freer, Eleanor. <u>Recollections and Reflections of an</u>
<u>American Composer.</u> New York: <u>Musical Advance</u>
<u>Pub. Co., 1929.</u> Autobiography.

FO   Friedland, Bea. "Louise Farrenc (1804-1875): Composer, Performer, Scholar." <u>Music Quarterly</u> 60
(April 1974), p257-74. Biography; discusses also
her output.

FP   Friskin, James, and Freundlich, Irwin. <u>Music for</u>
<u>the Piano: A Handbook for Concert and Teaching</u>

Material from 1850-1952. New York: Rinehart,
1954. 432p. List of works by genre and composer
is given within type section, with description of the
piece; some composers with brief biographies; list
of publishers, index, appendices.

FQ   Fuld, James J.   The Book of World-Famous Music.
New York: Crown, 1971. 688p. Traces lineage
of the most familiar compositions of the Western
world; thematic index includes detailed commen-
taries on sources, composers and history.

FR   Fürstenau, Moritz.   Die Musikalischen Beschäftigungen
der Prinzessin Amalie, Herzogin zu Sachsen.
Dresden: R. v. Zahn, 1874. 64 p.

GA   Gaume, Matilda.   Ruth Crawford Seeger: Her Life
and Works.   Ph.D. diss., Indiana University,
1973. 312p.

GB   Ginder, C. Richard.   "Great Musical Women of Yes-
terday."   Etude, September 1941, p603-32.   On
Clara Schumann and Wilhelmine Schroeder-Devrient.

GC   Gmelch, Dr. Joseph.   Die Kompositionen der Heil.
Hildegard.   Düsseldorf: L. Schwann, n.d.   37p.
+ 32p. kodex.

GD   Graham, Shirley.   "Spirituals to Symphonies."   Etude,
November 1936, p691-2+.   Brief survey of black
Music in America from primitive backgrounds; in-
formation on F. B. Price.

GE   "A Great American Lady Honored."   Congressional
Record--House.   Washington, D. C.:   U. S. Gov.
Printing Office, November 10, 1975.   Tribute to
Mana Zucca for her 50th year of membership in
ASCAP; includes an article on her published in the
Miami Herald regarding the anniversary.

GF   Green, Janet M.   Musical Biographies.   Vols. 5 & 6
of The American History and Encyclopedia of Music, W. L. Hubbard, ed.   Toledo: Irving Squire,
1908.   Biographical sketches in alphabetical order
emphasizing contemporary musicians; also includes
great composers, musicians, teachers, inventors
(musical), and others.

GG   Green, Miriam Stewart. "Consider These Creators."
      American Music Teacher 25 (July/August 1974),
      p9-12. Discusses American women's contributions
      to composing from 1776 to present; mixed media,
      classical form and electronic areas discussed with
      many names given; also discusses women who have
      collected Indian folk music.

GH   _____. "Women: From Silence to Song." Ameri-
      can Music Teacher 24 (September/October 1974),
      p5-7. Survey of women composers from Sappho to
      20th century; many names of women in music (not
      only composers).

GI   Grete von Zieritz: Werkverzeichnis. Berlin: Gesell-
      schaft der Freunde des Internationalen Musiker-
      Briefe-Archivs E. V., 1963. 11p. Short biographi-
      cal sketch, with complete list of works.

GJ   Grove's Dictionary of Music and Musicians. London:
      Macmillan, 1954. 9 vols. Cited only when
      Hixon/Hennessee (HL) did not include.

HA   Hackett, Karleton. "Some American Songwriters."
      Negro Music Journal 1 (July 1903), p213-7. Dis-
      cusses 10 American composers separately as song-
      writers (three women--Beach, Gaynor, Lang).

HB   Hall, Jacob Henry. Biography of Gospel Song and
      Hymn Writers. New York: AMS Press, 1971.
      419p. Biography of representatives of gospel song
      and hymn writers from around 1800-1900, in
      chronological order.

HC   Hall, Marnie. "Women's Work." Biographical notes
      accompanying the recording, "Woman's Work."
      New York: Gemini Hall Records, 1975. 41p.
      Biographical notes on 18 women composers repre-
      sented in the record; includes librettos to songs,
      and biographical sketches of the performers. Il-
      lustrated.

HD   Hanson, Dr. Howard, ed. The New Scribner Music
      Library. Vol. 11 (reference volume). New York:
      Scribner's, 1973. 137p. Biographical dictionary
      of composers represented in the complete NSML

(11 volumes) with complete index to NSML by composer and title; includes also a brief pictoral history of keyboard instruments and keyboard music,
and a reference dictionary of musical terms.

HE   Hare, Maud Cuney. Negro Musicians and Their Music.
Washington, D. C. : Associated Publishers, 1936.
439p. Traces music of blacks from African roots
to 1930's (folk and classical music); appendix of
African musical instruments, bibliography, and index included.

HF   Henahan, Donal. "Let's Hear It for Composer Per-
sons. " New York Times, August 31, 1975, pD-11.
An introduction to the idea of women composers,
drawing upon several of the more prominent women composers in compiling a brief history, and
discussing their leaguing together.

HG   Henderson, Robert. "Elisabeth Lutyens. " Musical
Times, August 1963, p551-5. Discusses her musical style.

HH   Henning, Laura. Die Freundschaft Clara Schumann
mit Johannes Brahms. Zürich: Lassen Verlag,
1952. 136p. Story of the relationship between the
two; bibliography included.

HI   Hines, Dixie, and Hanaford, Harry P. Who's Who in
Music and Drama. New York: H. P. Hanaford,
1914.

HJ   Hipsher, Edward Ellsworth. American Opera and Its
Composers. Philadelphia: T. Presser, 1927.
408p. History of the development of America's
operas.

HK   Hixon, Donald L. Music in Early America; A Bibliography of Music in Evans. Metuchen, N. J. :
Scarecrow Press, 1970. 607p. Index to music
published in the 17th and 18th centuries in America; includes biographical sketches, bibliography,
and indexes by title of pieces, composer and Evans
serial number.

HL   _____, and Hennessee, Don. Women in Music: A
Biobibliography. Metuchen, N. J. : Scarecrow

Press, 1975. 347p. An index to sources on women musicians with brief identification of each
woman.

HM Höcker, Karla. Clara Schumann. Regensburg: Bosse
Verlag, 1938. 93p. Biography, with works given;
illustrated.

HN Holbrooke, Joseph. Contemporary British Composers.
London: Cecil Palmer, 1925. 324p.

HO Honolka, Kurt. Die grossen Primadonnen. Stuttgart:
Cotto-Verlag, 1960. 287p. Biographies of singers
(Malibran included).

HP Howard, John Tasker. Our Contemporary Composers.
New York: Thomas Y. Crowell, 1941. 447p.
Supplementary volume to Our American Music deal-
ing with late 19th-century to mid-20th-century music and composers.

HQ Howard, John T., and Bellows, George Kent. A Short
History of Music in America. New York: Thomas
Y. Crowell, 1967. 496p. Concise history of
American music from Indian music to the present
including more noteworthy composers (with biographical sketches) and compositions, musical
events and institutions; more than half the book is
devoted to the 20th century. Supplementary readings and recordings of American music are given.

HR Howe, Ann Whitworth. Lily Strickland: Her Contribu-
tion to American Music in the Early Twentieth
Century. Ph.D. diss. Catholic University of
America. (Avail. from University Microfilms.)
1969. 185p. Very complete biography of her life,
with 14 appendices, and comprehensive bibliography.

HS Hughes, Eric, and Junge, Sylvia. "Recorded Music by
Elisabeth Lutyens." Recorded Sound 38 (April
1970), p599-600. Discography.

HT Hughes, Rupert. American Composers. Boston:
L. C. Page Co., 1914. 582p. Names some
women composers, with information on them.

HU _____. Contemporary American Composers. Boston:

L. C. Page Co. , 1900. 456p. Biographies of selected composers living around 1900; chapter on women composers p423-41.

HV   _____. Famous American Composers. Boston: L. C. Page Co. , 1900. Names some women composers, with information on them.

HW   _____. Music Lover's Encyclopedia. New York: Garden City Pub. Co. , 1947. 877p. General music dictionary with essays, stories of operas, biographies, and pronunciation keys; in alphabetical order.

HX   _____. "Woman Composers. " Century Magazine 55 (March 1898), p768-79. Discussion of women as composers, with information on 10 women composers and a list of other names.

HY   Hummel, Walter. Nannerl Mozarts Tagebuchblätter. Salzburg: Verlag das Berglandbuch, 1958. 135p.

IA   Indiana Federation of Music Clubs. Indiana Composers; Native and Adopted. Bloomington: Indiana University, 1936. 51p. Brief biographies of composers, titles to selected published pieces including publisher, and information at end on composers with unpublished manuscripts.

IB   Indiana University (Bloomington). Afro-American Arts Institute. Black Music Center--composer files.

IC   International Inventory of Musical Sources. Recueils imprimés XVIe-XVIIe siècles. Ouvrage publié sous la direction de François Lesure. Munich: G. Henle Verlag, 1960- . 639p. (RISM) Lists collections of music published between 1501 and 1700 with a summary of their contents and with the locations of copies in major European and American libraries. Index of editors, printers, and of titles and composers; alphabetical order.

ID   Ireland, Norma Olin. Index to Women of the World from Ancient to Modern Times. Westwood, Mass. : F. W. Faxon, 1970. 573p. Random selection of women of all centuries, from Irish beauties to

professional pilots. In the bibliography, the wrong
title is quoted for the Guy McCoy book: it should
read Portraits of the World's Best Known Musicians
(not ... Best Women Musicians). Also sources
are not cited consistently.

JA   Jacobi [Jacoby], Hugh William, comp. Contemporary
      American Composers Based at American Colleges
      and Universities. California: Paradise Arts Pub-
      lisher, 1975. 240p. Biographical sketches of uni-
      versity-based American composers in alphabetical
      order, including major works, articles by the com-
      posers and addresses.

JB   Jacobs-Bond, Carrie. The Roads of Melody. New
      York: D. Appleton, 1927. 223p. Autobiography.

JC   James, Edward T. Notable American Women 1607-
      1950: A Biographical Dictionary. Cambridge,
      Mass. : Belknap Press of Harvard University
      Press, 1971. 3 vols. Notable women from Vir-
      ginia Dare to women who died no later than the
      end of 1950; in alphabetical order.

JD   Johnson, H. Earle. Operas on American Subjects.
      New York: Coleman-Ross, 1964. 125p. Alpha-
      betical listing by composer of operas from the
      17th century to the present based on American
      subjects or characters.

JE   Johnson, Thomas Arnold. "The Pianoforte Music of
      Chaminade. " Musical Opinion 59 (1936), p678-9.

JF   Johnson, Tom. "Musician of the Month: Lucia Dlugos-
      zewski. " High Fidelity/Musical America, June
      1975, MA 4-5. Discusses style and technique of
      her works and her directions.

JG   Jones, F. O. A Handbook of American Music and Mu-
      sicians (1886). Reprinted, New York: Da Capo
      Press, 1971. 182p. Biographies of American
      musicians and histories of the main musical insti-
      tutions and societies, in alphabetical order.

KA   Kallmann, Helmut, ed. Catalogue of Canadian Com-
         posers. Toronto: Canadian Broadcasting Corpora-
         tion, 1972. 254p. (Hixon/Hennessee [HL] uses
         1952 edition.) Brief history of music in Canada,
         with short biographies of contemporary composers
         (Canadian-born and/or Canadian residents) in alpha-
         betical order and list of works including duration
         and publisher. Supplementary lists of composers
         (page numbers are cited with KA code for those
         composers).

KB   Kefalas, Elinor. "Pauline Oliveros: An Interview."
         High Fidelity/Musical America, June 1975, MA
         24-5. Discusses her attitude toward the problems
         of women composers.

KC   Knight, Janet. "For the First Time on the Great
         Stage." Ms., November 1975, p92-3. Biographi-
         cal sketches of five women composers, including
         some works and pictures.

KD   Krauss, Wilhelmine. "Die Musik der heiligen Hilde-
         gard von Bingen." Gregoriusblatt 61 (n.d.), p17-
         22.

KE   Kreuger, Karl. The Musical Heritage of the United
         States: The Unknown Portion. New York: Society
         for the Preservation of the American Musical
         Heritage, 1973. 237p. Chapters on composers
         who had works performed by major orchestras
         with biographical information and information on
         the work performed.

KF   Kühner, Hans. Grosse Sangerinnen der Klassik und
         Romantik. Stuttgart: Victoria Verlag, 1954. 326p.
         Biography of singers; names composers who wrote
         works for them; includes bibliographies by singers'
         names.

KG   Kupferberg, Herbert. The Mendelssohns: Three Gene-
         rations of Genius. New York: Scribner's, 1972.
         272p. Chapter on Fanny Mendelssohn.

LA   "Ladies of the Turntable." Stereo Review, May 1976,
         p124. Review of Gemini Hall Record album of
         women composers.

LB   Lahee, Henry Charles. Annals of Music in America.
        Boston: Marshall Jones Co., 1922. 298p. Chron-
        ological record of significant musical events from
        1640 to early 1900's.

LC   Landowski, W-L. "Propos du centenaire de 'Las Es-
        meralda.' " Le Menestrel 98 (n.d.), p313-4. On
        Louise Bertin.

LD   Larson, Margareta, and Hermelin, Carin. "Elfrida
        Andrée organiste et compositrice (1841-1929). "
        L'Orgue 157 (January-March 1976), p12-6. On
        Andrée's life as organist and difficulties in pre-
        senting compositions as a woman.

LE   Lebeau, Elisabeth. Lili Boulanger: 1893-1918. Paris:
        Bibliothèque Nationale, 1968. 16p. Chronology of
        Boulanger family, with biography of Lili including
        various items surrounding her life and death.

LF   "A List of Well-Known Woman Composers. " Etude,
        November 1918, p699-700. Brief paragraphs on
        women composers, plus a supplementary list of
        names in alphabetical order.

LG   Littlejohn, Joan. "Senior British Composers II: Eliz-
        abeth Poston. " Composer 56 (winter 1975/76),
        p15-8. Continued in spring 1976, p27-32. Bio-
        graphical sketch based on interview.

LH   Londeix, Jean Marie. 125 Ans de musique pour saxo-
        phone. Paris: Alphonse Leduc, 1971. 398p.
        General listing of works for saxophone (in alpha-
        betical order by composer), giving biographical in-
        formation for selected composers.

MA   MacMillan, Keith, and Beckwith, John, ed. Contempo-
        rary Canadian Composers. Toronto: Oxford Uni-
        versity Press, 1975. 248p. Biographical para-
        graphs including list of composition for composers
        with larger output, and additional bibliography; in
        alphabetical order; illustrated.

MB   Maconchy, Elisabeth. "A Composer Speaks. " Com-
        poser 42 (winter 1971/72), p25-9. Autobiographi-
        cal, on her development as a composer; names

other women composers on the scene.

MC   _____. "Who Is Your Favourite Composer?" Composer 24 (summer 1967), p20-1. Compares her
musical tastes as a student with those of today's
students.

MD   Mahler-Werfel, Alma. Mein Leben. Frankfurt/M:
S. Fischer, 1960. 375p. Autobiography; illustrated.

ME   Mahony, Patrick. "Alma Mahler-Werfel. " Composer
45 (autumn 1972), p13-7. Discusses her philoso-
phies and attitudes, especially regarding Mahler.

MF   Malone, Dumas, ed. Dictionary of American Biography.
New York: Scribner's, 1936. 22 vols. Alphabetical order; includes prominent Americans.

MG   Manfred, Willfort. "Clara Schumann. " Neue Zeitschrift für Musik 132 (May 1971), p239-43. Biographical, including bibliography and illustrations.

MH   Mannheimer Musiktage. Internationalen Wettbewerb
für Komponistinnen. zum III. Mannheim-Ludwig-
shafen, n.p., 1961. 17p. Brief summary of
women in music (in French and German) with information concerning the international music com-
petition.

MI   Mathews, William Smythe Babcock. A Hundred Years
of Music in America. Chicago: G. L. Howe,
1889. 715p. Covers American music during the
19th century with biographical sketches, and a
supplementary (biographical) list of musicians at
the end (naming several women).

MJ   Mathews, W. S. B. "A Great Pianist at Home. "
Music 9 (October 1895-April 1896), p1-10. On
Mme. Bloomfield-Zeisler.

MK   Matney, William C. , ed. Who's Who Among Black
Americans. Northbrook, Ill.: Who's Who Among
Black Americans, Inc. , 1975. 772p. Biographi-
cal articles, in alphabetical order.

ML   "A Matter of Art, Not Sex. " Time, November 10,

1975, p59. On women as composers, with information on four women.

MM   Mens en Melodie 30 (September 1975), p273. Biographical sketch of Betsy Jolas.

MN   Merrill, E. Lindsey. Mrs. H. H. A. Beach: Her
Life and Music. Ann Arbor, Mich. : University
Microfilms, 1963. Thorough study of Beach, with
statistical breakdown of the theoretical aspect of
her music.

MO   Metcalf, Frank Johnson. Stories of Hymn Tunes.
New York: Abingdon Press, 1928. 224p. A history of the writers and compilers of sacred music,
in chronological order by composer.

MP   Michigan State Council for the Arts. Annotated Directory of Michigan Orchestral Composers. Detroit:
The Council, 1967. 38p. Alphabetical listing of
composers with short biographical sketches and
list of compositions.

MQ   "MOMA: Women Composers: Summergarden Concert."
High Fidelity/Musical America 25 (December
1975), MA 27-8. Reviews concert of women's
music at Museum of Modern Art in New York,
August 15, 1975. Music by Bond, Semegen, Polin, and Chance.

MR   Moore, John Weeks. Complete Encyclopedia of Music.
Boston: J. P. Jewett & Co., 1854. 1004p.
American musical dictionary, with articles, biog-
raphies and definitions.

MS   Moore, Rebecca Deming. When They Were Girls.
Danville, N.Y. : A. Owen Pub. Co., 1937. 192p.
Biography of Mrs. H. H. A. Beach.

MT   "More Women Composers." Musical Courier 79 (1919),
p7.

MU   Mozart, Leopold. Nannerl Notenbuch (1759). Munich:
Rinn, 1956. A reprint.

MV   Mu Phi Epsilon. Composers and Authors. N.p.,
1962. Women only; selected works and their publishers.

MW Müller, Erich. Deutsches Musiker-Lexikon. Dresden:
         Wilhelm Limpert-Verlag, 1929. 1642p. Diction-
         ary of musicians, composers, and writers on mu-
         sic with background information on each (in alpha-
         betical order).

MX Müller von Asow, Hedwig. Komponistinnen-Disco-
         graphie. Berlin: Veroffentlichungen des Interna-
         tionalen Musiker-Brief-Archivs, 1962. 3p. Dis-
         cography of women composers.

MY Munte, Frank. Verzeichnis der deutschsprachigen
         Schrifttums über Robert Schumann 1856-1970.
         Anhang: Schrifttum über Clara Schumann. Ham-
         burg: Karl Dieter Wagner, 1972. 151p. Supple-
         ment contains bibliography and much information on
         Clara.

MZ Myers, Rollo. "Augusta Holmès: A Meteoric Career."
         Music Quarterly 53 (July 1967), p365-76. Bio-
         graphical essay.

NA National Music Council 35 (spring 1976), p18. Bio-
         graphical sketch of Daria Semegen.

NB "The New Etude Gallery of Musical Celebrities."
         Etude, July 1929, p511-2. Portraits of musicians
         with biographies on the back of the portraits.
         This particular month features Chaminade as one
         of the musicians.

NC "New Members: Ursula Mamlock." American Com-
         posers Alliance Bulletin 12 (spring 1964), p14.
         Biographical sketch.

ND Nisard, Theodore. "Reflexiens sur deux nouveaux
         trios inédits de Mme. J. L. Farrenc." Revue de
         Musique Ancienne et Moderne November 1856,
         p697-700.

NE Nolan, Dean Robert L. 'Dr. Eva Jessye 'The Mother
         of Black Music.' " Michigan Chronicle, Decem-
         ber 5, 1970, pB-8. Biographical sketch.

OA O'Day, Billie. "When Keyed Up Sound Off with 'Mana-

Zucca. ' " Miami News, April 30, 1965, p14-A.
On Mana-Zucca's career.

PA   Palmer, Christopher. "Lili Boulanger, 1893-1918. "
      Musical Times, March 1968, p227-8. Discusses
      her achievements in musical composition.

PB   Pan American Union. Compositores de America.
      Washington, D. C. : Pan American Union, 1955- .
      Catalog of selected composers throughout the
      Americas, with biographical sketches, and list of
      works with information on them; illustrated.

PC   Panzari, Louis. Louisiana Composers. New Orleans:
      Dinstuhl Printing and Pub. , 1972. 102p. Alpha-
      betical listing of composers active in Louisiana,
      with short biographical sketches.

PD   Patterson, Lindsay, comp. The Negro in Music and
      Art. New York: Publishers Company, Inc. (under
      the auspices of the International Library of Negro
      Life and History), (1967, 1968). 304p. Chapters
      by different writers on various areas of black mu-
      sic; includes biographical sketches on the writers;
      illustrated. Article by Margaret Bonds "A Remi-
      niscence, " p191-4 (autobiographical).

PE   Pavlakis, Christopher. The American Music Handbook.
      New York and London: Collier Macmillan Publi-
      shers, 1974. 836p. Contains chapter on (selected)
      composers active in America.

PF   Perreau, Robert. "Une Grande Pianiste colmerienne:
      Marie Kiené épouse Bigot de Morogues. " Annuaire
      de Colmar, 1962, p59-67. On Marie Bigot.

PG   "Pianist and Composer Who Helped Improvise the His-
      tory of Jazz: Mary Lou Williams. " Life, 1976
      issue, p54. Biographical sketch with picture.

PH   "Piano Keys Career--Julia Smith. " Music Clubs Mag-
      azine, May 1956, p17+. Brief biographical sketch
      on her present accomplishments; picture.

PI   Polansky, Hannah. "Mana Zucca: Grande Dame of
      Miami Music. " The Reporter (Miami), April 11,

1971, pA-14. Reviews her career and life.

PJ   Politikens Musikbibliotek. Musikkens Hven Hvad Hvor:
      Biografier. Copenhagen: Politikens Forlag, 1961.
      2 vols. Biographical sketches of men and women
      in music, in alphabetical order.

PK   Porter, A. "Musical Events: N. Y. Philharmonic
      Concert. " New Yorker, November 24, 1975, p151-
      5. On women's concert.

PL   Pratt, Waldo Seldon. American Supplement to Grove's
      Dictionary of Music and Musicians. New York:
      Macmillan, 1930. 438p. Many women composers
      given.

PM   Prieberg, Fred K. Lexikon der neuen Musik. Munich:
      Verlag Karl Albert Freiburg, 1958. 495p. Biog-
      raphies of selected (20th-century) composers, in
      alphabetical order.

PN   "Profiles. " New Yorker, May 2, 1964, p52+. Story
      of Mary Lou Williams as pianist, composer and
      arranger up to the 1960's; illustrated.

QA   Quednau, Werner. Clara Schumann. Berlin: Altber-
      liner Verlag Groszer, 1955. 318p. Biography;
      no index.

RA   Raney, Carolyn. Francesca Caccini, Musician to the
      Medici, and Her Primo Libro (1618). Ph.D. dis-
      sertation, New York University, 1971.

RB   _____. "Francesca Caccini's 'Primo Libro. ' "
      Music and Letters 48 (October 1967), p350-7.
      Gives a biography of her life up to 1618 and then
      a discussion of the volume of songs "Il Primo
      Libro. "

RC   _____. "Introduction to Francesca Caccini. " Bul-
      letin of the National Association of Teachers of
      Singing, 1966, n. p.

RD   _____. "A Solution to a Lute Tablature of Isabella
      de Medici (c. 1540-1576). " Memorie e contributi

alla musica di Frederico Ghisi, ed. by Guiseppe
Vecchi. Bologna: University of Bologna Press,
1974.

RE _____. "Vocal Style in the Works of Francesca
Caccini. " Bulletin of the National Association of
Teachers of Singing, 1966, n. p.

RF "Rare Treat for Retiree: Adieu by Concert. " Clavier
11 (November 1972), p43. Announced a concert
given for Undine S. Moore upon her retirement
with a biographical sketch on her.

RG Reis, Clare R. American Composers. 2nd ed. New
York: International Society for Contemporary Music, U. S. Section, 1932. 128p. Biographical information on composers who wrote larger works
between 1912 and 1932, with emphasis on the works;
in alphabetical order.

RH Riemann, Hugo. Musik Lexikon. Berlin: Max Hesses
Verlag, 1929. 2 vols.

RI Rimmer, Frederick. "Scottish Composers 1974. "
Composer 53 (winter 1974-75), p10-3. Scottish
and British representatives of the contemporary
music scene discussed.

RJ Robinson, Wilhelmina. Historical Negro Biographies.
New York: Publishers Company, Inc. , 1968.
291p. Biographical articles of selected blacks in
various areas of accomplishment; in alphabetical
order with supplementary index of names by major
activity.

RK Rokseth, Yvonne. "Antonia Bembo, Composer to
Louis XIV. " Music Quarterly 23 (April 1937),
p147-69. In-depth biographical essay on her life
and works; illustrated.

RL not used

RM Rosen, Judith, and Rubin-Rabson, Grace. "Why
Haven't Women Become Great Composers ?" High
Fidelity/Musical America 23 (February 1973),
MA 47-50. Two separate articles under the same
title on women's struggle against the odds of

becoming a composer and on those who have become recognized.

RN   Rosenstiel, Leonie.   The Life and Works of Lili Bou-
       langer.   Ph. D. dissertation, Columbia University,
       1974.   Based on family possessions and other ma-
       terials less accessible.

RO   Rostand, Claude.   Dictionnaire de la musique con-
       temporaire.   Paris: Librairie Larousse, 1970.
       255p.   Brief biographical paragraphs on musicians
       and composers in alphabetical order; illustrated.

RP   Russell, Thomas A.   "Nadia Boulanger. "   Musical
       Opinion 61 (n. d.), p214-5.

SA   Saal, Hubert.   "Sound of Women. "   Newsweek 86 (No-
       vember 24, 1975), p83-4.   Review of women's
       concert conducted by Sarah Caldwell.

SB   _____ .   "The Spirit of Mary Lou. "   Newsweek 78
       (December 20, 1971), p67.   Talks about Williams
       and the score to her mass as adapted to a ballet
       performance.

SC   St. John, C.   Ethel Smyth.   New York: Longmans,
       Green, 1959.   316p.   Biography; with chapters by
       V. Sackville-West and Kathleen Dale.

SD   "A Salute to Women Composers. "   Pan Pipes of Sigma
       Alpha Iota, January 1975, p4-7.   Looks at 15 wo-
       men composers of the 20th century.

SE   Schafer, Murray.   British Composers in Interview.
       London: Faber & Faber, 1963.   187p.   Interviews
       with 16 British composers, with pictures.

SF   Schneider, Hans.   Musik zum Jahr der Frau.   No. 196.
       Tutzing: Musikantiquariat Hans Schneider, 1975.
       77p.   Selected music and letters by composers
       and musicians to or about a woman, including date,
       publisher, etc.; illustrated.

SG   Schumann, Robert.   Music and Musicians; Essays and
       Criticisms.   Translated by Fanny Raymond Ritter.
       London: William Reeves, n. d.   418p.   Selected

essays by musicians close to Schumann; information on Clara Schumann.

SH   Schuyler, George Samuel.   Black and Conservative:
       The Autobiography of George S. Schuyler.   New
       York: Arlington House, 1966.   362p.   Information
       on Philippa D. Schuyler.

SI   Schuyler, Philippa Duke.   Adventures in Black and
       White.   New York: Robert Speller and Sons, 1960.
       302p.   Autobiography.

SJ   _____ .   Good Men Die.   New York: Twin Circle
       Pub. Co. , 1969.   256p.   Autobiography.

SK   Schweizer Musiker-Lexikon.   Dictionnaire des musi-
       ciens suisses.   Zurich: Atlantis Verlag, 1964.
       421p.   Biographical articles on musicians, com-
       posers and writers on music in Switzerland, in
       alphabetical order.

SL   Scott, Marion M.   "Maddalena Lombardini, Madame
       Syrmen. "   Music and Letters 14 (n. d.), p149-63.
       Biographical essay with a look at her works.

SM   Searle, Humphrey, and Layton, Robert.   Britain,
       Scandinavia and the Netherlands.   Vol. 3 of
       Twentieth Century Composers, ed. by Anna Kal-
       lin and Nicolas Nabokov.   New York: Holt, Rine-
       hart & Winston, 1972.   280p.

SN   Smith, Julia Francis.   Directory of American Women
       Composers with Selected Music for Senior and
       Junior Clubs.   Chicago: National Federation of
       Music Clubs, 1970.   51p.   Alphabetical ordering
       of women composers with their addresses, types
       of works composed and publisher; supplementary
       list of selected music.

SO   Smith, Warren Storey.   "The Songs of Alma Mahler. "
       Chord and Discord 2 (1930), p74-8.

SP   Smyth, Ethel Mary.   As Time Went On.   London:
       Longmans, Green, 1936.   339p.   Autobiographical
       essays.

SQ   _____ .   A Final Burning of the Boats.   London:

Longmans, Green, 1928. 263p. Chapter on Augusta Holmès.

SR   Southeastern Composers League Catalogue. Hatties-
        burg, Miss.: Tritone Press, 1962. Unpaginated.
        Biographical sketches and list of works in alpha-
        betical order (by composer).

SS   Southern, Eileen. The Music of Black Americans: A
        History. New York: W. W. Norton, 1971. 552p.
        Chapter on composers from post-World War I to
        present.

ST   Springer, Hermann; Schneider, Max; and Wolffheim,
        Werner. Miscellanea Musicae Bio-Bibliographica.
        New York: Musurgia, 1947. 435p. Biographies
        at the end of selected people with lists of works
        and their locations.

SU   Stanford, Patric, comp. "Living British Composers
        on Record 1975." Composer 56 (winter 1975/76),
        p19-23. Discography.

SV   Stephenson, Kurt. Clara Schumann. Bonn: Inter
        Nationes, 1969. 83p.

TA   "Tete-A-Tete." The Composer 6 (1975), p33-7. On
        Heidi von Gunden.

TB   Thompson, Oscar, ed. The International Cyclopedia
        of Music and Musicians. 9th ed. New York:
        Dodd, Mead, 1964. 2511p. Cited only when
        Hixon/Hennessee left it out.

TC   Thomson, Virgil. American Music Since 1910. Vol.
        1 of Twentieth Century Composers, ed. by Anna
        Kallin and Nicolas Nabokov. New York: Holt,
        Rinehart & Winston, 1971. 240p. History of
        20th-century American music with 106 American
        composers' biographies.

TD   Tick, Judith. "Tuning Out Women Composers." Wo-
        men: A Journal of Liberation 3 (1972), p61-3.

TE   _____. "Women as Professional Musicians in the
        United States, 1870-1900." Yearbook for the

Inter-American Musical Research 9 (February 1973), p95-133. Covers history of women in the general music area, as instrumentalists, in orchestras, and as composers; contains statistical tables, a large bibliography and a chronology of significant events in the history of American women in composition.

TF   Tracey, James M.   "Some of the World's Greatest Women Pianists; Short, Interesting Biographies of Great Performers from Clara Schumann to the Present Day. " Etude, 1907, p773-4.

TG   Tuthill, Burnet C.   "The Works of Mrs. H. H. A. Beach. " Music Quarterly 26 (1940), p297-310. Includes lists of works by medium, with publisher and date of composition.

UA   Ullrich, Hermann.   "Das Stammbuch der blinden Musikerin Maria Teresa Paradis. " Bonner Geschichtsblatter 15 (1961), p341-84.

UB   Upton, William Treat.   Art-Song in America.   Boston: Oliver Ditson, 1930.   279p.   Analysis of American songs from 1750-1930, by periods.

VA   Valéry, Paul.   "Nadia Boulanger. " La Revue Internationale de Musique 93 (October-November 1938), p607-8.   Talks about how talented she is.

VB   "Violet Archer: Important Commission; Many Hearings of Works. " Pan Pipes of Sigma Alpha Iota, March 1958, p. 29.   Announces world premier of a chamber piece and discusses other works of hers.

WA   Walch-Schumann, Kathe, ed.   Friederich Wieck, Briefe: Aus den Jahren 1830-1838.   Cologne: Arno Volk-Verlag, 1968.   103p.   Letters of the Schumanns; contains biographical sketch of Clara.

WB   Weissmann, John S.   "Current Chronicle: Italy. " Music Quarterly 49 (April 1963), p225-47.   Discusses influence of Palermo on Norma Beecroft and other composers.

WC   Weller, S. "Carla Bley and All Her Jazz." Ms. 4
        (Aug. 1975), p35-7. Biographical essay.

WD   not used

WE   Williams, Ora. American Black Women in the Arts
        and Social Sciences: A Bibliographic Survey. Me-
        tuchen, N.J.: Scarecrow Press, 1973. 141p.
        Bibliographies divided by fields; list of selected
        works accompany composers; table of contents con-
        tains a paging error.

WF   Wilson, John S. "Mary Lou Takes Her Jazz Mass to
        Church." New York Times, February 9, 1975,
        p20. Talks about her career up to writing of the
        mass.

WG   Winer, Linda. "Kenwood High's Little Lady of Music"
        in Lena McLin: 'In This World.' Ed. by General
        Words and Music Co. N.p.: Neil A. Kjos, Jr.,
        1970. 4p. Biographical article.

WH   Winters, Kenneth. "A Composer Who Doesn't Wear
        Music Like a Straitjacket." Canadian Composer
        64 (November 1971), p4-8. On Norma Beecroft.

WI   Wisconsin Federation of Music Clubs. Wisconsin Com-
        posers. Wisconsin: Wisconsin Federation of Mu-
        sic Clubs, 1948. 87p. In two sections: major
        composers whose birth or residence in Wisconsin
        is documented, and minor composers missing
        necessary information.

WJ   Wolfe, Richard J. Secular Music in America 1800-
        1825. New York: New York Public Library, 1964.
        3 vols. Lists songs and piano pieces printed in
        the U.S. between 1801 and 1825 in alphabetical
        order by composer, or title where there is no
        composer, with detailed descriptions of the music,
        and biographical sketches of composers.

WK   Wolff, Konrad. 'Dika Newlin." American Composers
        Alliance Bulletin 10 (December 1962), p1-6. Ex-
        amines her background and musical style, as well
        as several of her compositions; includes a com-
        plete list of her works.

WL   "The Woman Who Inspired Wagner." Musician 8 (1903),
        p332-3.   On Wilhelmine Schroder-Devrient.

WM   "Women Composers: En Route." High Fidelity/Musi-
        cal America, June 1975, MA p21.   Survey of wo-
        men composers in the major North American con-
        servatories; also surveys the major orchestras re-
        garding their performing works by women.

WN   "Women Composers Honored--Commissions--Composi-
        tions Featured in Concert--Women and American
        Song--Concert for International Women's Year."
        Pan Pipes of Sigma Alpha Iota 68 (January 1976),
        p7-8.   Information on various women composers.

WO   "Women in Music/Festival of Northwest Composers."
        Pan Pipes of Sigma Alpha Iota 67 (January 1975),
        p2.   Program presented by North Seattle Commu-
        nity College of women's music.

WP   "Women in the Pit." Newsweek, August 21, 1972,
        p82-3.   Biographical, on composer/conductor
        Margaret Harris.

YA   Young, Percy M.   A History of British Music.   New
        York: W. W. Norton, 1967.   641p.   Covers ori-
        gins of British music through modern times; many
        names given.

YB   Yuhasz, Sister Marie Joy, O. P.   "Black Composers
        and Their Piano Music." American Music Teach-
        er 19 (February/March 1970), p24-6.   Biographi-
        cal sketches of five composers (two women) with
        list of works and publishers' names.

THE HANDBOOK

ABBOTT, Jane. Mrs. Jane Bingham Abbott. fl. 1894,
England. 1 song. EA*

ABRAMS, Harriet. b. 1760, London? d. ca. 1825, London.
soprano. songs. EA* FG* (Henriette) HK p1,
294, 399, 499* HL IC* WJ

ACKLAND, Jeanne Isabel Dorothy. b. Calgary, Alberta,
Can., 20th cent. pianist, organist, violinist. 1
opera, organ, piano. HL KA

ACKLAND, Jessie Agnes. b. Ontario, Can., 20th cent.
pianist, music teacher. songs. HL KA

ADAIEWSKY, Ella see SCHULTZ-ADAIEVSKY, Ella

ADAIR, Mildred. b. ?, Clayton, Ala. d. 1943.
teacher. piano. EK Feb 1932 p84 +pict FO July
1934 p443* +pict

ADAMS, Carrie Belle (Mrs.). nee Wilson. b. July 21,
1859, Oxford, Ohio. d. 1940. organist, educator,
conductor. choral. BE p34 (b. Oxford, Ind.) EG
p258 (b. Oxford, Ind.) EK May 1940 p354 +pict
HB p368-71* +pict IA p7* (b. Terre Haute, Ind.)
ID LF

ADAMS, Mrs. Crosby. nee Juliette Graves. b. 1858,
Niagara Falls, N.Y. d. ? organist, teacher, writer,
pianist, lecturer. piano, songs. AB BE p6* EA*
EK Feb 1932 p84 +pict LF PL SN

---

*An asterisk indicates the given source contains titles of
compositions by the composer; +pict means a portrait is included; +biblio means a bibliography is included.

ADAMS, Elizabeth Kilmer. b. Jan. 8, 1911, Oconto Falls, Wis. piano, organ, songs. WI p3*

AGNESI, Maria Teresa. Mrs. Pinottini. b. Oct. 17, 1720, Milan. d. Jan. 19, 1795, Milan. pianist. choral, orchestra. piano, 4 operas. EG p213-4 HL ST p341

AHLEFELDT, Maria Theresia, Grafin von. (German) (Countess of). b. Feb. 28, 1755, Regensburg, Ger. d. Nov. 4, 1823, Prague. pianist. 1 opera, 1 choral, 1 incidental. EA* EG p168* HL IC*

AKIYOSHI, Toshiko. b. Dec. 12, 1929, Dairen, Manchuria. pianist. songs. AJ p495*

ALDRIDGE, Amanda Ira. pseud., Montague Ring. b. March 16, 1866, Upper Norwood, Eng. d. March 15, 1956. pianist, teacher. songs. CO p314-318

ALEOTTI, Raffaela. b. ca. 1570, Ferrara, Italy. d. (after 1638), Ferrara. organist. songs. BK p29 FG Rafella-Argenta Aleotti HL IC*

ALEOTTI, Vittoria. b. ca. 1575, Ferrara, Italy. d. ? harpsichordist, nun. madrigals, motets. BK p29-30 ("she may have been Raphaela's sister or the same woman using different names for secular publications") EA* EG p64 HL IC*

ALESSANDRA, Catherine. b. Pavia, Italy, 16th cent. d. Pavia. motets. FG HL

ALLARD-DEMERS, Cecile. b. 1904, Canada. d. 1949. music teacher. songs. KA

ALLITSEN, Frances. Mary Frances Bumpus. b. 1849, London. d. Oct. 2, 1912, London. singer. songs, orchestra. EA* EG p148-9, 238* EK Feb 1932 p84 +pict* HL ID LF

ALT, Hansi. b. Feb. 25, 1911, Vienna. teacher, pianist. piano. HD p49* SN

ALTER, Martha A. b. 1904, New Bloomfield, Pa. teacher, pianist. choral, chamber. 2 operas, orchestra. AJ HL SN

ALTMAN, Adella C.   fl. 20th cent. , America.   choral,
    operas, incidental.   AJ   SN

AMALIE, Marie Charlotte.   Duchess of Saxe-Gotha.   fl. 18th
    cent. , Germany.   songs.   EG p155

AMALIE FRIEDERIKE, Marie.   Princess of Saxony.   b. Aug.
    10, 1794, Dresden.   d. Sept. 18, 1870, Dresden.   14
    operas.   EA*   EG p155-6*   HL (Marie A. Fred-
    erike Amalia) (Grove: "Amalie Heiter, penname of
    M. A. Fredericke, Princess of Saxony")   RH* +biblio

AMANN, Josephine.   nee Weinlich.   b. 1848, Vienna.   d. ?
    piano.   EA*

AMERSFOODT-DYCK, Hermine.   b. June 26, 1821, Amster-
    dam.   d. ? 1 choral.   EA*

AMES, Mrs. Henry.   fl. 19th cent. , England.   songs.   EA*

AMES, Marie Mildred.   b. June 20, 1867, England.   cham-
    ber.   HL

ANDERSON, Beth.   b. Jan. 3, 1950, Lexington, Ky.   or-
    ganist, pianist.   1 opera, electronic, mixed media.
    AJ*   GG p11

ANDERSON, Ruth.   b. March 21, 1928, Kalispell, Mont.
    flutist, teacher, author.   choral, vocal, chamber,
    electronic, mixed media.   AJ*   SN

ANDREOZZI, Maria.   Marquise de Bottini.   fl. 19th cent. ,
    Italy.   1 opera, orchestral, songs, choral, piano,
    harp.   EG p214*

ANDREWS, Mrs. Alfred Burritt   see   ETTEN, Jane van

ANDREWS, Mrs. John Holman.   Jenny Constant.   b. 1817,
    England.   d. April 29, 1878, London.   singer, teacher.
    songs, piano.   EA*   HL

ANDREWS, Katherine.   fl. 20th cent. , America.   songs.
    SN

ANDREWS, Virginia.   fl. 20th cent. , America.   piano.   SN

ANDRUS, Helen Josephine.   b. Poughkeepsie, N.Y. , 19th

cent. organist. organ, piano, songs.   BE p34   EA*
EG p207   LF

ANNA AMALIA. Duchess of Saxe-Weimar. b. Oct. 24,
1739, Wolfenbüttel, Germany. d. April 10, 1807,
Weimar. incidental, chamber.   BK p31   EA*
(Amalia Anna) EG p155*   FG*   HC p7-8, 29*   HL
IC*   RH* +biblio

ANNA AMALIA. Princess of Prussia. b. Nov. 9, 1723,
Berlin. d. Sept. 30, 1787, Berlin. clavecinist.
instrumental, choral, chamber, orchestra.   BK p31
EA*   EG p154-5*   FG*   FR*   HC p6-7   HL   RH*
+biblio

ANSPACH (Ansbach), Elizabeth, Margravine of. Mrs. Crav-
en. b. Dec. 17, 1750, London. d. Jan. 13, 1828,
Naples. 2 operas, incidental.   HL   IC*

ANTOINETTE, Marie (same as Marie Antoinette Kingston?).
fl. 19th cent. songs.   EG p114-16 +pict

APPELDOORN, Dina. b. Feb. 26, 1884, Rotterdam. d.
Dec. 4, 1938, The Hague. pianist, teacher. chamber,
orchestra, songs.   HL

APPIANI, Eugenia. fl. 19th cent., Italy. piano.   EA*
EG p216

APPLEDORN, Mary Jeanne van. b. Oct. 2, 1927, Holland,
Mich. teacher. piano.   AJ p449*   HD p49   JA*
(under V)

APPLETON, Adeline Carola. b. Nov. 29, 1886, Waverly,
Iowa. teacher. songs, piano, operas.   BE p34
BF p805   EG p259-60 (Appleton)   HJ p69-70*

AQUA, Eve dell'. fl. 20th cent., Italy. songs, operas.
EA* (under D)   EG p212*, 238

ARAGO, Victoria. fl. 19th cent., France. songs.   EA*

ARBUCKLE, Dorothy Fry. fl. 20th cent., America. songs.
KA   SN

ARCHER, Violet. nee Balestreri. b. April 24, 1913,
Montreal. pianist, teacher. orchestra, piano,

chamber, songs, choral.   CB* + pict.   HL   MA*
+ biblio   PB p7-12* + pict   SN   VB* + pict

ARENA, (Mrs.) Iris Mae.   fl. 20th cent., Louisiana.   pianist, organist.   piano.   PC* pict

ARKWRIGHT, Marian.   b. Jan. 25, 1863, Norwich, England.
d. March 23, 1922, Highclere, England.   chamber,
songs, choral, orchestra, 1 opera.   HL

ARKWRIGHT, Mrs. Robert.   nee Kemble.   b. ?   d. 1849,
England.   actress.   songs.   EA*   HL

ARMSTRONG, Annie.   fl. 19th cent., England.   songs.
EA*

ARNETT, Frieda (Mrs.).   b. Lafayette, Ind., 20th cent.
songs.   IA p46

ARNIM, Bettina von (Mrs.).   nee Elisabeth Brentano.
pseud. Beans Beor.   b. April 4, 1785, Frankfort.
d. Jan. 20, 1859, Berlin.   songs.   EA*   FG   HL
(under B)

ARRIEU, Claude.   b. Nov. 30, 1903, Paris.   pianist.   incidental, songs, chamber, 3 operas.   HL

ASHFORD, Mrs. Emma Louise.   nee Hindle.   b. March 27,
1850, Newark, Del.   d. 1930.   teacher.   choral,
organ, piano.   EK Feb 1932 p84* + pict   FD July
1935 p432* + pict   HB p288-92* + pict   ID   LF

ASPERI, Ursula.   b. 1807, Rome.   d. Sept. 30, 1884,
Rome.   conductor, singer.   operas.   EA*   EG p215
FG*   HL (Orsola Aspri [Asperi] stage name of Ade-
laide Appignani)

ASSANDRA, Caterina.   b. ca. 1580, Italy.   d. ?, Pavia,
It.   vocal.   EA*   EG p65 (Catterina)   HL   IC*

ATHERTON, Grace.   fl. 19th cent., America.   songs.   EA

ATWOOD, Olive.   fl. 20th cent., Wisconsin.   songs.   WI
p78*

AUERNHAMMER, Josepha Barbara   see   AURENHAMMER,
J.

AUGUSTA MARIE LOUISE, Empress. fl. 19th cent. , Ger-
     many. b. 1811. orchestra, songs. EA* EG p155-
     6*

AURENHAMMER, Josepha. Mme. Bosenhonig. b. 1776,
     Vienna. d. 1841, Vienna. pianist. piano. EA
     HL (J. Barbara von Auernhammer, nee Bessenig,
     Sept. 25, 1758-Jan. 30, 1820)

AUS DEM WINKEL, Therese Emile Henrietta see WINKEL,
     Therese Emile Henrietta aus dem

AUS DER OHE, Adele see OHE, Adele aus der

AUSPITZ-KOLAR, Augusta. b. 1843, Prague. d. 1878,
     Vienna. pianist. songs, piano. EA EG p227

AUSTEN, Augusta Amherst. Mrs. T. Anstey Guthrie. b.
     Aug. 2, 1827, London. d. Aug. 5, 1877, Glasgow.
     organist. songs. EA EG p134 HL

AUSTIN, Frances. fl. 20th cent. , America. choral. SN

AUSTIN, Roberta Martin see MARTIN, Roberta

AXTENS, Florence E. b. London, 20th cent. songs, piano.
     HL

AYLWARD, Florence. b. 1862, Sussex, England. d. ?
     songs. BF p805 EA* LF

B. , Countess of. fl. 19th cent. , America. 1 piano. WJ*

BABITS, Linda. b. July 28, 1940, New York, N. Y. or-
     chestra. AJ* AN

BABNIGG, Emma Mampe see MAMPE-BABNIGG, Emma

BACH, Maria. b. March 11, 1896, Vienna. orchestra,
     chamber. HL PJ*

BACHE, Constance. b. March 11, 1846, Edgbaston, Eng-
     land. d. June 28, 1903, Montreux, Switzerland.
     writer. songs. EA EG p240 (Bach) (not as

composer except in appendix)   HL (not as composer)

BACHELLER, Mildred Thomas. b. Jan. 10, 1911, Richmond, Ind. teacher. 1 chamber.   MP*

BACHMANN, Charlotte Christine. nee Stowe. b. Nov. 2,
1757, Berlin. d. Aug. 19, 1817, Berlin. singer, pianist. songs.   FG   HL (Grove: Charlotte [Caroline
Wilhelmine] Bachmann)

BACHMANN, Elise. b. 1838, Naumburg, Germany. d. ?
songs, piano.   EA*   EG p168

BACHMANN, Judith. fl. 18th cent., Vienna. pianist. organ.   EA*   EG p172

BADALLA, Rose Giancinta. fl. 17th cent., Italy. motets.
IC*   RK p150

BAER, Louisa. fl. 19th cent., Germany. songs.   EA

BAGLIONCELLA, Francesca. b. Perugia, Italy, 16th cent.
madrigals.   EA   EG p64

BAHMANN, Marianne E. b. Dec. 1, 1933, Schuylkill
County, Pa. singer, teacher, accompanist. choral,
organ.   AJ*

BAIL, Grace Shattuck. b. Jan. 17, 1898, Cherry Creek,
N.Y. chamber, choral, piano, organ, orchestra.
AJ*

BAIRD, Lorine Chamberlain. fl. 20th cent., America.
songs, piano.   SN

BAKER, Gertrude Tremblay. fl. 20th cent., America.
songs, piano, choral.   SN

BALL, Frances de Villa (Mrs.). b. 1875, Schenevus, N.Y.
pianist, teacher.   LF

BALL, Ida W. (Mrs.). b. 1851, Dallas County, Ala. d. ?
pianist. songs.   EA   MI p703

BALLASEYUS, Virginia. b. March 14, 1893, Hollins, Va.
d. 1969, Calif. author. songs, piano, orchestra.
AJ   AN   SN

BALLOU, Esther Williamson. b. July 17, 1915, Elmira,
    N.Y. d. March 12, 1973, Washington, D.C. teacher.
    orchestra, choral, chamber, organ. AJ   HL   PB
    v9, 1963 p13-8* +pict   PE p320   SD p5   SN

BAMPTON, Ruth. b. March 7, 1902, Boston. choral di-
    rector, organist. choral. AJ   ID   SN

BARBLAN-OPIENSKA, Lydia. b. April 12, 1890, Morges,
    Switzerland. writer. piano, songs. HL   SK*

BARBOUR, Florence Newell (Mrs.). b. Aug. 4, 1867,
    Providence, R.I. d. July 24, 1946, Providence, R.I.
    pianist. piano, songs, choral. AL p154 (Bardour)
    BE p7-8*   EG p270*   EH p390*   EK Mar 1932
    p160 +pict   GG p10   HL (b. 1866)   ID   LF   PL

BARD, Vivien. b. Terre Haute, Ind. , 20th cent. piano.
    IA p7, 46*

BARIL, Jeanne. Soeur M. Louise-Andrée. b. 1913, Prov.
    Quebec, Can. music teacher. piano, choral. KA
    p250

BARIONA, Madelka. fl. 16th cent. , Germany. psalms.
    EA*   EG p66

BARKER, Laura Wilson. Mrs. Tom Taylor. b. 1819,
    Thirkleby, Yorkshire, England. d. 1905, Coleshill,
    England. songs, piano, chamber, choral. EA* (un-
    der Barker and Taylor)   EG p144*   HL

BARKIN, Elaine. b. Dec. 15, 1932, New York, N.Y.
    piano, chamber. AJ*   SN   JA*

BARNARD, Mrs. Charles. née Charlotte Alington. pseud.
    Claribel. b. Dec. 23, 1830, London. d. Jan. 30,
    1869, Dover. songs.   EA   EG p135 (b. 1834)   FQ
    p151*   GF*   HD p50   HL   LF

BARNES, Bertha L. fl. 19th cent. piano.   EA*

BARNES-WOOD, Zilpha. b. Killbuck, Ohio, 19th cent.
    conductor, teacher.   BF p805   LF

BARNETT, Alice. Mrs. George Roy Stevenson. b. May
    26, 1886, Lewiston, Ill. teacher. songs. AJ*

AN*   BE p34*   HL   SN   UB p182, 214-24

BARNETT, Clara Kathleen see ROGERS, Clara Kathleen

BARNETT, Emma. fl. 19th cent. , London. pianist. piano,
     songs.   EA   HL

BARNS, Ethel. b. 1880, London. d. Dec. 31, 1948, Maid-
     enhead, England. violinist. chamber, orchestra.
     EG p145   HL

BARONI, Eleonora. "L'Adrianetta. " b. Dec. 1611, Mantua,
     Italy. d. April 1670, Rome. singer, theorbist, vio-
     lade gambist.   HL (Basile-Baroni, Leonora) (not com-
     poser) (Grove lists her as composer)

BARONI-CAVALCABO, Julie von. b. 1805, Vienna. d. ?
     pianist. piano, songs.   EA*   EG p228-9*   HL

BARRAINE, Elsa. b. Feb. 13, 1910, Paris. orchestra,
     piano, songs, chamber, incidental, 1 opera.   EM*
     +pict   HL (Jacqueline Elsa Barraine)   LH*   PJ*
     +pict   PM*   RO*

BARTALOTTI, Signora. fl. 18th cent. , Italy. 1 orchestra.
     EA*   EG p215*

BARTHELEMON, Cecilia Maria. Mrs. Henslowe. b. 1770?
     d. ? harpsichordist, singer, harpist. songs, harpsi-
     cord.   HL +biblio (not as composer)   IC* (also un-
     der Maria Barthelemon)   ST p167-8*

BARTHELSON, Joyce Holloway. b. May 18, 1908, Yakima,
     Wash. conductor, vocal & ensemble coach. choral,
     operas, orchestral, piano.   AL p25*   AJ*   SN

BARTHOLOMEW, Ann Shepard see MOUNSEY, Ann Shep-
     ard

BARTLETT, Floy Little. b. 1883, Burlington, Iowa. vio-
     linist. songs, choral.   AJ   BE p12*   EG p262
     SN

BASSETT, Karolyn Wells. b. Aug. 2, 1892, Derby, Conn.
     d. June 8, 1931, New York, N.Y. pianist, soprano.
     songs, choral.   AJ (d. June 2)   AN*   HL   SN

BASTIEN, Jane Smisor. b. Hutchinson, Kansas, 20th cent.
author. piano.   PC* +pict   SN

BATES, Anna Craig. fl. 20th cent., America. piano,
songs.   SN

BATTA, Clementine. fl. 19th cent., Germany. 1 song.
EA*   EG p166*

BAUDISSIN, Sophie (Countess). fl. 19th cent., Germany.
pianist. piano.   EA*   EG p171

BAUER, Catharina. b. 1785, Wurzburg, Germany. piano.
EA*

BAUER, Charlotte. fl. 19th cent., Germany. songs, piano.
EA*

BAUER, Emilie Frances. pseud. Francisco di Nogero.
b. March 5, 1865, Walla Walla, Wash. d. March 9,
1926, New York, N.Y. critic, pianist, piano teacher,
editor. songs.   HL

BAUER, Marion Eugenie. b. Aug. 15, 1887, Walla Walla,
Wash. d. Aug. 9, 1955, South Hadley, Mass. teacher, author. orchestra, chamber, songs, choral, incidental.   AJ   AL p153*   BE p19*   CF p523*   EG
p267   EK March 1932 p160 +pict   FP p253*   GG
p11   HL +biblio (Grove: b. Aug. 15, 1897)   HP
p192-3*   HQ p300, 431   ID   PJ   PM*   RM p48
SN   UB p144-45

BAUM, Katherine. fl. 19th cent., Germany. songs.   EA*

BAUMGRAS, Irene see HALE, Mrs. Philip

BAUR, Constance Maud de see MAUD DE BAUR, Constance

BAWR, Alexandrine Sophie, Comtesse de. b. 1776, Stuttgart. d. 1860, Paris. songs.   EA   FG +biblio

BAXTER, Lydia. b. Sept. 2, 1809, Petersburg, N.Y.
d. June 23, 1874, N.Y. hymns.   JG

BAYER, Mlle. A. fl. 18th cent., Austria. songs, piano.
EA

BAYLIS, Lilian Mary. b. May 9, 1874, London. d. Nov.
25, 1937, London. philanthropist, theatre manager.
ID (Grove, not as composer)

BAYON-LOUIS, Mme. fl. 18th cent. , France. clavecinist,
singer. chamber. FG*   HL   IC*

BEACH, Amy Marcy (Cheney). Mrs. Henry Harris Aubrey.
b. Sept. 5, 1867, Henniker, N. H. d. Dec. 28, 1945,
New York, N. Y. pianist. piano, songs, chamber,
choral. AA   AF   AI p11   AL p152*   AM*   AN*
AO p111*   BC   BE p2-3*   BH   BR   BT p32-3*
CF p378*   CM   EA*   EG p195-01, 235-7, 242,
243* + pict   EH p294-05* + pict   EJ Sept 1910 p583-4
EK March 1932 p160 + pict   FA p237-8 + pict   FC
FD Sept 1937 p610* + pict   FM*   FP p342*   GF*
+ pict   GG p10-1   HA p213*   HD p51   HI   HL
HP p10, 16-7*   HQ p163-4, 431   HT p425-32, 433,
519-20   HU p425-32   HV   HW   HX p773, 777-8*
+ pict   ID   JC* + biblio   KE p188-90* + pict   LB
p110, 121, 196-7   LF   MN   MS   PL   RG   RH*
+ biblio   SN   TE p112, 114, 116, 122, 125*   TG*
UB p134-8

BEAN, Mabel. fl. 20th cent. , America. piano, songs.
AJ   SN

BEATON, Isabella. b. May 20, 1870, Grinnell, Iowa. d.
Jan. 19, 1929, Mt. Pleasant, Iowa. 1 opera, songs,
chamber. AJ   BC   BE p8*   EH p397   EK April
1932 p236 + pict   HL   ID   LF   PL

BEATRICE, Mary Victoria Feodore, Princess of Battenberg.
b. 1857. songs. EA*   EG p156

BEAU, Louise Adolpha Le see LE BEAU

BEAUCHEMIN, Marie. Soeur St. -Marie Cecile du Sacre-
Coeur. b. 1892, Prov. Quebec, Can. music teacher.
"Religious works. "   KA p250

BEAUMESNIL, Henriette Adelaide Villard de. b. Aug. 31,
1758, Paris. d. 1813, Paris. singer. 3 operas.
EA* (b. 1738)   EG p187* (b. 1748, d. 1803)   FG   HL
IC*

BEAUMONT, Vivian. fl. 20th cent. , America.   AJ   SN

BECK, Martha. Mrs. G. Howard Carragan. b. Jan. 19,
    1900, Sodaville, Ore. author. piano, chamber, choral.
    AJ* (b. 1902)   AN   HD p51*   SN

BECKER, Ida. fl. 19th cent., Germany. songs.   EA*
    EG p172

BEECROFT, Norma M. nee Marian. b. 1934, Oshawa,
    Ontario, Can. chamber, choral, electronic, orchestra.
    HL   MA* +biblio   PB v17 1971 p33-8* +pict   WB
    p243-4*   WH

BEHNKE, Kate Emil. b. London, 20th cent. lecturer,
    teacher.   BF p805   LF

BEHR, Louise. fl. 19th cent., Germany. songs.   EA*

BEHREND, Jeanne. b. May 11, 1911, Philadelphia. pianist,
    teacher. songs, chamber, choral, orchestra.   AJ*
    FP p253-4*   HL   SN

BELL, Lucille Anderson. fl. 20th cent., America. pianist.
    songs, instrumental.   AJ*   AN   SN

BELLAMY, Marian Meredith. b. March 17, 1927, Wood-
    bury, N.J. chamber, piano.   AJ*

BELLAVANCE, Ginette. b. June 30, 1946, Lévis, Quebec.
    electronic (theatre), film.   MA*

BELLEROSE, Sister Cecilia CSC. b. Nov. 8, 1897, Sun-
    cook, N.H. piano, choral, violin.   AJ*   SN   JA*
    (b. Pembroke, N.H.)

BELLEVILLE-OURY, Emilie (Anna Caroline). (Mrs. An-
    tonio James Oury.) b. June 24, 1808, Landshut,
    Bavaria. d. July 22, 1880, Munich. pianist, arrang-
    er. piano.   EA*   EG p169   FG (says cf. Oury
    but has no such entry)   HL (under Oury, Anna Caro-
    line)   RH +biblio

BELOW-BUTTLAR, Gerda von. b. Nov. 9, 1894, Saleske,
    author. lute songs.   MW

BEMBO, Antonia. b. ca. 1670, Venice. d. ? court mu-
    sician. songs.   BK p30-1   GH p5   HL   RK*
    RM p51

BENDA, Juliana. b. 1752, Potsdam. d. May 9, 1783,
    Berlin. pianist. songs, piano. FG* HL

BENFEY-SCHUPPE, Anna. b. Landeck, Germany, 19th
    cent. incidental, chamber. EA* EG p162*

BENNETT, Wilhelmine. b. June 14, 1933, Carmi, Ill.
    chamber, orchestra, instrumental, songs. AJ* SN

BENOIT, Francine. Germaine van Gool. b. July 30, 1894,
    Perigueux, France. critic. orchestra, chamber,
    songs, piano. HL

BENTLEY, Bernice Benson. b. Jan. 2, 1887, Oskaloosa,
    Iowa. d. April 2, 1971, Claremont, Calif. piano,
    songs. AJ* (Berenice) BE p26*

BERBERIAN, Cathy. b. July 4, 1925, Attleboro, Mass.
    soprano. songs. HL RO

BERCKMAN, Evelyn. b. Oct. 18, 1900, Philadelphia.
    writer. chamber, orchestra. AJ* HL HP p197*

BERESFORD, Florence King. fl. 20th cent., Wisconsin.
    songs. WI p78*

BERNARD, Vincenzia. b. 1840, Krischanovitz, Moravia,
    Germany. d. ? organist, music teacher. EA

BERNARDONE, Anka. penname of Sister Mary Ann Joyce.
    b. Oct. 3, 1937, Champaign, Ill. pianist. choral,
    piano. HD p51-2*

BERNOUILLY, Agnes. b. 1825, Berlin. songs, piano,
    orchestra. EA EG p162

BERRY, Margaret Mary Robinson. b. 1918, Alberta, Can.
    piano, choral, vocal. KA p250

BERTIN, Louise Angelique. b. Feb. 15, 1805, Les Roches,
    France. d. April 26, 1877, Paris. poet, contralto,
    pianist, painter. 3 operas, songs, choral, chamber.
    EA* EG p182, 183 FG HL ID LC RH*
    +biblio RM p47

BERTINI, Natalie. fl. 19th cent., Italy. piano. EA*
    EG p216

BERTINOTTI, Teresa. b. 1780, Savigliano, Italy. d. 1852,
    Bologna, Italy. singer. songs. EA   EG p216   FG
    HL (not as composer)

BERTRAND, Aline. b. 1798, Paris. d. March 13, 1835,
    Paris. harpist. harp. FG*   HL

BEZDEK, Jan. pseud. of Sister John Joseph Bezdek, Julia
    Derleth. b. Aug. 29, 1896, St. Louis, Mo. pianist.
    piano. HD p52*

BIEHLER, Ludmilla. fl. 19th cent., Germany. piano.
    EA*

BIENVENU, Lily. b. 1920, France. 1 saxophone symphony.
    LH*

BIGOT, Mme. Marie (de Morogues). nee Kiene. b. March
    3, 1786, Kolmar, Alsace. d. Sept. 16, 1820, Paris.
    pianist. piano. EA   EG p192   FG*   HL (not as
    composer) (b. Colmar) PF   RH + biblio

BILBRO, Anna Matilde. b. 1880, Tuskegee, Ala. piano.
    operas, incidental. BE p13*   EK April 1932 p236*
    + pict   FD Aug 1932 p499* + pict   ID   LF   SN

BILLINGTON, Elizabeth. b. 1765 (1765 or 1768), London.
    d. Aug. 25, 1818, Venice. soprano. harpsichord.
    FG   GF   HL   IC*

BILLSON, Ada. fl. 20th cent., America. choral. SN

BILTCLIFFE, Florence. b. Yorkshire, England, 20th cent.
    pianist, teacher. piano, choral. HL   KA*

BINDE, Martha. fl. 20th cent., America. choral. SN

BINET, Jocelyne. b. Sept. 27, 1923, East-Angus, P.Q.
    violinist, teacher. orchestra, choral, chamber. HL
    KA*

BINFIELD, Hanna. Elizabeth Anne Binfield. b. 1810,
    Reading, England. d. 1887, Reading, England. or-
    ganist, harpist, teacher. organ, harp. EA (Hannah
    R. Binfield) EG p135*

BISHOP, Dorothy. fl. 20th cent., America. piano, choral.

SN

BISLAND, Margaret Cyrilla. b. Sept. 30, 1839, Brooklyn.
    d. ? pianist. piano. MI p704

BISSET, Elizabeth Anne. b. 1800, London. d. ? harpist.
    chamber. EA* EG p135 HL

BITGOOD, Dr. Roberta. Mrs. J. G. Wiersma. b. Jan. 15,
    1908, New London, Conn. conductor, violist, organist.
    choral, organ, songs. AJ AN* SN

BIXBY, Allene K. (Mrs.). b. ? d. 1947. organist, teach-
    er. songs, piano, choral. EK April 1932 p236 + pict
    ID SN

BLACK, Jennie Prince. b. Oct. 10, 1868, New York, N. Y.
    d. Sept. 20, 1945. songs. AN* EA*

BLAHETKA, Marie Leopoldine. b. Nov. 15, 1811, Gunt-
    ramsdorf, Austria. d. Jan. 12, 1887, Boulogne.
    pianist, teacher, physharmonica player. piano, songs,
    chamber, 1 opera. EA* EG p160-1* FG* GF
    HL

BLAIR, Kathleen. Mrs. J. A. Foster. songs published al-
    so under name Kathleen Blair Clarke. b. San Antonio,
    Texas, 20th cent. d. Louisiana. songs. PC*

BLAKE, Dorothy Gaynor. b. Nov. 21, 1893, St. Joseph,
    Mo. d. ?, Webster Groves, Mo. teacher, pianist.
    piano, songs, 2 operas. AJ BE p24-5* EG p271
    EK April 1932 p236 + pict FD Sept 1935 p557* + pict
    HL ID SN

BLAKE, Myrtle. fl. 20th cent. , America. songs. SN

BLAND, Dora [Dorothea] see JORDAN, Mrs. [pseud.]

BLAND, Maria Theresa. b. 1769, Italy. d. Jan. 15, 1838,
    London. singer. 1 song. Grove (not as composer)
    IC* WJ

BLASIS, Teresa de. b. ? d. 1868, Florence, Italy. piano.
    EA EG p216 FG (Blasis-Virginie)

BLAUHUTH, Jenny. b. 1862, Leipzig. d. ? piano. EA*

BLEY, Carla. née Berg. b. 1938, Oakland, Calif. pianist.
1 opera, orchestra.   AJ*   WC* + pict

BLIESENER, Ada Elizabeth Michelmann. b. Oct. 9, 1909,
Quincy, Ill. piano, chamber, orchestra, songs.   SN
JA*

BLISS, Alice. fl. 20th cent. , America. songs, choral.
SN

BLISS, Mrs. J. Worthington see LINDSAY, Miss M.

BLOCK, Isabelle McKee. b. McKee Settlement, Iowa, 19th
cent. pianist. piano.   BF p805   LF (Bloch)

BLOMFIELD-HOLT, Patricia. b. Sept. 15, 1910, Lindsay,
Ontario. pianist. orchestra, songs, chamber.   HL
KA

BLOOD, Esta. b. March 25, 1933, New York, N.Y. piano
teacher, pianist. chamber, songs.   AJ*

BLOOMFIELD-ZEISLER, Fannie. Mrs. Sigmund Zeissler.
b. July 16, 1863, Bielitz, Austria. d. Aug. 20, 1927,
Chicago. pianist. piano, songs.   BC (under Z)   BR
CI   EA   EH p309*   EK April 1940 p282 (under Z)
GF   HL (under Z) (not as composer)   JC + biblio
LF (under Z)   MI p145-8 + pict

BOCARD, Sister Cecilia Clair. b. 1899, New Albany, Ind.
piano, organ, choral.   IA p10-1*

BOCK, Berta. b. March 15, 1857, Hermannstadt. 1 opera,
songs, choral.   MW

BOCKHOLTZ-FALCONI, Anna. b. 1820, Frankfurt.   d.
1879, Paris. singer, teacher. songs.   EA*   FG*

BOERNER-SANDRINI, Marie. fl. 19th cent. , Germany.
pianist, teacher, singer. songs.   EA*   EG p172

BOESE, Helen. b. 1896, Toronto. pianist, administrator.
choral, songs.   HL

BOESENHOENIG, Josepha. fl. 19th cent. , Vienna. pianist.
piano.   EA

BOLZ, Harriet Hallock (Mrs.). fl. 1975. b. Cleveland.
pianist, teacher, lecturer, author. songs, choral,
chamber, piano. AJ* SN

BOND, Carrie Jacobs (Mrs.). b. Aug. 11, 1862, Janesville,
Wis. d. Dec. 28, 1946, Riverside, Calif. songs,
piano. AL p151* AN* BE p13* EA* EG
p265-6 EK May 1932 p314* +pict FQ p238, 352-3*
(d. Hollywood) GF HL HW ID JB JC
+biblio PJ* PL SN WI p7-8*

BOND, Victoria. b. May 6, 1945, Los Angeles. conductor.
chamber, songs. AJ*

BONDS, Margaret. b. March 3, 1913, Chicago. d. April
26, 1972, Los Angeles. educator, pianist, historian.
piano, songs, orchestra. AJ* AN GG p7, 12*
HE p263-4 LF MK* PD p190-3* +pict SS p474
WE p97-8, 101-3* +biblio YB p24*

BONIS, Melanie, pseud. Mme. Albert Domange. b. Jan.
21, 1858, Paris. d. March 18, 1937, Sarcelles.
chamber, piano, choral. HL

BOORN-COCLET, Henriette van den. b. Jan. 15, 1866,
Liège, Belgium. d. March 6, 1945, Liege. teacher.
orchestra, chamber, songs, piano. HL

BOOZER, Patricia P. b. March 14, 1947, Atlanta. teacher. choral. AJ

BORDEWIJK ROEPMAN, Johanna. b. Aug. 4, 1892, Rotterdam. orchestra, choral. HL

BOREK, Minuetta. b. Calgary, Alberta, Can., 20th cent.
pianist, teacher. orchestra, piano, songs. HL
KA*

BORROFF, Edith. b. Aug. 2, 1925, New York, N.Y.
teacher. chamber, 1 opera. AJ*

BORTON, Alice. fl. 19th cent., England. pianist. choral,
songs, piano. EA* EG p139* HL

BOSMANS, Henriette Hilda. b. Dec. 6, 1895, Amsterdam.
d. July 2, 1952, Amsterdam. pianist. chamber,
songs. HL ID

BOSTELMANN, Ida. b. 1894, Corning, N.Y. piano, songs,
1 opera. BE p25*   EG p272

BOTIANO, Helene von. fl. 19th cent., Germany. musician.
piano. EA

BOTTINI, Marianne A. (Marquise de). b. 1802, Lucca,
Italy. d. 1858, Lucca, Italy. 1 opera, choral, songs,
orchestra. EA*

BOUCHER, Lydia. Soeur Marie Therese. b. Feb. 28,
1890, St. Ambroise de Kildare, Prov. Quebec, Can.
Instrumentalist, teacher, singer. piano, choral, songs.
HL   KA*

BOULANGER, Juliette Nadia. b. Sept. 16, 1877, Paris.
organist, teacher, conductor. 1 opera, piano, orchestra, songs, cello. BC   BT p33   EG p248-9   EK
June 1940 p426   EN +pict   GH p6   HL   RM p48
RO   RP   VA

BOULANGER, Lily (Juliette Marie Olga). b. Aug. 21, 1893,
Paris. d. March 15, 1918, Mezy, Seine-et-Oise.
musician. songs, choral, orchestra, chamber.   AO
p111*   BC   CA*   DD p11-23* +pict   EG p249
FG*   GH p6   HC p25-7* +pict   HL   KC p93* +pict
LE   MX*   PA   PJ*   RH* +biblio   RN   RO*
RM p48, 52   SA p83*

BOURGES, Clementine de. b. ? d. Sept. 30, 1561, Lyons,
France. poet, musician. 1 choral. EA*   EG p66-
7   HL   ID   RM p51*

BOVET, Hermine. b. 1842, Hoxter, Westphalia, Germany.
d. ? author. songs, piano. EA

BOYCE, Ethel Mary. b. Oct. 5, 1863, Chertsey, Surry,
England. d. ? pianist. choral, songs, piano. EA
EG p143, 238*   HL

BOYKIN, Helen. b. Nov. 5, 1904, River Falls, Ala. pianist, teacher. piano. AJ*   SN

BRADLEY, Ruth. b. 1894, New Jersey. d. ? choral,
songs, 1 opera, piano. AJ*   SN

BRAMBILLA, Marietta Cassano D'Adda. b. June 6, 1807,

Cassano, Italy. d. Nov. 6, 1875, Milan. contralto, teacher. songs. EA* EG p216 FG HL (not as composer) RH (under Brambilla, Paolo)

BRANDENSTEIN, Charlotte von. b. 1750, Ludwigsburg, Wurtemberg, Germany. piano. EA FG IC* (Caroline)

BRANDES, Charlotte Wilhelmina Francesca. b. May 21, 1765, Berlin. d. June 13, 1788, Hamburg. musician. songs, piano. EA (b. 1756) FG IC* (Minna Brandes)

BRANDHURST, Elise. fl. 19th cent., Germany. piano, songs. EA*

BRANDT, Dorothea. b. May 1, 1896, Frewsburg, N.Y. teacher. piano, choral. AJ*

BRANHAM, Norma Wood. b. Brazil, Ind., 19th cent. "church music" IA p11*

BRANNING, Grace. b. Oct. 10, 1912, Washington, D.C. piano teacher. 1 opera, chamber, songs, piano. AJ*

BRANNON, Gertrude Legler. b. Muscatine, Iowa, 20th cent. songs. SN

BRANSCOMBE, Gena. Mrs. John F. Tenney. b. Nov. 4, 1881, Ontario, Can. author, conductor, pianist, teacher. orchestra, chamber, choral, songs. AJ AL p58* AN BC BE p13-4* EG p249-51 EH p398* EK May 1932 p314* +pict HL HP p72-3* ID LG PJ* SN

BRAUER, Johanna Elisabeth. b. April 27, 1861, Lahr, Baden, Germany. d. ? teacher, pianist. choral, songs. MW

BRECK, Carrie Ellis. Mrs. Frank A. Breck. b. 1855, Walden, Vermont. d. 1934. songs. AN SN

BRENET, Therese. b. 1935, France. 1 saxophone. LH*

BRES, Dorothy. fl. 20th cent., America. piano. SN

BRESSON, Mlle. see BRISSON, Mlle.

BRIGGS, Cora Skillings. Mrs. George A. Briggs. b. 1859,
South Paris, Maine. d. 1935. organist, teacher.
songs, choral. BE p34* EG p267 EK June 1932
p390* +pict ID LF SN

BRIGGS, Dorothy Bell. b. 1895, St. Louis. choral, piano.
BE p31-2* ID

BRIGHAM, Helena (Mrs.). b. Chicago, 19th cent. songs.
EG p269

BRIGHT, Dora Estella. b. Aug. 16, 1863, Sheffield, England. d. Nov. 16, 1951, Babington, Somerset, England.
teacher, pianist. piano, chamber, songs, orchestra,
3 operas. EA* EG p138-9, 237 GF* HL

BRILLON DE JOUY, Mlle. fl. 18th cent., France. pianist.
piano. EA FG

BRINGUER, Estela. b. June 3, 1931, Argentina (American).
conductor. orchestra, piano, violin, chamber, choral.
AJ SN

BRINKMAN, Minna. b. 1831, Osterwieck, Germany. piano.
BF p805 EA* EG p171 LF

BRISSON, Mlle. b. 1785, Paris. d. ? pianist. harp,
piano, chamber. EA EG p191 LF

BRITAIN, Radie. b. March 17, 1903, Amarillo, Texas.
orchestra, chamber, choral, 2 operas. AJ AN
AL p154* BB HL HP p232* ID PJ* SD p4
SN

BRITTON, Dorothy Guyver. b. 1922, America. chamber.
AJ*

BRIZZI GIORGI, Maria. b. Aug. 7, 1775, Bologna. d.
July 26, 1811, Bologna. organist, pianist. HL

BROADWOOD, Lucy E. b. Aug. 9, 1858, London. d. Aug.
22, 1929, London. editor, folksong collector. songs.
EA* HL

BROCK, Blanche Kerr. b. Feb. 3, 1888, Greenfork, Ind.
d. Jan. 3, 1958, Winowa Lake, Ind. songs. AJ*
AN* SN

BROCKMAN, Jane. b. March 17, 1949, Schenectady, N.Y.
orchestra, piano, chamber.   AJ   WN p7*

BRÖES, Mlle. b. 1791, Amsterdam. d. ?, Paris. pianist.
piano.   EA   EG p216   FG*

BROGUE, Rosalyn. b. Feb. 16, 1919, Chicago. instrumentalist, soprano, artist, poetess, teacher. songs,
chamber, orchestra.   AJ   BB   CK p8-9*   HL
SN

BRONSON, Margaret. fl. 20th cent., America. piano,
choral.   SN

BROOKS, Alice M. fl. 20th cent., America. choral, piano.
SN

BROUK, Joanna. b. Feb. 20, 1949, St. Louis, Mo. radio
announcer. electronic.   AJ*

BROWN, Elizabeth Bouldin. Mrs. J. Stanley Brown. b.
Jan. 11, 1901, Halifax, Va. choral, flute, string,
piano.   AJ   SN

BROWN, Elizabeth Van Ness. b. June 12, 1902, Topeka,
Kan. violinist, organist, choir director, supervisor.
violin, piano, choral.   AJ*

BROWN, Mary Helen. b. ?, Buffalo, N.Y. d. 1937.
songs, choral, operas.   EG p263   EK June 1932
p390 + pict   ID

BROWNE, Augusta. Mrs. Garrett Browne. fl. 19th cent.,
America? songs, choral.   MR

BRUCKEN-FOCK, Emilie von. fl. 19th cent., Germany.
piano, songs.   EA*

BRUCKENTHAL, Bertha von (Baroness). fl. 19th cent.,
Germany. choral, piano.   EA*   EG p166

BRUCKSHAW, Kathleen. b. Jan. 5, 1877, London. d. Oct.
10, 1921, London. pianist. piano.   HL

BRUSH, Ruth J. b. Feb. 7, 1910, Fairfax, Okla. pianist.
organ, violin, choral, piano, orchestra.   AJ*   AN*
SD p5*   SN

BRUSSELS, Iris. fl. 20th cent., America. piano, 1 chamber. AL p155* SN

BUCHANAN, Annabel Morris. b. Oct. 22, 1888, Groesbeck, Texas. folklorist, author, organist. songs, choral. AJ AN* HL HP p276 SN

BUCK, Era Marguerite. b. Manitoulin Island, Ontario, Can., 20th cent. pianist, violinist, organist. choral, songs. HL KA*

BUCKLEY, Beatrice Barron. b. Sarnia, Ontario, Can., 20th cent. singer, pianist, author. songs. HL KA*

BUCKLEY, Caroline Kemper (Mrs.). b. Louisiana, 20th cent. ? songs. PC

BUCKLEY, Dorothy Pike. b. April 26, 1911, Glens Falls, N.Y. teacher. chamber, piano, songs. AJ*

BUCKLEY, Helen Dallam see DALLAM, Helen

BUCKLEY, Olivia (Mrs.) see DUSSEK, Olivia

BÜLOW, Charlotte von. fl. 19th cent., Germany. songs. EA

BUGBEE, L. A. Mrs. Davis. b. ?, America. d. 1917. piano. FD Feb 1934 p132* +pict EK June 1932 p390 +pict* LF

BUGGE, Magda. b. Norway, 19th cent (American). pianist. piano, songs. EA EG p225

BULLARD, Carrie. fl. 20th cent., America. operas. BE p35-6* (Lewis, Carrie Bullard) EG p260 (under L in index)

BUMSTEAD, Gladys (Mrs.). b. ca. 1900, near Macon, Mo. singer. songs. PC*

BURCHELL, H. Louise. b. Sydney, Nova Scotia, Can., 20th cent. organist, choirmaster, teacher. 1 organ, 1 piano, 2 songs, string. HL KA*

BURDE, Jeanette. b. 1799, Vienna. d. ?, Berlin.

teacher. songs. EA*

BURDICK, Elizabeth Tucker. b. Milwaukee, 20th cent.
songs, operas. WI p9*

BUREN, Alicia Van. b. Kentucky, 19th cent. singer, poet.
songs. BE p38* (under V) EA p140* (under V) EG
p206 EK June 1939 p358 +pict

BURKE, Lora Miller. fl. 20th cent., America. songs.
SN

BURKE, Loretto. b. May 23, 1922, Parkersburg, W. Va.
teacher. 1 orchestra, 1 chamber, 2 choral. AJ*

BURROUGHS, Jane Johnson (Mrs.). b. Martinsville, Ill.,
20th cent. teacher. songs, organ, violin. IA p47

BURROWES, Katherine. b. Kingston, Ontario, Can., 19th
cent.? pianist, teacher, author. BF p806 LF

BURT, Virginia M. b. April 28, 1919, Minneapolis.
teacher, organist, choir director. 1 choral. AJ*

BUSH, Grace E. b. April 25, 1884, America. poet,
pianist, lecturer. songs, piano. AJ ID SN

BUTLER, Lois. b. May 25, 1912, Stockdale, Texas. violinist, organist. choral, chamber. AJ* SN

BUTT, Thelma. nee Van Eye. fl. 20th cent., America.
author, publisher. songs. AN* SN

BUTTENSTEIN, Constance von. fl. 19th cent., Germany.
songs, piano, instrumental. EA* EG p163*

BUTTERFIELD, Hattie May. b. ?, America. d. 1969.
choral. SN

BYERS, Roxana. b. San Francisco, 20th cent. pianist.
songs. AJ*

CACCINI, Francesca. "la Cecchina". b. Sept. 18, 1587,
Florence. d. ca. 1640, Lucca. singer, poet. 2

operas, songs.   BK p30   BT p17   EA*   EG p64-
5, 211, 238   HC p4-5, 28*   HL   IC*   RA   RB
RC   RE   RM p50

CADORET, Charlotte. Soeur St. Jean du Sacre Coeur. b.
    Feb. 29, 1908, Newark, N.J. pianist. choral, songs.
    HL

CADY, Harriette. b. N.Y. city, 20th cent. pianist, teach-
    er.   BF p806   LF

CADZOW, Dorothy Forrest. Dorothy Cadzow Hokanson.
    b. Aug. 9, 1916, Edmonton, Alberta, Can. arranger,
    teacher. songs, chamber, piano.   AJ* (under H)
    HL   KA*   SN

CAESAR, Shirley. b. 1939, Durham, N.C. songs.   WE
    p104*

CALDWELL, Mary Elizabeth (Mrs.). b. Aug. 1, 1909, Ta-
    coma Wash. conductor, organist. songs, operas (at
    least 1), choral.   AJ*   AN*   SN

CALEGARI, Cornelia Maria Caterina. b. 1644, Bergamo,
    Italy. d. 1662? singer, organist. motets, madrigals.
    EA*   EG p65-6   FG*   HL

CALVIN, Susan. fl. 20th cent., America. choral.   AJ*

CAMMACK, Amelia. fl. 19th cent., America. piano, songs.
    EA*

CAMPBELL, Aline see MONTGOMERY, Merle

CAMPBELL, Edith Mary. b. Sept. 1, 1912, St. Luc, St.
    Johns County, Prov. Quebec, Can. organist, choral
    conductor. chamber, organ, choral.   HL   KA*

CAMPBELL, Mary Maxwell. b. 1812, Fife, Scotland. d.
    Jan. 15, 1886, St. Andrews, Scotland. songs.   EA*
    HL

CAMPOLIETI, Virginia Mariani see MARIANI

CANAL, Marguerite. b. Jan. 29, 1890, Toulouse, France.
    pianist. piano, violin, cello, songs.   EG p257   HL
    PJ*

CANDEILLE, Emilie (Amélie) Julie. Mrs. Simons. b. July 31, 1767, Paris. d. Feb. 4, 1834, Paris. operatic soprano, actress, poetess. piano, songs, 2 operas. EA* (b. 1766)   EG p187*   FG* (under S)   GF   HL IC*

CANNING, Effie see CROCKETT, Effie I.

CANTELO, Annie. Mrs. Harry Cox. b. 1881, Nottingham, England. piano.   EA (Cantello)   HL   IC*

CAPERTON, Florence Tait. Mrs. G. A. Dornin. b. April 21, 1886, Amherst County, Va. violinist. anthems. AJ*

CAPPIANI, Luisa. fl. 1814. teacher. songs.   EA*

CAPSIR-TANZI, Mercedes. b. July 20, 1895, Barcelona. d. March 13, 1969, Suzzara, Lombardy, Italy. soprano.   HL

CAREW, Lady Henry. fl. 19th cent., England. songs. BF p806   EA*   EG p256   LF

CARISSAN, Celanie. b. Nancy, France, 19th cent. 1 opera, choral, songs, piano.   EA*   EG p186*, 237

CARMICHAEL, Mary Grant. b. 1851, Birkenhead, England. d. March 17, 1935, London. pianist. 1 opera, songs, piano, orchestra.   EA*   EG p141, 237*   GF*   HL LF

CARMON, Helen Bidwell. fl. 20th cent., America. 1 anthem, 1 opera.   SN

CARNO, Zita. fl. 20th cent., America. 1 percussion. AJ*

CAROLINE, Mlle. fl. 18th cent., France. 1 opera.   EA*

CAROLSFELD, Malvina Schnorr von see SCHNORR VON CAROLSFELD, Malvina

CARON-LEGRIS, Albertine. b. Louiseville, Quebec, Can., 20th cent. pianist. piano, songs.   KA*

CARR, Bess Berry. fl. 20th cent., America. choral.   SN

CARREAU, Margaret Stiver (Mrs.). b. Jan. 23, 1899,
Bedford, Pa. organist, pianist. songs, instrumentals. AJ* AN* SN

CARRINGTON-THOMAS, Virginia. b. Oct. 27, 1899, Bristol, Conn. organist, teacher. organ. HL

CARROLL, Barbara. Barbara Coppersmith. b. Jan. 25,
1925, Worcester, Mass. pianist. songs, instrumentals. AN* SN

CARSON, Ruby B. b. Aug. 15, 1892, Cowan, Ind. piano.
IA p13* SN

CARTER, Buenta MacDaniel. b. 1883, Golden City, Mo.
teacher, organist, pianist. piano, orchestra, choral.
BE p24* SN

CARTWRIGHT, Mrs. Robert. fl. 19th cent., England.
songs. EA*

CASADESUS, Regina Patorni. b. 1866, Paris. pianist,
teacher. 1 opera, piano, songs. HL

CASE, Anna. b. Clinton, N.J., 20th cent. singer. songs.
BF p806

CASELLA, Signora. fl. 1865, Italy. 1 opera. EA* EG
p215*

CASSEL, Flora Hamilton (Mrs.). b. 1852, Otterville, Ill.
songs. HB p304-7* + pict

CASSON, Margaret. b. ca. 1775, London? d. ? vocalist,
harpsichordist. songs. EA FQ p263* HL IC*

CASTAGNETTA, Grace. b. June 10, 1912, New York, N.Y.
pianist. piano, songs. ID SN

CASULANA DE MEZARI, Maddalena. "La Casulana". b.
ca. 1540, Brescia, Italy. d. ? madrigals. EA
EG p63-4 FG* HL (under M)

CATALANI, Angelica. b. May 10, 1780, Sinigaglia, Italy.
d. June 12, 1849, Paris. singer. songs. EA*
(b.1783) EG p216 HL (not as composer)

CATO, Jane Dickson. fl. 20th cent. , America. organ.
    SN

CAVENDISH, Georgiana (Spencer) see DEVONSHIRE,
    duchess of

CAWKER, Lenore H. fl. 1900, Wisconsin. songs. WI
    p13*

CECCONI, Monique Gabrielle. b. 1936 ? 1 saxophone.
    LH*

CERRINI DE MONTE-VARCHI, Anna von. b. 1833, Geneva,
    Switzerland. d. ? piano. EA*   EG p230

CEVEE, Alice De see De CEVEE, Alice

CHADBOURNE, Grace see WASSALS, Grace

CHAMBERLAYNE, Miss Edith A. fl. 19th cent. , England.
    songs, orchestral, chamber. EA*   EG p139, 236
    HL

CHAMINADE, Cécile Louise Stéphanie. b. Aug. 8, 1857,
    Paris. d. April 13, 1944, Monte Carlo. published
    under "C. Chaminade". pianist, conductor. orches-
    tra, piano, songs, saxophone, 1 opera. BC   BR
    EA*   EG p174-7, 234, 236, 238, 273   EH p293-4
    EJ July 1929, p511-12* +pict   EK July 1932 p460*
    +pict   FP p100, 366*   FQ p397-8*   GF*   GH p6
    HC p24*   HD p54   HL   HX p769, 770-5*   ID   JE
    LF*   MW*   RH* +biblio   RM p47

CHAMPION, Constance MacLean. b. Independence, Kan. ,
    20th cent. piano, choral, songs. WI p13, 83*

CHANCE, Nancy Laird. b. March 19, 1931, Cincinnati.
    chamber, orchestra, songs. AJ*   CK* (1975)   SN

CHARLOTTE Frédericke Wilhelmine Louise. Princess of
    Saxe-Meiningen. b. June 27, 1831, Berlin. d. March
    30, 1855. songs, piano, orchestra. EA   EG p156

CHARLOTTE, Princess of Saxe-Meiningen. b. July 24,
    1860, Germany. d. ? chamber, orchestra. EA*
    EG p156

CHAZAL, Mrs. Elizabetta de Gambarini. b. 1731, England.
d. ? conductor, soprano, organist. orchestra, piano, violin. EA* EG p133, 246 HL (under de)
IC* (under G.)

CHEATHAM, Kitty. Catherine Smiley Bugg. b. 1864,
Nashville. d. 1946, Greenwich, Conn. singer, author,
lecturer. songs, choral. ID LF TB

CHERTOK, Pearl. b. June 18, 1918, Laconia, N.H. harpist. harp, incidental. AJ SN

CHERUBIM, Sister Mary Schaefer, CSF. b. Jan. 11, 1886,
Slinger, Wis. songs, choral, organ. WI p13-5*

CHESTER, Isabel. fl. 20th cent., Wisconsin. hymns.
WI p15*

CHEVALIER DE MONTREAL, Julia. b. April 20, 1829,
Paris. d. ? poet. FG

CHICKERING, Mrs. C. F. fl. 19th cent., America. songs.
EA*

CHITTENDEN, Kate Sara. b. April 17, 1856, Hamilton,
Ontario, Can. d. Sept. 16, 1949, New York. pianist,
teacher, writer. piano. EA* EK Aug 1932 p532
+pict HL LF PL

CHOQUET, Louise. fl. 19th cent., France. piano. EA*

CHRETIEN-GENARO, Hedwige. fl. 19th cent., France.
teacher, musician. 1 orchestra. EA* EG p189*

CHRIST, Fanny. fl. 19th cent., Germany. zither player.
zither. EA EG p173

CHRISTOPHER, Mary. fl. 20th cent., America. songs.
SN

CIBBINI, Katherina. née Kozeluch. b. 1790, Vienna.
d. 1858, Vienna. pianist. piano. EA EG p205

CINTI-DAMOUREAU, Laura. née Montalant. "Cinti."
b. Feb. 6, 1801, Paris. d. Feb. 25, 1863, Paris.
singer, teacher. songs. EA* FG* GF HL
(under D) (not as composer)

CLAMAN, Dolores Olga. b. 1927, Vancouver, B. C. , Can.
    pianist. 2 orchestra, 1 piano, 1 song.   HL   KA*

CLARIBEL see BARNARD, Mrs. Charles

CLARK, Elizabeth Mary. b. June 5, 1917, Placerville,
    Calif. songs, chamber, orchestra.   HD p54

CLARK, Florence Durell. b. April 29, 1891, Rochester,
    N. Y. pianist, violinist, violist, organist. string,
    organ.   HL   KA*

CLARK, Helen Archibald. b. Philadelphia, 19th cent.
    editor, lecturer. piano, songs.   BE p34   EG p263

CLARK, June Leland. fl. 20th cent. , America. chamber,
    songs.   BE p34* (Jane)   EG p266 (Jane)

CLARK, Mary Gail. b. 1914, Berlin. teacher. piano,
    songs.   EG p269   EK Aug 1932 p532* + pict   ID

CLARK, Ruth Scott. fl. 20th cent. , America. choral,
    songs.   SN

CLARKE, Jane. fl. 1808, England. organist. psalms.
    EG p266

CLARKE, Rebecca. Mrs. James Friskin. b. Aug. 27,
    1886, Harrow, England. violist, violinist. chamber,
    songs.   AJ*   AN*   EG p256-7   HL

CLARKE, Rosemary. b. June 23, 1921, Daytona Beach,
    Fla. pianist. chamber, orchestra, choral, piano,
    organ.   AJ   CK* 1975   JA*   SJ   SR*

CLEMENT, Mary. b. 1861, Stettin, Germany. songs,
    piano.   EA   EG p169

CLOSTRE, Adrienne. b. Oct. 9, 1921, Thomery, France.
    saxophone, chamber, songs.   HL   LH   RO*

COATES, Gloria Kannenberg. b. Oct. 10, 1938, Wausau,
    Wis. critic, music director. songs, piano, chamber.
    AJ*   CK   SN

COATES, Kathleen Kyle. fl. 19th cent. , America. piano.
    EA

COBB, Hazel. b. July 15, 1892, Groesbeck, Tex. d. Sept. 8, 1973, Dallas. teacher. piano, songs, 2 operas. AJ* SN

COCCIA, Maria Rosa. b. Jan. 4, 1759, Rome. d. Nov. 1833, Rome. musician. "church music." EA EG p216 HL ID

COLBRAN, Isabella Angela. Sra. Gioacchino Rossini. b. Feb. 2, 1785, Madrid. d. Oct. 7, 1845, Bologna. singer. songs. EA EG p230 FG HL (d. Castenaso [near Bologna])

COLE, Charlotte. fl. 19th cent., England. teacher, soprano. songs. EA HL

COLE, Elizabeth Shirk (Mrs.). b. June 6, 1859, Peru, Ind. d. Oct. 7, 1927, Peru, Ind. songs. IA p14*

COLE, Ulric. b. Sept. 9, 1905, New York, N.Y. pianist. chamber, piano, orchestra. AJ* BA FP p258* HP p196* ID SN TB p420

COLEMAN, Ellen. b. 1884, ? piano, chamber. EG p267 MX*

COLERIDGE-TAYLOR, Avril Gwendolen. b. March 8, 1903, South Norwood, [near London], England. conductor. orchestra, instrumental, songs. HL

COLLET, Sophia Dobson. b. 1822, London. d. March 27, 1894, Highbury Park, England. songs, choral. EA HL

COLLI, Adelina Muri see MURI-COLLI, Adelina

COLLIN, Helene. fl. 19th cent., France. pianist. piano. EA EG p193

COLLINET, Clara. fl. 19th cent., America. songs. EA*

COLLINS, Laura Sedgwick. fl. 19th cent., America. songs, violin, chamber. BE p34 EA* EG p206 HT p441

COLONNA, Vittoria. duchess of Amalfi and Marchesa of Pescara. b. 1490, Marino, Italy. d. Feb. 25, 1547,

Rome. "church music." HL

CONSTANT, Jenny see Mrs. John Homan ANDREWS

CONTIN, Mme. fl. 19th cent. , Italy. 1 piano.   EA*

CONWAY, Olive. fl. 20th cent. , America. songs, choral.
SN

COOK, Eliza. b. 1818, London. d. ? poetess. songs.
EA

COOK, Rosalind. fl. 20th cent. , America. songs. SN

COOKE, Edith. fl. 19th cent. , England. songs.   EA*
EG p152

COOLIDGE, Elizabeth Sprague (Mrs.). b. Oct. 20, 1864,
Chicago. d. Nov. 4, 1953, Cambridge. patroness,
pianist. songs. EK July 1940 p498   GG p10   HL
MX*   PJ

COOLIDGE, Peggy Stuart. b. Swampscott, Mass. , 20th
cent. conductor, pianist. songs, instrumentals, piano.
AJ   AN*   SN

COOMBS, Mary Woodhull. fl. 19th cent. , America. songs.
EA

COOPER, Esther Sayward. fl. 20th cent. , America.
choral, songs. SN

COOPER, Rose Marie. b. Feb. 21, 1937, Cairo, Ill.
choral, songs.   AJ   AN*   SN

COPLAND, Berniece Rose. b. Lynnville, Iowa, 20th cent.
teacher. piano.   EK July 1940 p498   ID

CORDULA, Sister M. Sister of the Holy Cross. fl. 20th
cent. , Mich. teacher, writer. piano.   IA p28-9*

CORRER, Comtess Ida. b. Padua, Italy, 19th cent. 1
opera.   EA*   EG p215*

CORRI, Sophia. Mme. Dussek. b. May 1, 1775, Edinburgh. d. 1847, London. pianist, harpist, singer.
harp, piano.   EA   HL (under D: "Dussek, S. G.

[Mrs. Jan Ladislav, later Mrs. John Alvis Moralt, born
Corri"]) WJ* (Sophia Guistina Corri Dussek)

CORY, Eleanor. b. Sept. 8, 1943, Englewood, N.J. cham-
    ber. JA*

COSWAY, Mrs. fl. 1790. songs. GG p10

COSWAY, Maria. songs, chamber. IC*

CÔTE, Hélène (Dr.). Soeur Marie-Stéphane. b. Jan. 9,
    1888, St. Barthelemi, Prov. Quebec, Can. pianist,
    writer, administrator. 1 chamber, 1 choral, 1 organ.
    HL   KA*

COTTON-MARSHALL, Grace see MARSCHAL-LOEPKE,
    Grace

COULOMBE-SAINT-MARCOUX, Micheline. b. Aug. 9, 1938,
    Notre Dame-de-la-Doré, Prov. Quebec, Can. teacher.
    electronic, orchestra, chamber, piano. HL   MA*
    +biblio

COULTHARD, Jean. b. Feb. 10, 1908, Vancouver. pianist.
    orchestra, chamber, piano, choral, songs.   BB
    CB* +pict   GH p6-7   HL   MA* +biblio   PB v. 6
    p47-54* +pict   PJ*

COUPER, Mildred. b. Dec. 10, 1887, America. piano,
    orchestra, chamber. SN

COUTURE, Priscilla. fl. 20th cent. , America. choral,
    vocal, orchestra, band. SN

COWLES, Cecil Marion. b. Jan. 14, 1898, San Francisco.
    pianist. piano, songs.   AJ*   BA (not in Hixon)   ID
    (b. 1901)   PJ* (b. 1901)   TB (not in Hixon)

COWLES, Darleen. b. Nov. 13, 1942, Chicago. teacher.
    chamber, choral.   AJ*

COZZOLANI, Chiara Margarita. b. ?, Milan. d. ca. 1653,
    Italy. nun. motets.   EA   EG p65   FG*   HL
    IC

CRANE, Joelle Wallach. b. June 29, 1946, New York,
    N. Y. teacher. chamber, songs, piano.   AJ

CRAVEN, Elizabeth see ANSPACK, Elizabeth

CRAWFORD, Dawn C. b. Dec. 19, 1919, Ellington Field, Texas. teacher, accompanist, music dept. chairman. 1 opera, chamber, songs. AJ* JA*

CRAWFORD, Louise. fl. 20th cent., America. songs, chamber. AJ* SN

CRAWFORD-SEEGER, Ruth Porter (Mrs.). nee Crawford. b. July 3, 1901, East Liverpool, Ohio. d. Nov. 18, 1953, Chevy Chase, Md. author, teacher, folklorist. chamber, songs, piano, choral, flute, orchestra. AJ* AL p155 AO p114* BE p25* CA* FP p259* GA HF* HL HP p240* ID KC p92* +pict PB v2 1956 p36-40* +pict PJ RM p52 SA p83 SN TC p135* WN p7*

CRETI, Mariana. fl. 19th cent., Italy. harpist. harp, chamber. EA* (Mariana de Rocchis Creti) EG p216

CREWS, Lucile. Mrs. Lucile Marsh. b. Aug. 23, 1888, Pueblo, Col. singer, accompanist. chamber, orches-tra, songs, piano, 1 opera. AJ* BF Feb 1930 p92 (under M) HJ p312-3, 271-2 (under M) HL (under M) ID (under M) SN (under M)

CROCKETT, Effie I. pseud. Effie I. Canning. b. 1857, Rockland, Me. d. 1940, Boston. 1 song. FQ p469* SN

CROFTS, Inez. fl. 20th cent., America. choral, vocal, chamber. SN

CROKER, Catherine Munnell. fl. 20th cent., America. songs. SN

CRONENTHAL, Louise Augusta Hänel von. b. June 18, 1839, Naumber, Germany. d. March 9, 1896, Paris. piano, chamber, 1 opera, orchestra. EA* (under H) EG p186* GF* (Julie) HL (under H)

CROWE, Bonita. fl. 20th cent., America. organist, pian-ist. songs, choral, piano, orchestra. ID SN

CROWNINSHIELD, Mary Bradford (Mrs.). fl. 20th cent., America. songs, carols, church music. BE p34*

  EA* EG p266 LF

CURRAN, Pearl Gildersleeve. b. June 25, 1875, Denver.
  d. April 16, 1941, New Rochelle, N. Y. songs, choral.
  AJ* AN* BE p13* EK Oct 1932 p686* + pict
  HL ID SN

CURTIS-BURLIN, Natalie (Mrs. Paul). b. April 26, 1875,
  New York. d. Oct. 23, 1921, Paris. pianist, lecturer,
  Indian music specialist. songs, choral. HL (not as
  composer) HT p571 ID JC + biblio PL SN

CURTRIGHT, Carolee. fl. 20th cent. , America. choral.
  SN

CUTLER, Mary J. fl. 20th cent. , America. choral. SN

CZANYI. pseud. for Mrs. Alois Schmitt. fl. 19th cent. ,
  Germany. songs. EA*

DALE, Kathleen. née Richards. b. June 29, 1895, London.
  pianist, musicologist, teacher, author. songs, piano,
  chamber. HL

DALLAM, Helen. b. Oct. 4?, 1899, Macomb, Ill. author,
  violinist, teacher. orchestra, piano, songs, violin,
  chamber. AJ* AN* BE p26* EK Oct 1932
  p686 + pict ID SN

DAMCKE, Louise. fl. 19th cent. , Germany. piano. EA*

DAMOREAU, Laura Cinthie Montalant see CINTI-
  DAMOUREAU

DANCLA, Alphonsine-Géneviève-Lore. Mme. Deliphard.
  b. June 21, 1824, Bagneres-de-Bigorre, France.
  d. March 22, 1880, Tarbes, France. teacher. piano,
  songs. HL

DANEAU, Suzanne. b. Aug. 17, 1901, Tournal, Belgium.
  pianist. orchestra, chamber, songs. HL (b. Tour-
  nai, France) PJ*

DANIELS, Mabel Wheeler. b. Nov. 27, 1878, Swampscott,

Mass. d. March 10, 1971, Cambridge. music director. orchestra, chamber, choral, 3 operas. AJ*
AL p153*   AN*   BE p19*   EG p246-8   EH p307,
398*   EK Oct 1932 p686 +pict   GG p11   HL   HP
p72*   HT p523-4   ID   LF   PJ*   SN

DANZI, Margarete. née Marchand. b. 1768, Frankfurt/
Main. d. June 11, 1800, Munich. singer. piano.
HL (not as composer)   IC*

DAUNCH, Virginia Obenchain see OBENCHAIN, Virginia

DAVENPORT, Gladys Goertz. b. Oct. 11, 1895, Croyden,
England. violinist. chamber, songs. HL   KA*

DAVIES, Llewela. b. Brecon, South Wales, 19th cent.
pianist. orchestra, chamber, songs.   EA   EG p153*
HL

DAVIS, Miss. fl. 19th cent., England. songs. EA*   HL

DAVIS, Eleanor. fl. 20th cent., America. songs, choral,
organ, piano, harp, cello, chamber. SN

DAVIS, Fay Simmons. d. Feb. 3, 1943, Glen Ridge, N.J.
b. ?, Cambridge. pianist, teacher. anthems.   EK
Oct 1932 p686 +pict   ID

DAVIS, Genevieve. b. Dec. 11, 1889, Falconer, N.Y.
d. Dec. 3, 1950, Plainfield, N.J. singer, pianist.
songs. AJ p498   AN*

DAVIS, Hazel E. b. Feb. 14, 1907, Bucklin, Kan. author,
publisher. sacred songs. AN*   SN

DAVIS, Jean Reynolds (Mrs.). b. Nov. 1, 1927, Cumber-
land, Md. author, pianist, editor, teacher. choral,
2 operas, orchestra, songs. AJ*   AN*   SN

DAVIS, Katherine K. b. June 25, 1892, St. Joseph, Mo.
author, teacher. choral, songs, piano. AJ*   AN*
SN

DAVIS, Margaret. b. July 22, 1908, Spencer, Iowa.
teacher, accompanist, organist, pianist. chamber,
choral, vocal. AJ*   SN

DAVIS, Marianne. Mrs. Gabriel. d. July 18, 1888, Little-more, Oxford, England. songs. EA* HL

DAVIS-BERRYMAN, Alice. fl. 20th cent., America. songs. SN

DAVISON, Martha Taylor. fl. 20th cent., America. piano, choral. SN

DAWSON, Alice E. fl. 20th cent., America. choral. SN

DEACON, Mary Conner. b. Feb. 22, 1907, Johnson City, Tenn. pianist, organist. choral, piano, songs. AJ p498* AN* HL KA*

DECARIE, Reine. Soeur Johane d'Arcie. b. Jan. 4, 1912, Montreal. teacher. songs, choral. HL

De CEVEE, Alice. b. Feb. 25, 1904, Harrisburg, Pa. pianist, teacher. songs, piano, orchestra. AJ* AN* SN

DECKER, Pauline von (Mrs.). nee Schätzell. b. 1812, Berlin. d. ? singer. songs. EA* FG (under S; not as composer)

DEE, Margaret see DIEFENTHALER, Margaret

DEERING, Lady see HARVEY, Mary

De GAMBARINI, Elisabetta see CHAZAL, Mrs.

DEGRAFF, Grace Clark. fl. 20th cent., America. songs. SN

DEICHMANN, Julie. fl. 19th cent. (?), Germany. songs. EA*

DEJAZET, Hermine. fl. 19th cent., France. 1 opera. EA* EG p189

De LARA, Adelina. real name Tilbury. b. Jan. 23, 1872, Carlisle, England. pianist. songs, orchestra. HL

DELAVAL, Mme. fl. 18th cent., France. harpist. choral, harp, songs, chamber. EA* EG p190 IC*

De LEATH, Vaughn. b. 1897, Mt. Pulaski, Ill. singer.
    songs.   BE p26*

DELORME, Isabelle. b. Nov. 14, 1900, Montreal. pianist,
    violinist, teacher. chamber, organ, choral.   HL
    KA*

DEL RIEGO, Teresa Clotilde. Mrs. Leadbetter. b. April
    7, 1876, London. d. Jan. 23, 1968, London. songs.
    EA*   EK Nov 1932 p762* +pict   HL   ID   LF

DE MALLEVILLE, Charlotte Tardien see MALLEVILLE,
    Charlotte Tardien de

DE MANZIARLY, Marcelle see MANZIARLY, Marcelle de

DEMAR, Theresa. b. 1801, Paris. d. ? harpist.   harp,
    songs.   EA   EG p194   FG   IC* (Demars)

DEMARQUEZ, Suzanne. b. July 5, 1899, Paris. d. Oct.
    23, 1965, Paris. pianist, critic, musicologist, teach-
    er. chamber, piano, songs.   HL   PJ* +pict   RO

DEMESSIEUX, Jeanne. b. Feb. 14, 1921, Montpellier,
    France. d. Nov. 11, 1968, Paris. organist, teach-
    er. orchestra, organ, chamber, choral.   HL   PJ*

DENBOW, Stefania Bjornson. b. Dec. 28, 1916, Minneota,
    Minn. teacher, organist. choral, songs, piano, or-
    gan.   AJ*

DE NEUVILLE, Mme. Alphonse see NEUVILLE, Mme.
    Alphonse de

DE PESADORE, Antoinette see PESADORE, Antoinette de

DE POLIGNAC, Armande see POLIGNAC, Armande de

DEPPEN, Jessie L. Mrs. J. D. McLeod. b. July 10,
    1881, Detroit. d. Jan. 22, 1956, Los Angeles. pi-
    anist. songs, piano.   AJ p498   AN*   BE p34*

DERHEIMER, Cecile. d. 1896, Paris. soprano. organ,
    choral.   EA   EG p190

DERING, Lady see HARVEY, Mary

DERLETH, Julia see BEZDEK, Jan

DESPORTES, Yvonne. b. July 18, 1907, Cobourg, France.
    teacher. saxophone, 1 opera, orchestra, chamber,
    songs, incidental.   HL (Y. Bertha Melitta Desporte)
    LH*   MH p163*   PJ* +pict   RO*

DE THEIS SALM-DYCK, Constance Marie see THEIS
    SALM-DYCK, Constance Marie de

DE TRAVENET, Mme. see TRAVENET, Mme. de

DE VILLARD, Nina see VILLARD, Nina de

DEVONSHIRE, Georgiana (Spencer) Cavendish, duchess of.
    b. June 9, 1757. d. March 30, 1806, Piccadilly.
    songs.   HK p56, 319, 417, 522*   IC*   WJ (under
    C)*

DEYO, Ruth Lynda. b. April 20, 1884, Poughkeepsie, N.Y.
    d. March 4, 1960, Cairo, Egypt. pianist. operas.
    AJ*   BB   HL

DEZEDE, Florine. fl. 18th cent. 1 opera.   GJ*

D'HARCOURT, Marguerite Beclard see HARCOURT, Mar-
    guerite Becland d'

D'HARDELOT, Guy see HARDELOT, Guy d'

DIA, Beatrix de. fl. 1160, France?   trobairitz (female
    troubadour). songs.   BK p28

DIAMOND, Arline. b. Jan. 17, 1928, New York. teacher.
    chamber, piano.   AJ*   JA*   SN

DIBDIN, Isabelle Perkins (Mrs.). nee Palmer. b. Jan. 19,
    1828, Southwold, Suffolk, England. d. ? soprano.
    songs.   HL   IC* (Mrs. Dibdin)

DICK, Edith A. fl. 19th cent., England. songs, piano.
    EA*   LF

DICK, Ethel A. fl. 20th cent., England. songs, piano.
    BF p806

DICKSON, Ellen. pseud. Dolores. b. 1819, Woolwich,

England. d. July 4, 1878, Lyndhurst, England. songs.
EA*   EG p135*   HL   LF

DIEFENTHALER, Margaret Kissinger. Margaret Dee. fl.
20th cent. , America. teacher, pianist. songs, piano.
SN   WI p19

DIEMER, Emma Lou. b. Nov. 24, 1927, Kansas City, Mo.
piano, organ, choral, orchestra, opera.   AJ   AN*
CK 1974 p12-3*   HD p56*   JA*   SN

DIETRICH, Amalia. b. 1838, Dresden, Germany. d. ?
pianist. piano, songs.   EA*

DILLER, Angela. b. Aug. 1, 1877, Brooklyn, N.Y. d.
April 30, 1968, Stamford, Conn. pianist, teacher,
writer, editor. songs, piano.   BE p35*   EA*   EG
p271   HL (not as composer)   LF

DILLER, Saralu C. b. June 3, 1930, Ohio. violinist,
(music) director. songs, choral.   AJ*

DILLON, Fannie Charles. b. March 16, 1881, Denver.
d. Feb. 21, 1947, Altadena, Calif. pianist. orchestra, piano, chamber, songs, choral.   AJ   AN*
BE p14*   EG* p270   EK Dec 1932 p877 +pict   HL
ID   SN (Frances)

DI SIRMEN, Maddalena see SIRMEN, Maddalena di

DITTENHAVER, Sarah Louise. b. Dec. 16, 1901, Paulding,
Ohio. d. Feb. 4, 1973, Asheville, N.C. teacher.
piano, choral, songs.   AJ*   SN

DIXON, Esther. fl. 20th cent. , America. songs, choral.
SN

DLUGESZOWSKI, Lucia. b. June 16, 1925, Detroit. pianist, teacher. chamber, songs.   AJ*   HL   JF
SN   TC p139*

DOANE, Dorothy. b. Leesburgh, Ind. , 20th cent. author,
pianist, publisher. songs, instrumentals.   AN*   SN

DODD, Ruth Carrell. b. Cincinnati, 20th cent. songs.
AN*   SN

DODGE, Cynthia. Mrs. Cynthia D. Crawford. fl. 20th
    cent., America. 1 opera.   EG p260   EK June 1933
    p4* +pict   ID

DODGE, May Hewes. fl. 20th cent., Wisconsin. violinist,
    pianist, teacher. operas.   EK June 1933 p4 +pict

DOLAN, Hazel. fl. 20th cent., America. songs, piano.
    SN

DOLBY, Charlotte Helen Sainton see SAINTON-DOLBY,
    Charlotte Helen

DOLLEY, Betty Grace. fl. 20th cent., America. songs,
    piano, choral.   SN

DOMANGE, Madame Albert see BONIS, Melanie

DONAHUE, Bertha Terry. choral.   AJ*

DONALDS, Belle. fl. 19th cent., America. piano, songs.
    EA*

DONALDSON, Elizabeth. fl. 19th cent. instrumental, songs.
    EA*

DONALDSON, Sadie. b. July 2, 1909, New York, N.Y.
    teacher. 1 opera, songs.   AJ*

DORIA, Clara see ROGERS, Clara Kathleen Barnett

DORTCH, Eileen Wier. fl. 20th cent., America. choral,
    songs.   AJ SN

DOUGAN, Vera Warnder. b. July 7, 1898, Chicago. songs,
    piano.   SN WI p79*

DOWNEY, Mary E. b. 1897, St. Paul, Minn. organist.
    choral, organ.   BE p26-7*   EK Dec 1932 p877*
    +pict   ID

DOWNING, Lula Jones. b. Peru, Ind., 20th cent. "musi-
    cal settings."   IA p16*

DRAPER, Mrs. J. T. fl. 19th cent., America. songs.
    EA*

DREIFUSS, Henrietta. fl. 19th cent. , Germany. songs.
EA*

DRENNEN, Dorothy Carter. b. March 21, 1929, Hankinson,
N.D. teacher. trombone, choral. AJ* (D. E.
Drennen) CK*

DRETKE, Leora N. fl. 20th cent. , America (Ohio). choral.
SN

DRIEBURG, Louise von. fl. 18th cent. , Germany. songs.
EA* (von Drieburg)

DROSTE, Doreen (Mrs.). b. May 29, 1907, Tacoma, Wash.
choral. AJ*

DROSTE-HULSHOFF, Annette von. b. Jan. 1, 1797, Kreis
Roxel bei Munster/Westfalen. d. 1848, Meerburg.
artist, poetess. songs, 3 (incomplete) operas. FF
ID SF p32

DRYE, Sarah Lynn. fl. 20th cent. , America. choral.
SN

DRYNAN, Margaret. b. Dec. 10, 1915, Toronto. choral.
HL

DUCELLE, Paul (pseud.) see KROGMAN, Mrs. Carrie W.

DUCHAMBGE, Pauline. née du Montet. b. 1778, Marti-
nique, France. d. April 23, 1858, Paris. pianist,
teacher. songs. EA* EG p193 FG* HL
(Charlotte Antoinette Pauline)

DUDLEY, Marjorie Eastwood. fl. 20th cent. , South Dakota.
chamber, songs, orchestra. AJ p498 SN

DUFFENHORST, Irma Habeck. fl. 20th cent. , America.
piano. WI p20*

DUFFERIN, Lady Helen Selina (Countess of). nee Sheridan.
b. 1807, Ireland. d. June 13, 1867, ? songs. EA*
EG p152 HL

DUGAL, Madaleine. b. June 3, 1926, Chicoutimi, Prov.
Quebec, Can. pianist. piano. HL KA*

DUHAN, Mme. fl. 19th cent., France. writer. instrumental. EA*

DULCKEN, Sophie see LEBRUN, Sophie

DUMESNIL, E. L. see LEHMAN, Evangeline

DUNGAN, Olive. Mrs. Claude Pullen. b. July 19, 1903, Allegheny, Pa. teacher, pianist. piano, songs, organ, choral. AJ* AN* BE p35* SN

DUNLOP, Isobel. Violet Skelton. b. March 4, 1901, Edinburgh. violinist. choral, piano, songs. HL

DUNN, Rebecca Welty. b. Sept. 23, 1890, Guthrie, Okla. author, pianist, arranger. 7 operas, songs, choral. AJ* HN* SN

DU PAGE, Florence. b. Sept. 20, 1910, Vandergrift, Pa. author, pianist, organist. 1 opera, orchestra, chamber. AJ* AN* SN

DUSHKIN, Dorothy. b. July 26, 1903, Chicago. music director. chamber. AJ* SN

DUSSEK, Mme. see CORRI, Sophia

DUSSEK, Olivia. Mrs. Buckley. b. Sept. 29, 1801, London. d. 1847, London. pianist, writer, harpist, organist. songs, harp, piano. EA* (under Buckley; b. 1799) EG p135 FG HL

DUTTON, Theodora. pen name for Blanch Ray Alden. b. ?, Springfield, Mass. d. (Nov. 14), 1934, Northampton, Mass. pianist. chamber, piano. EG p272 EK Jan 1933 p4 + pict FD March 1936 p191* + pict ID LF SN

DUVAL, Mlle. b. ? d. 1769, Paris. singer. 1 orchestra. EA EG p187* FG HL IC*

DU VERGER, Virginie Morel see VERGER, Virginie Morel du

DVORKIN, Judith. b. 1930, New York. pianist. chamber, songs, piano, choral, orchestra, 1 opera. AJ* HD p57 SN

DWIGHT, Catherine McFarland.   fl. 20th cent. , America.
    songs.   SN

EAKIN, Vera O.   b. Aug. 6, 1890, Emlenton, Pa.   pianist,
    organist.   songs.   AJ*   AN* (b. 1900)   SN

EAMES, Juanita.   pseud. Juan Masters.   fl. 20th cent. ,
    America.   pianist, teacher.   instrumentals.   AN*
    SN

EASTES, Helen M.   b. April 21, 1892, Galesburg, Ill.
    author, teacher.   choral, songs, chamber.   AN*
    SN

EATON, Frances.   fl. 19th cent. , England.   1 choral.
    EA*

EBERLIN, Maria Cäcilia Barbara.   b. Nov. 17, 1728, Salz-
    burg.   d. ?   HL

ECKHARDT-GRAMATTE, Sophie Carmen.   née de Frid-
    man-Kotschewskoj.   b. Jan. 6, 1902, Moscow.
    d. Dec. 2, 1974, Stuttgart.   Austrian.   pianist,
    violinist.   orchestra, chamber, piano, violin,
    choral.   HL (since 1939 known as Sonia Friedman-
    Gramatté)   MA* +biblio   MH +pict   PB p51-6
    PJ* +pict

EDWARDS, Clara.   pseud. Bernard Haigh.   b. April
    18, 1887, Mankato, Minn.   d. Jan. 17, 1974,
    New York City.   author, singer.   songs, choral.
    AJ*   AL p154*   AN*   BB   BE p14-5*   EG
    p265   EK March 1933 p148 +pict   HL (b. 1879)
    ID   SN

EDWARDS, Jessie B.   fl. 20th cent. , America.   choral.
    AJ   SN

EGGAR, Katharine Emily.   b. Jan. 5, 1874, London.   pi-
    anist.   chamber, songs.   HL

EGGLESTON, Anne.   b. Sept. 6, 1934, Ottawa, Ontario.
    pianist, teacher.   1 opera, orchestra, chamber, piano,

songs, choral. HL MA*

EICHNER, Maria Adelheid. b. 1762, Mannheim. d. April
5, 1787, Potsdam. pianist. songs. FG (Adelaïde)
GJ (Adelheid Marie; not in Hixon) IC*

EICHORN, Hermene W. b. April 3, 1906, Hickory, N. C.
organist, choirmaster, writer. choral. AJ p498*
SN

EILERS, Joyce Elaine. b. July 28, 1941, Mooreland, Okla.
teacher. choral. AJ*

EISENSTEIN, Stella Prince. b. Feb. 16, 1886, Glasgow,
Mo. d. March 28, 1969, Moberly, Mo. violinist,
teacher. violin, organ, piano, choral. SN

ELLICOTT, Rosalind Frances. b. Nov. 14, 1857, Cambridge, England. d. April 5, 1924, London. pianist.
orchestra, choral, chamber, songs, piano. EA*
EG p140, 237, 239* GF* HL

ELLIOTT, Janice Overmiller. b. Feb. 5, 1921, Atchison,
Kan. songs, piano. JA*

ELLIOTT, Marjorie Reeve (Mrs.). b. Aug. 7, 1890, Syracuse, N. Y. teacher. piano, choral, songs, operas.
AJ SN

ELLIS, Cecil Osik. b. 1884, Chicago. songs, choral.
EK March 1933 p148* + pict ID

ELMORE, Catherine. b. July 4, 1930, Wilson, N. C.
piano. JA*

ELVYN, Myrtle. b. 1886, Sherman, Texas. pianist. piano. GF

EMERY, Dorothy Radde. b. 1901, Cleveland, Ohio. choral,
piano, organ, chamber, songs. BE p33-4* SN

EMERY, Emma Wilson (Mrs.). fl. 20th cent. , Louisiana.
songs. PC*

EMIG, Lois Myers (Mrs.). b. Oct. 12, 1925, Roseville,
Ohio. teacher, organist. choral. AJ* (L. Myer
Emig) SN

ENDRES, Olive. b. Dec. 23, 1898, Johnsberg, Wis. or-
    ganist, teacher. chamber, choral, piano. AJ*   SN
    WI p21-2*

ENGBERG, M. Davenport. b. 1880, Spokane, Wash. vio-
    linist, conductor.   EK March 1933 p148 +pict   ID

ERDMANNSDÖRFER, Pauline. née Fichtner Oprawill.
    b. June 28, 1847, Vienna. d. 1916. pianist. piano,
    songs, chamber.   EA*   EG p168   HL (not as com-
    poser; "born Oprawnik, called Fichtner after her adop-
    tive father")

ERHART (Ehrhardt), Dorothy (Agnes Alice). b. Jan. 5,
    1894, London. d. April 1971, England. harpsichord-
    ist, conductor, writer. piano, choral.   HL

ERNEST, Sister M. fl. 20th cent., America. vocal, in-
    strumental.   SN

ERVIN, Emily L. fl. 20th cent., America. songs.   SN

ESCHBORN, Nina. fl. 19th cent., Germany. harpist.
    harp, songs.   EA*   EG p173

ESCOT, Pozzi. b. Oct. 1, 1933, Lima, Peru. teacher.
    piano, orchestra, chamber, songs.   AJ*   CA   KC
    p93* +pict   ML*   PB p63-9* +pict (b. 1931?)   SA
    p83   WN p7*

ESTABROOK, Miss G. fl. 19th cent., America. songs.
    EA*   EG p206

ETTEN, Jane van. b. St. Paul, Minn., 20th cent. singer.
    opera, songs.   BE p11*   EG p250   HJ p353-5   RG

EVERSOLE, Rose M. fl. 20th cent., America. songs.
    EA

EZELL, Helen Ingle. b. May 18, 1903, Marshall, Okla.
    piano, songs.   AJ*   HD p58*   SN

FABRE, Marie. fl. 19th cent., France. piano.   EA*

FAHRBACH, Henrietta. b. Jan. 22, 1851, Vienna. d. Feb. 24, 1923, Vienna. choral conductor, teacher. songs, piano. EA* HL

FAIRCHILD, Helen. fl. 20th cent., Wisconsin. songs. WI p23*

FAIRLIE, Margaret. b. March 27, 1928, Atlanta, Ga. pianist, teacher, author. chamber, piano. AJ SN SR*

FAISST, Clara Mathilde. b. June 22, 1872, Karlsruhe, Germany. d. Nov. 22, 1948, Karlsruhe. songs. EA* (Faist) HL

FALTIS, Evelyn. b. Feb. 20, 1890, Trautenau, Bohemia. d. May 13, 1937, Vienna. chamber, songs, choral, orchestra. HL

FARE, Florence. fl. 19th cent., England. dances. EA

FARLEY, Marion. fl. 19th cent., America. songs. EA*

FARMER, Emily Bardsley. Mrs. Arthur W. Lambert. fl. 19th cent., England. 1 opera, songs. HL

FARRENC, Jeanne Louise. (Mrs. Jacque-Hippolyte Aristide.) née Dumont. b. May 31, 1804, Paris. d. Sept. 15, 1875, Paris. pianist, teacher. chamber, orchestra, piano. EA* EG p181-2, 236 FG* FO GF* HC HL ND* RH* +biblio

FARRENC, Victorine Louise. (daughter of above.) b. Feb. 23, 1826, Paris. d. Jan. 3, 1859, Paris. pianist. piano, songs. EA EG p182 FG HL

FELDMAN, Joanne E. b. Oct. 19, 1941, New York, N.Y. teacher. piano, songs, choral, chamber. AJ JA* SN

FELSENTHEL, Amalie. b. 1841, Iserlohn, Germany. d. ? piano, songs. EA*

FERGUS-HOYT, Phyllis. b. Chicago, 20th cent. pianist. choral, songs, opera, chamber, piano, violin. BE p20* EK April 1933 p222 +pict ID SN

FERRARI, Carlotta.   b. Jan. 27, 1837, Lodi, Italy.   d.
    Nov. 23, 1907, Bologna.   3 operas, choral, piano,
    songs.   EA*   EG p212-3, 234, 238*   HL   RH*
    +biblio

FERRARI, Mme. Gabriella.   née Colombari de Montegre.
    b. Sept. 14, 1851, Paris.   d. July 4, 1921, Paris.
    pianist.   songs, orchestra, piano, 3 operas.   EA*
    EG p185*   HL   RH* +biblio

FERRIS, Isabel D.   fl. 20th cent. , America.   choral.   SN

FICHTNER, Pauline see ERDMANNSDÖRFER, Pauline

FILIPOWICZ, Elise.   née Mayer.   b. 1794, Rastadt.   d. ?
    chamber.   FG*

FINE, Vivian.   b. Sept. 28, 1913, Chicago.   pianist, teach-
    er.   piano, orchestra, chamber, songs, choral.   AJ*
    FP p261*   HL   ID   PJ*   SN   TC p142-3*

FINK, Emma C.   fl. 20th cent. , Wisconsin.   piano, organ,
    band, chamber.   WI p23-4*

FINLEY, Lorraine Noel.   Mrs. Theodore F. Fitch.   b. Dec.
    24, 1899, Montreal.   D. Feb. 13, 1972, Greenwich,
    Conn.   songs, piano, choral, chamber, violin, orches-
    tra.   AJ*   AN*   SN

FIRESTONE, Idabelle (Mrs.).   b. Nov. 10, 1874, Minnesota
    City, Minn.   d. July 9, 1954, Akron, Ohio.   songs.
    AJ*   AN* (b. July 7)

FISCHER, Edith.   b. Jan. 9, 1922, Portland, Ore.   songs,
    chamber.   AJ   SN

FISHER, Charlotte E. (Carlotta).   fl. 19th cent. , England.
    violinist, pianist, editor.   songs.   HL   KA*

FISHER, Doris.   b. May 2, 1915, New York, N. Y.   author,
    producer, singer.   songs, incidental.   AJ   AN*
    SN

FISHER, Gladys W.   b. May 16, 1900, Klamath Falls, Ore.
    teacher.   songs, piano, organ, choral.   AJ*   SN

FISHER, Katharine Danforth.   fl. 20th cent. , America.

choral.   SN

FISHMAN, Marian.   b. Dec. 7, 1941, Brooklyn.   teacher.
chamber, choral, songs.   AJ*   CK*

FITZGERALD, Sister Florence Therese.   b. Chicago, 20th
cent.   teacher.   choral.   IA p18-9*

FLEMING, Shari Beatrice.   b. St. Johnsbury, Vt. , 20th
cent.   teacher.   1 choral.   AJ p341*

FLICK-FLOOD, Dora.   b. Cleveland, Ohio, 20th cent.
author, pianist, teacher.   piano, songs, choral.   AJ
p499*   AN*   SN

FLORING, Grace Kenny (Mrs.).   b. Tipton, Ind. , 20th cent.
teacher, pianist.   chamber, piano, songs.   IA p48

FLOWER, Eliza.   b. April 19, 1803, Harlow, England.
d. Dec. 12, 1846, London.   poetess.   songs, choral.
EA*   HL

FOLVILLE, Juliette (Eugénie Emilie).   b. Jan. 5, 1870,
Liège, Belgium.   d. Oct. 28, 1946, Dourgne, Tarn,
France.   violinist, teacher, conductor, pianist.   opera,
orchestra, piano, organ, songs, violin.   EA*   EG
p218*   GF*   HL   LF   RH* +biblio (b. Lüttich)

FONTYN, Jacqueline.   Mrs. Schmit.   b. Dec. 27, 1930,
Antwerp, Belgium.   orchestra, chamber, songs.   CD
HL   MH* +pict

FOOT, Phyllis Margaret.   b. Oct. 15, 1914, London.
teacher.   piano.   HL   KA*

FORD, Mrs. Raymond C.   fl. 20th cent. , Wisconsin.
opera, songs.   WI p79

FORMAN, Joanne.   b. June 26, 1934, Chicago.   1 opera,
incidental, chamber, songs.   AJ*

FORMAN, Mrs. R. R.   b. Aug. 1, 1885, Brooklyn.   d. 1947.
piano, songs, choral, operas.   EG p261   EK June
1933 p364 +pict   FD Aug 1933 p558* +pict   ID

FORREST, Sidney see STAIRS, Louise E.

FORSTER, Dorothy. b. Feb. 20, 1884, Carshalton, London.
d. Dec. 25, 1950, England. pianist. songs, piano.
AN*   EK June 3 1933 p364* +pict (born Surrey)   ID

FORSYTH, Josephine. Mrs. P. A. Meyers. b. July 5,
1889, Cleveland, Ohio. d. May 24, 1940, Cleveland,
Ohio. choral. BE p27*   HL   SN

FORTEY, Mary Comber. b. ca. 1860, England. d. ?
pianist. songs. EA*   HL

FORTMAGUE, Baroness de. fl. 19th cent. 1 opera.   EA*
EG p189

FOSSEY, Elizabeth Jarrell. fl. 20th cent. , America. piano,
chamber, songs. SN

FOSTER, Dorothy. b. Wolcottville, Ind. , 20th cent. songs.
EG p265   IA p48

FOSTER, Dorothy. b. Sept. 17, 1930, Melrose, Mass.
teacher. songs, choral. AJ*   LF

FOSTER, Fay. b. Nov. 8, 1886, Leavenworth, Kan. d.
April 17, 1960, Bayport, N. Y. pianist, teacher.
songs, 5 operas, piano. AJ*   AL p154*   AN*
BE p15*   EG p266   EK June 1933 p364* +pict   GG
p11   HL   HT p571   ID   LF   SN

FOWLER, Marje. b. Jan. 8, 1917, New Haven, Conn.
violinist, choir director, teacher. songs. AJ*

FOWLES, Margaret F. b. Ryde, Isle of Wight, England,
19th cent. organist, pianist, conductor. songs,
choral. EA   HL

FOX, Doris H. b. Sept. 9, 1894, Oshkosh, Wis. songs.
WI p24*

FRACKER, Cora Robins. b. Aug. 11, 1849, Iowa City,
Iowa. d. ? guitarist, teacher. guitar, piano.
MI p706

FRANCO, Clare J. fl. 20th cent. , America. 1 piano, 1
vocal, 1 chamber. AJ*   SN

FRANCHERE-DesROSIERS, Rose de. b. Jan. 6, 1863,

Roede Lima, Montreal. d. ? pianist, teacher. piano, songs. HL KA*

FRANCOIS, Emmy von. fl. 19th cent. , Germany. band, piano. EA

FRANK, Jean Forward (Mrs.). b. Aug. 13, 1927, Pitts-burgh, Pa. 2 operas, choral, piano. AJ*

FRANKEL, Gisela. fl. 19th cent. , Germany. choral, piano. EA*

FREEHOFF, Ruth Williams. b. April 9, 1893, Genesee Township, Waukesha County, Wis. choral, songs. SN WI p24*

FREER, Eleanor Warner. nee Everest. b. May 14, 1864, Philadelphia. d. Dec. 13, 1942, Chicago. songs, piano, 10 operas. AL p151-2* AN* BE p8-9* EC* EG p259 EK July 1933 p434* +pict FK FN HJ p183-9* +pict HL HP p73 HT p572 HW ID JD LF PL SN

FRICKER, Anne. Mrs. Mogford. b. 1820, England. d. ? poetess. songs. EA* HL

FROMM-MICHAELS, Ilse. b. Dec. 30, 1888, Hamburg. pianist. orchestra, chamber, piano, songs. HL MH* +pict MW p374 RH* +biblio

FRUGONI, Bertha. fl. 19th cent. , Italy. piano. EA EG p216

FRUMKER, Linda. b. Dec. 11, 1940, Geneva, Ohio. chamber, songs, orchestra. AJ*

FRYXELL, Regina Holmen. b. Nov. 24, 1899, Morganville, Kan. organist, teacher. choral, songs, chamber. AJ SN

FUCHS, Lillian. b. Nov. 18, 1910, New York, N.Y. vio-linist, teacher, violist. chamber, viola. AJ* HL

FULLER, Jeanne Weaver. b. Oct. 23, 1917, Regina, Sask. , Can. teacher. choral, songs, piano. AJ*

GABLER, Jeannette. b. 1820. d. ? pianist. piano, songs.
FG (under Christophe-Auguste Gabler)

GABRIEL, Mary Ann Virginia. Mrs. George E. March.
b. Feb. 7, 1825, Banstead, Surrey. d. Aug. 7, 1877,
London. pianist. operas, choral, songs, piano.
EA*   EG p136   GF*   HL   ID   LF

GAIL, Edmée Sophie (Mrs.). née Garre. b. Aug. 28, 1775,
Paris. d. July 24, 1819, Paris. soprano. 5 operas,
songs, piano.   EA*   EG p187-8*   FG*   GF*   HL
ID   RH* + biblio   SF p20

GALAJIKIAN, Florence (Mrs.). b. July 29, 1900, Maywood,
Ill. pianist, teacher. orchestra, piano, choral,
chamber.   AJ*   AL p154*   BE p27-8*   HL   HP
p230*   ID   SN

GALLENHOFER, Josepha Müller see MÜLLER-GALLEN-
HOFER, Josepha

GALLOIS, Mme. Phillipe. fl. 19th cent. , France. ballets,
songs, piano.   EA   EG p189-90

GALLONI, Adolfa. fl. 19th cent. , Italy. opera, songs,
instrumental.   EA*   EG p215*

GAMBARINI, Elisabetta see CHAZAL, Mrs.

GANNON, Helen C. b. April 13, 1898, Baltimore. pianist, teacher. piano, songs.   HL

GARDNER, Mildred Alvine. b. Oct. 12, 1899, Quincy, Ill.
pianist, teacher. chamber, songs.   AJ*

GARELLI DELLA MOREA, Vincenza. b. Nov. 1859, Valeg-
gio, Pavia, Italy.   HL

GARTENLAUB, Odette. b. 1922, Paris. pianist. piano,
songs.   PJ*

GARWOOD, Margaret. b. March 22, 1927, New Jersey.
pianist, teacher. songs, 2 operas, orchestra.   AJ*
SN

GASCHIN DE ROSENBERG, Fanny (Countess). b. March 9,
1818, Thorn, Germany. d. ? pianist. piano.   EA*

FG*

GASTON, Marjorie Dean.   fl. 20th cent., America.   songs,
    organ, chamber.   SN

GATES, Alice Avery.   fl. 19th cent., America.   songs.
    EA*

GAUTHIEZ, Cecile.   b. March 8, 1873, Paris.   d. ?
    organ, piano, choral, chamber.   BF p806   EG p256-
    7   TB (not in Hixon)

GAY, Addie Seldon.   b. Milwaukee, 20th cent.   piano, songs.
    WI p24-5*

GAY, Marie Sophie.   b. July 1, 1776, Paris.   d. March 5,
    1852, Paris.   pianist.   piano, choral.   EA   EG p190
    FG*

GAYNOR, Jessie Lovel (Mrs.).   née Smith.   b. Feb. 17,
    1863, St. Louis, Mo.   d. Feb. 20, 1921, Webster
    Groves, Mo.   pianist, teacher.   songs, piano, operas.
    AL p151*   BC*   BE p9*   EA*   EG p208   EH
    p307   EK Sept 1933 p568* + pict   FC p355   GF
    HA p216*   HL   HT p441   HU   HX p779*   ID
    LF   PL   SN

GEBUHR, Ann K.   b. May 7, 1945, Des Moines, Iowa.
    teacher.   choral, songs.   AJ*

GEIGER, Constanze.   b. 1836, Vienna.   d. ?   piano, songs,
    instrumental.   EA*   EG p171*   FG*

GENET, Marianne.   b. 1876, Watertown, N.Y.   organist.
    songs, opera, choral.   BE p14*   EG p264   EK
    Sept 1933 p568 + pict   ID   SN

GENLIS, Comtesse de.   Stephanie Felicite Genlis, Marquise
    de Sillery.   b. Jan. 25, 1746, Champcerie, France.
    d. Dec. 31, 1830.   harpist.   harp.   EA   EG p194
    FG* (Stephanie-Felicite Ducrest de Saint-Aubin, Com-
    tesse de Genlis)   HL (not as composer)

GENTEMANN, Sister Mary E.   b. Oct. 4, 1904, Fredericks-
    burg, Texas.   teacher.   choral, piano.   AJ   JA*
    (b. 1909)   SN

GEORGE, Anna E. b. Enterprise, Miss. , 20th cent. pianist.   EK Sept 1933 p568 +pict   ID

GEORGE, Grace (Mrs.). b. Ft. Wayne, Ind. , 20th cent. accompanist.   IA p19*

GEORGE, Lila Gene. b. Sept. 25, 1918, Sioux City, Iowa. choral, organ, chamber, songs.   AJ*   SN

GERE, Florence Parr see PARR-GERE, Florence

GERRISH-JONES, Abbie see JONES, Abbie Gerrish

GESSLER, Caroline. b. March 7, 1908, Indiana, Pa. teacher. choral.   AJ*   SN

GEST, Elizabeth. fl. 20th cent. , America. pianist, teacher, editor, lecturer. songs, piano.   BE p15-6* EG p272   EK Oct 1933 p640 +pict   ID   SN

GHIGLIERI, Sylvia M. b. March 13, 1933, Stockton, Cal. teacher. piano, choral.   AJ*   SN

GIACOMELLI, Geneviève-Sophie Billé. b. ? d. Nov. 11, 1819, Paris. singer. songs.   FG*

GIBSON, Isabella Mary (Mrs. Patrick). née Scott. b. 1786, Edinburgh. d. Nov. 28, 1838, Edinburgh. singer, harpist. songs.   HL

GIDEON, Miriam. b. Oct. 23, 1906, Greeley, Colo. teacher, musicologist. chamber, choral, 1 opera, orchestra, piano, songs.   AJ*   EL p221-3*   FP p264* GH p7   HL   PE*   PJ*   SN

GIGNOUX, Mlle. fl. 19th cent. , France. 1 incidental. EA*   EG p189*

GILBERT, Florence. fl. 19th cent. , England. songs. EG p151, 238*

GILBERT, Pia. b. June 1, 1921, Germany. teacher. incidental, orchestra.   AJ*

GILBERTSON, Virginia M. b. Dec. 2, 1914, Memphis, Tenn. author, pianist, teacher, accompanist. songs. AJ*   AN*   SN

GIPPS, Ruth. b. Feb. 20, 1921, Bexhill-on-Sea, England.
pianist, oboist. choral, orchestra, chamber, songs.
HL   PJ*

GISELA, Sister Mary, SSND. M. G. Hornback. b. Amity,
Ore. , 20th cent. teacher. songs. WI p26*

GIURANNA, Barbara Elena. b. Nov. 18, 1902, Palermo,
Italy. pianist. 2 operas, orchestra, chamber. HL
(Th: Elena Barbara) PJ* + pict

GLANVILLE-HICKS, Peggy. b. Dec. 29, 1912, Melbourne,
Australia. writer, critic, Am. citizen 1948. 4 operas,
chamber, choral, orchestra, songs, incidental.   AG*
+ pict   AJ*   AK   AL p148, 155   EB   EL*   HF*
HL   MX*   PB v. 13 1967 p53-9* + pict   PE p332*
PJ*   SN

GLASER, Victoria M. b. Sept. 11, 1918, Amherst, Mass.
teacher. songs, choral, chamber, orchestra.   AJ*
SN

GLEN, Irma. fl. 20th cent. , America. author, actress,
organist, minister. songs, choral, piano, organ.
AJ*   AN*   SN

GLEN, Katherine A. b. Philadelphia, 20th cent. pianist.
songs.   EK Nov 1933 p728* + pict   ID

GLICKMAN, Sylvia. b. Nov. 8, 1932, New York, N. Y.
teacher, pianist, lecturer. chamber.   AJ*

GLUCK, Hulda. fl. 20th cent. , America. choral.   SN

GLYN, Margaret Henrietta. b. Feb. 28, 1865, Ewell, Surrey, England. d. June 3, 1946, Ewell, Surrey, England. musicologist, organist, author, editor. organ.
HL

GOATLEY, Alma. fl. 20th cent. , France. songs.   EG
p266 (Goatleg)   EK Nov 1933 p728 + pict   ID

GOBER, Belle Baird. b. Bonham, Texas, 20th cent. pianist, teacher. songs, choral.   EK Nov 1933 p728
+ pict   ID

GODDARD, Arabella. b. Jan. 12, 1836, St. Servan, France.

d. April 6, 1922, Boulogne-sur-Mer, France. pianist.
piano. EA (b. nr. St. Malo) EG p146 (b. 1838)
GF   HL

GODWIN, Joscelyn. b. Jan. 16, 1945, Kelmscott, England.
teacher. instrumental, choral. AJ*

GOERRES, Maria Vespermann. fl. 19th cent., Germany.
songs, instrumental. EA*

GOERTZ, Gladys Davenport see DAVENPORT, Gladys

GOETSCHIUS, Marjorie. b. Sept. 23, 1915, Raymond, N.H.
author, pianist, cellist, singer. piano, songs, choral,
chamber. AJ* AN* SN

GOETZE, Auguste. b. Feb. 24, 1840, Weimar, Germany.
d. April 29, 1908, Leipzig. singer, teacher. 3 operas,
songs. EA* EG p167-8* HL (not as composer)

GOLLAHON, Gladys. b. April 8, 1908, Cincinnati. songs.
AJ p500* AN* SN

GOLLENHOFER-MULLER, Josephine. fl. 19th cent., Germany. harpist. harp. EA*

GOLSON, Florence. Mrs. W. W. Bateman. b. Dec. 4,
1891, Fort Deposit, Ala. soprano. songs, chamber,
choral. AJ* EK Nov 1935 p728* +pict ID SN

GOODE, Blanche. b. 1889, Warren, Ind. pianist. songs,
piano. ID p20* LF

GOODEVE, Mrs. Arthur. fl. 19th cent., England. songs.
EA* EG p256 LF

GOODSMITH, Ruth B. b. Sept. 27, 1892, Chicago. teacher. 1 opera, orchestra, piano. AJ*

GOODWIN, Amina Beatrice. Mrs. W. Ingram-Adams.
b. Dec. 5, 1867, Manchester, England. d. March 10,
1942, East Moseley, England. pianist, teacher, author.
piano. EA EG p146 GF HL LF

GOREAU, Laurraine R. fl. 20th cent., America. editor,
playwright, lyricist, author, music publisher. songs.
PC*

GOSSLER, Clara von. fl. 19th cent., Germany. piano, songs. EA

GOTKOVSKY, Ida. b. Aug. 26, 1933, Paris. orchestra. HL (b. Calais)   LH* (b. Aug 8)

GOULD, Elizabeth Davies. b. May 4, 1904, Toledo, Ohio. pianist, teacher. songs, chamber, orchestra, piano, organ, 1 opera, choral.   AJ*   AN* (b. March 4) GH p7   MH* +pict   SN

GOULD, Octavia. fl. 20th cent., Florida. songs, opera, choral.   SN

GRAB, Isabella von. fl. 19th cent., Germany. piano. EA*

GRAEF, Marie Madeleine see KAUTH, Marie Madeleine

GRAF, Grace. fl. 20th cent., Pennsylvania. choral, songs. SN

GRAHAM, Shirley Lola. Mrs. McCanns, Mrs. W. E. B. DuBois. b. Nov. 11, 1904, Evansville, Ind. author. 1 opera, songs, incidental.   GD*   HE p345   HJ p218-20*   ID (b. 1907)   MK* (b. 1906)   WE p105*

GRAMMONT, Mme. de. née Renaud d'Alleu. b. 1790, Paris. d. ? piano, songs.   FG

GRANDVAL, Mme. la Vicomtesse de Marie Felicie Clemence de Reiset. b. Jan. 21, 1830, la Cour du Bois, France. d. Jan. 15, 1907, Paris. songs, choral, chamber, orchestra, 7 operas.   EA*   EG p180-1, 236, 237* GF* (pseud. Tesier, Valgrand, Jasper, Banger and others)   HL (b. Saint-Rémy-des-Monts, Sarthe, France)   HX p771, 775*   LF   RH* +biblio

GRANT, Miki. b. Chicago, 20th cent. singer. songs, musicals.   MK   WE p106*

GRAY, Dorothy. fl. 20th cent., America. choral, songs. SN

GRAY, Louisa. Mrs. Abingdon Compton. fl. 19th cent., England. 1 opera, songs.   EA*   EG p142*   HL

GREEN, Dorothy Haslam. b. 1887, Germany. teacher.
    songs.   KA p251*

GREEN, Edith Noyes see PORTER, Edith Rowena Noyes

GREEN, Elizabeth A. H. fl. 20th cent., America. choral.
    SN

GREENE, Edith. fl. 19th cent., England. 1 symphony,
    "smaller works. " EA*   EG p138

GREENE, Flora. fl. 20th cent., America. choral.   SN

GRETRY, Lucille. b. Dec. 1, 1770, Paris. d. March
    1790, Paris. 2 operas.   EA* (d. 1794)   EG p187
    FG* (d. 1793)   GJ* (Angelique Dorothée Lucie)   HL
    (did not include Grove; b. July 16, 1772, d. Aug 25,
    1790)   IC*

GREVILLE, Ursula. fl. 20th cent. ?, England. soprano,
    editor.   EK Jan 1934 p4 +pict

GRIEBEL, Thekla. fl. 19th cent., Germany. 1 opera.
    EA*   EG p168*

GRIEF, Marjorie. fl. 20th cent., America. vocal, orches-
    tra.   SN

GRIGSBY, Beverly Pinsky. fl. 20th cent., America. elec-
    tronic, chamber, orchestra.   SN

GRIMANI, Maria Margherita. fl. 18th cent., Vienna.
    court musician. choral.   HL

GRIMAUD, Yvette. b. Jan. 29, 1922, Alger, France.
    pianist. electronic.   HL (b. 1920)   PJ* +pict

GRIMES, Doreen. b. Feb. 1, 1932, Weatherford, Texas.
    teacher, music school director. choral, 1 opera,
    chamber, orchestra.   AJ*   SN

GRINDELL, Clara Kyle. b. Grant County, Platteville, Wis.,
    20th cent. 2 operas, 2 songs.   WI p27*

GRISWOLD, Gertrude. fl. 19th cent., America. songs.
    EA*   LF

GRISWOLD, Henrietta Dippman. b. Broad Brook, Conn.,
20th cent. pianist, teacher. piano, songs. EK Jan
1934 p4 +pict ID

GRO, Josephine. fl. 19th cent., America. songs, piano.
EA* EG p210

GROH, B. Jeanie. pseud. B. J. Rosco. fl. 20th cent.,
America. piano, chamber. SN

GROOM, Mrs. née Wilkinson. b. ? d. 1867, England.
singer. songs. EA*

GRÜNBAUM, Therese (Mrs. Johann Christoph). nee Müller.
b. Aug. 24, 1791, Vienna. d. Jan. 30, 1876, Berlin.
soprano. HL

GUBITOSI, Emilia. b. April 4, 1887, Naples. pianist.
2 operas, orchestra, violin, piano, songs. HL (Th:
b. 1889)

GUCHY, Gregoria Karides. fl. 20th cent., America. piano,
vocal, choral, orchestra. SN

GUDAUSKAS, Giedra. b. July 10, 1923, Kaunas, Lithuania.
teacher, accompanist. chamber, songs. AJ*

GUEDON, Mlle. de Presles. fl. 18th cent., France?
songs. BK p31 IC*

GUENIN, Mlle. b. 1791, Amiens, France. d. ? 1 opera.
EA* EG p188*

GUERRE, Elisabeth de la see LA GUERRE, Elisabeth de

GUEST, Jeanne Marie. Mrs. Miles. b. 1769, Bath.
organ, piano. EA* EG p133 IC*

GUIDI, Teresa. fl. 19th cent., Italy. operas. EA*
EG p215

GULDBRANDSEN, Yvonne. b. 1892, Quebec. pianist, singer. songs. HL (different person--Swedish singer
named) KA p251

GULESIAN, Grace Warner (Mrs.). b. May 16, 1884,
Lawrence, Mass. author, pianist, teacher, choral

director.   songs, operas, orchestra, piano.   AJ*
EG p265   ID   SN

GUMMER, Phyllis Mary.   b. March 12, 1919, Kingston,
Ontario.   instrumentalist.   songs, chamber.   HL
KA*

GUNDEN, Heidi Von.   b. April 13, 1940, San Diego, Cal.
teacher.   chamber.   AJ p454*   TA*

GYDE, Margaret.   b. London, 19th cent.   pianist.   piano,
songs, organ, violin.   EA   EG p144   HL

GYRING, Elizabeth.   fl. 20th cent., America.   piano,
choral, chamber, orchestra, organ.   SN

HAAS, Maria Catherina.   b. 1844, Ottweiler, Germany.
d. ?   piano, songs, harmonium.   EA* (Haass)

HABAN, Sister Teresine M.   b. Jan. 15, 1914, Columbus,
Ohio.   teacher, chairman music dept.   chamber,
choral.   AJ*   JA*

HACKLEY, Emma Azalia Smith.   b. June 29, 1867.   d. Dec.
13, 1922.   singer, teacher.   1 song.   DA   GG p12
HE p241-2, 226   JC   WE

HADDEN, Frances.   b. Aug. 24, 1910, Kuling, Kiangsi,
China (American).   author, pianist.   musicals, songs.
AJ* (b. Hankow, China)   AN*

HAGAN, Helen Eugenia.   b. 1895, New Haven, Conn.
organist, pianist.   piano.   HL   WE p107*

HAGUE, Harriet.   b. 1793, England.   d. 1816, England.
pianist.   songs.   HL

HAHN, Sandra Lea.   b. Jan. 5, 1940, Spokane, Wash.
pianist, teacher.   chamber.   AJ*

HAIK-VANTOURA, Suzanne.   b. July 12, 1912, Paris.
orchestra.   LH*

HALE, Irene (Mrs. Philip).   née Baumgras.   pseud. Victor

René. b. Syracuse, N.Y., fl. 19th cent. songs, piano. BE p6* EA* (under Renne and Hale; nee Baungros) EG p209 GF* HT p$\overline{434}$-40 HU p439-40* HV

HALL, Beatrice May. fl. 19th cent., America. piano. EH p398

HALPERN, Stella. b. May 18, 1923, Austria. teacher. chamber. AJ* JA

HAMILTON, Anna Heuermann. b. ca. 1868, Chicago. pianist, teacher. songs. BE p6-7* EK March 1934 p144 +pict ID

HAMMER, Marie von. fl. 19th cent., America. cello, songs. BE p38* (under V) EA* EG p207

HAMMOND, Fanny Reed (Mrs.). b. Springfield, Mass., 20th cent. pianist, teacher. songs, violin. EK March 1934 p144 +pict ID

HANCHETT, Sybil Croly. fl. 20th cent., Wis. opera. WI p80*

HANEL VON CRONENTHAL, Marquise see CRONENTHAL, Marquise Hanel von

HANKS, Sybil Ann. b. March 5, 1908, Madison. saxophone, songs, choral, piano, orchestra. WI p29-30, 83*

HANSON, Fay S. fl. 20th cent., America. brass. SN

HARCOURT, Marguerite Beclard, d' (Mm. Raoul). b. Feb. 24, 1884, Paris. d. Aug. 2, 1964, Paris. folklorist, ethnomusicologist, writer. opera, orchestra, chamber, songs. HL PJ*

HARDELOT, Guy d'. Mrs. W. L. Rhodes. nee Helen Guy. b. 1858, near Boulogne-sur-Mer, France. d. July 7, 1936, London. songs, 1 operetta. BA* EA* EG p149-50, 238 (under D and Rhoades [sic]) EK March 1934 p144 +pict GF* HL (doesn't include BA or TB) BA* LF* TB*

HARDIMAN, Ellena B. b. 1890, Canada. d. 1949. pianist. 1 opera, orchestra, songs. HL KA*

HARKNESS, Rebekah. Mrs. B. H. Dean. b. April 17, 1915, St. Louis, Mo. director ballet company. songs, orchestra. AJ* AN*

HARLAND, Lizzie. fl. 19th cent., England. conductor. choral, piano. EA* EG p143* ID

HARNDEN, Ethel. b. Syracuse, Kan., 20th cent. songs. SD p5*

HARPER, Marjorie. b. St. Paul, Minn., 20th cent. author, pianist. songs, piano, choral. AJ p501 AN* SN

HARRADEN, Beatrice. fl. 19th cent., England. cellist. songs. HL

HARRADEN, R. Ethel. Mrs. Frank Glover. fl. 19th cent., England. 2 operas, songs, choral, violin. EA* EG p141* HL LF*

HARRINGTON, Amber Roobenian. Mrs. W. Clark. b. May 13, 1905, Boston. organist. orchestra, choral, songs. AJ*

HARRIS, Ethel Ramos (Mrs. Chester). b. Aug. 18, 1908, Newport, R.I. author, pianist, singer, lecturer. songs, instrumentals, piano, choral. AJ* AN*

HARRIS, Letitia Radcliffe. b. Germantown, Philadelphia, 20th cent. pianist. songs, piano, chamber. EK May 1934 p272 + pict ID

HARRIS, Margaret R. b. Sept. 15, 1943, Chicago. conductor, pianist. orchestra, songs. MK WE p107* WP

HARRISON, Annie Fortescue. Lady Arthur Hill. b. 1851, England. d. 1944. 2 operas, piano. EA EG p142* FQ p299* HD p61 HL LF*

HARRISON, Pamela. b. 1915, Orpington, Kent, England. songs, chamber. PJ* + pict TB* (not in Hixon)

HARRISON, Susie Frances. pseud. Seranus. b. 1859, Toronto. d. 1935. poetess. songs, piano. KA p251

HARROD, Beth Miller. fl. 20th cent., America. piano, choral, instrumental. SN

HARTER, Louise C. fl. 20th cent., America. songs, piano, choral. SN

HARTLAND, Lizzie. fl. 19th cent., England. accompanist, teacher. songs, choral, piano. HL

HARTLEY, Evaline. fl. 20th cent., America. songs. SN

HARVEY, Mary. Lady Dering. b. Aug. 1629, England. d. 1704, England. songs. GG p5-6* HL (under D)

HASKELL, Doris Burd. fl. 20th cent., Louisiana. violinist, teacher. PC

HAUSENFLUCK, Frances W. fl. 20th cent., America. songs, choral. SN

HAWES, Maria. M. Billington-Hawes. b. April 1816, London. d. April 24, 1886, Ryde, Isle of Wight. contralto. songs. HL

[HAWTHORNE, Alice: pseud. for Septimus Winner, 1827-1902, male; found as female in SN p41]

HAYS, Doris Ernestine. b. Aug. 6, 1941, Memphis, Tenn. teacher, author. mixed media. AJ*

HAYWARD, Mae Shepard. fl. 20th cent., America. piano, chamber, songs. AJ*

HAZEN, Sara. Sally Hazen Evans. b. July 14, 1935, Sarasota, Fla. chamber, piano, choral. AJ*

HEALE, Helene. b. Feb. 14, 1855, London. d. ? pianist, teacher. choral, piano, violin. EA EG p143* HL

HEARDING, Elizabeth. b. Detroit, fl. 20th cent. songs. WI p32*

HECKSCHER, Celeste de Longre. née Massey. b. Feb. 23,

1860, Philadelphia. d. Feb. 18, 1928, Philadelphia.
administrator. songs, piano, 1 opera. BE p3*
EA* EG p254-5 EK May 1934 p272* +pict GG
p10 HJ p225-6 HL ID LF* PL

HEFNER, Leah. fl. 20th cent., America. songs. SN

HEGGE, Mrs. M. H. b. Stoughton, Wis., 20th cent.
choral. WI p32*

HEIDENREICH, Henrietta. fl. 19th cent., Germany. violin.
EA EG p169

HEIMLICH, Florentine. b. Calumet, Mich., 20th cent.
teacher. songs, operas. WI p32*

HEINDRICH-MERTA, Marie. b. 1842, Salzburg. d. ?
piano, songs. EA* (b. 1852) EG p168-9

HEINKE, Ottilie. b. Breslau, Germany, 19th cent. cello,
piano. EA* EG p172

HEINRICH, Adel. b. July 20, 1926, Cleveland. organist,
teacher. choral. AJ*

HEINRICHS, Agnes. b. July 26, 1903, Köln-Deutz. teacher, pianist. piano, songs, choral, chamber. MX
p519

HEINSIUS, Clara. b. 1801, Berlin. d. 1823, Berlin.
songs. EA*

HEITMANN, Mathilde. fl. 19th cent., Germany. songs.
EA*

HELLER, Barbara. b. 1936, Ludwigshafen/Rhein. chamber, songs. MH* +pict

HELLER, Ottilie. fl. 19th cent., Germany. songs, piano.
EA*

HEMINGWAY, Mme. Clara Edwards. fl. 20th cent., Michigan. contralto, teacher, author. songs. EK June
1934 p332 +pict ID

HEMMENT, Marguerite E. b. April 19, 1908, Carlyle, Ill.
songs. AN* SN

HENDERSON, Elizabeth. fl. 20th cent., America. choral, songs. SN

HENDERSON, Rosamon (Mrs. Stanley). b. July 13, 1894, Shellman, Ga. choral. AJ*

HENN, Angelica. b. Pforzheim, Germany, 19th cent. 1 opera, songs, instrumental. EA* EG p166-7

HENSEL, Fanny M. see MENDELSSOHN-HENSEL, Fanny

HERBERT, Dorothy. fl. 20th cent., America. songs, choral, 1 opera. SN

HERITTE-VIARDOT, Louise Pauline Marie see VIARDOT, Louise Pauline Marie

HERMANN, Johanna Müller see MÜLLER HERMANN, Johanna

HERRESHOFF, Constance. fl. 19th cent., ? songs. EG p262*

HERTZ, Hedwig. fl. 19th cent., Germany. choral, songs, piano. EA

HERZOGENBERG, Elizabeth. née von Stockhausen. b. April 13, 1847, Paris. d. Jan. 7, 1892, San Remo, Italy. pianist. piano. EA HL (not as composer)

HEUBERGER, Jenny. b. 1831, Cassel, Germany. d. ? singer, teacher. songs. EA* ("author of songs")

HEYMAN, Katherine Ruth Willoughby. b. 1877 (1877/79), Sacramento. d. Sept. 18, 1944, Sharon, Conn. pianist, writer. songs. BE p35* EG p257 HL LF

HIER, Ethel Glenn. b. June 25, 1889, Cincinnati. d. Jan. 14, 1971, New York City. pianist, teacher. chamber, orchestra, choral, piano. AJ* BE p20* EK July 1934 p392 +pict HL HP p202* ID SN

HIGGINBOTHAM, Irene. Mrs. Moetahar Padellan. pseud. Hart Jones. b. June 11, 1918, Worcester, Mass. pianist. songs, instrumentals. IB

HILDEGARD von Bingen. b. 1098, Böckelheim, Germany.
   d. Sept. 17, 1179, Rupertsberg, near Bingen, Germany.
   poet. church songs. BG* +biblio BT p17* GC*
   +biblio HL KD p17-22 RH +biblio

HILDRETH, Daisy Wood. fl. 20th cent. , America. piano,
   songs. SN

HILER, Charlotte Ailene. b. Jan. 9, 1910, Junction City,
   Kan. d. June 3, 1958, Hohokus, N.J. songs. AN*
   SN

HILL, Mabel Wood see WOOD-HILL, Mabel

HILL, May. fl. 20th cent. , America. songs, piano. SN

HILL, Mildred J. b. June 27, 1859, Louisville. d. June
   5, 1916, Chicago. author, pianist, organist. songs,
   piano. AN* BE p35* EA* EG p209 FQ p267*
   GG p11 ID SN

HILLER, Phyllis. b. Aug. 5, 1927, California. author.
   songs, choral. AN* SN

HINEBAUGH, Bessie. fl. 20th cent. , Pennsylvania. anthems. SN

HINKLE, Daisy Estelle. b. Bloomington, Ind. , 20th cent.
   piano, chamber. IA p48

HINRICHS, Marie. b. 1828, Germany. d. May 5, 1891,
   Halle, Germany. songs. EA* HL

HODGES, Faustina Hasse. b. 182?, New York City. d.
   Feb. 4, 1895, New York City. organist. organ, pi-
   ano, songs. BE p35* EA* EG p207 HL (d. 1896)
   LF (b. 1896)

HOFF, Elizabeth von. née Chamberlaine. fl. 19th cent.
   pianist, organist, teacher. piano. HL

HOFFMANN, Peggy (Mrs. Arnold E.). b. Aug. 25, 1910,
   Delaware, Ohio. organist. choral, organ. AJ*
   SN

HOFFRICHTER, Bertha Chaitkin (Mrs. Maurice J.). b.
   Dec. 8, 1915, Pittsburgh. piano, songs, choral. AJ*

HOKANSON, Dorothy Cadzow see CADZOW, Dorothy

HOKANSON, Margrethe. b. Dec. 19, 1893, Duluth, Minn.
organist, pianist, arranger, educator, conductor.
choral, organ, orchestra. AJ* AN* SN

HOLDEN, Anne Stratton see STRATTON, Anne

HOLLAND, Caroline. fl. 19th cent. , England. conductor.
choral. EA* EG p143* HL

HOLLIS, Ruby Shaw. fl. 20th cent. , Ohio. choral. SN

HOLLWAY, Elizabeth L. fl. 20th cent. , America. songs,
piano. SN

HOLMES, Augusta Mary Anne. pseud. Hermann Zenta.
b. Dec. 16, 1847, Paris. d. Jan. 28, 1903, Paris.
pianist, singer, poetess. orchestra, choral, 4 operas,
songs. BC BT p32 DB p6, 7, 140, 161, 243,
251-8 EA* (b. 1850) EG p178-80, 235, 236, 238*
+pict EJ June 1910, p375-6 +pict EK Aug 1934
p448 +pict GF* GH p6 HL (Pratt: 1849-1903)
HX p775-6, 770* +pict ID LF MZ RH* +biblio
SQ

HOLMES, Mary. fl. 19th cent. , England? author. 1 piano.
EA* HL

HOLST, Agnes Moller. fl. 20th cent. , Pennsylvania.
anthems. SN

HOLST, Imogen Clare. b. April 12, 1907, Richmond, Surrey, England. pianist, teacher. piano. FJ p50
HL

HOLST, Marie Seuel. b. 1877, Hochheim, Wis. pianist,
teacher. piano, songs, choral. AL BE p20-1*
EG p271 (Senel-Holst) ID SN (under S) WI p34-6*

HOLT, Patricia Blomfield. b. Sept. 15, 1910, Lindsay,
Ontario. teacher, pianist. chamber. MA*

HOLTHUSEN, Anita Saunders. b. Milwaukee, 20th cent.
teacher. 1 piano, 1 choral. WI p36*

HOME, Ann see HUNTER, Ann

HOOD, Helen Francis. b. June 28, 1863, Chelsea, Mass.
d. Jan. 22, 1949, Brookline, Mass. teacher. songs,
chamber, violin, choral.   AL p152   BC   BE p4-5*
EA*   EG p207   EH p306-7*   EK Aug 1934 p448
+pict   GF   HL   HT p441   HW   ID   LF   PL

HOPEKIRK, Helen. Mrs. William Wilson. b. May 20,
1856, Edinburgh, Scotland. d. Nov. 19, 1945, Cam-
bridge, Mass. pianist, teacher. piano, songs, violin.
AL p58*   BC   BE p5* (Mrs. Wm. Wilson)   EA*
(English)   EG p204   EH p303, 307-8, 397* +pict (nee
Wilson; Scottish)   EK Sept 1934 p506 +pict   HL   HW
ID   JC* +biblio   LF   PL

HORROCKS, Amy Elsie. b. Feb. 23, 1867, Rio de Grande
de Sul, Brazil. (British) pianist, teacher. chamber,
songs, piano, violin.   EA*   EG p138*, 238   HL
LF*

HORSLEY, Imogene. b. Oct. 31, 1931, Seattle. musicologist, writer. "all types. "   HL (not as composer)
SN

HORTENSE, Eugenie de Beauharnais, Queen of Holland
(French-Dutch). b. April 10, 1783, Paris. d. Oct.
5, 1837, Viry, France. musician. songs.   EA
EG p193   FG   HL (not as composer)

HOTCHKISS, Evelyn Dissmore. fl. 20th cent., America.
songs, opera.   SN

HOUSE, L. Marguerite. b. St. Louis, Mo. , 20th cent.
teacher. 4 operas, choral.   SN   WI p36-7*

HOUSMAN, Rosalie. b. June 25, 1888, San Francisco.
d. Oct. 28, 1949, New York City. pianist, lecturer,
musicologist. songs, choral, piano.   AJ*   EK
Sept 1934 p506 +pict   HL   ID

HOWE, Mary (Mrs. Walter Bruce). b. April 4, 1882,
Richmond, Va. d. Sept. 14, 1964, Washington, D. C.
pianist. orchestra, chamber, choral, songs.   AJ*
AL p152-3*   AN*   BE p28-9*   CF p523*   GG p11
HD p63   HL   HP p193-4*   HQ p300, 443*   ID
MX*   PJ*   SN

HOWELL, Dorothy. b. Feb. 25, 1898, Handsworth, England.

pianist, teacher. orchestra.   EK Sept 1934 p506 + pict
HL   HN*   ID   PJ*

HOY, Bonnie. b. Aug. 27, 1936, Jenkintown, Pa. teacher,
music consultant. chamber, choral.   AJ*

HOYLAND, Janet. fl. 20th cent., America. choral.   SN

HOYT, Marie Mack. b. 1893, Maine. d. 1965. songs,
choral.   SN

HSU, Wen-Ying. b. May 2, 1909, Shanghai, China. U.S.
citizen 1972. teacher. chamber, piano, songs.   AJ*
SN

HUBER, Nanette. fl. 19th cent., Germany. writer. piano.
EA*

HÜBNER see HUEBNER

HUDSON, Mrs. H. B. b. Aug. 15, 1854, Ludlow, Vt.
d. ? soprano, organist, teacher.   EK Oct 1934
p570 + pict

HUDSON, Mary. b. ?, London. d. March 28, 1801, London. organist. hymns.   BF p806 (b. 1801)   EA
HL   LF

HUEBNER, Ilse. b. 1898, Vienna. d. 1969. teacher. piano.   EK Oct 1934 p570 + pict   ID
SN

HUGHES, Mother Martina. b. Sept. 2, 1902, Hibbing,
Minn. head of music department. choral, chamber.
AJ*   SN

HUGHEY, Evangeline Hart. fl. 20th cent., America.
songs, choral.   SN

HULL, Anne. b. Jan. 25, 1888, Brookland, Pa. pianist.
songs, piano.   AJ*   HD p63   SN

HUNDT, Aline. b. 1849, Germany. d. 1873. conductor.
choral, songs, piano.   EA*   EG p162-3, 236*

HUNKINS, Eusebia Simpson. b. June 20, 1902, Troy, Ohio.
author, teacher. choral, operas, chamber, incidental.

AJ*   AN*   SN

HUNTER, Alberta. b. April 1, 1897, Memphis, Tenn.
    author, singer. songs.   AN*   SN   WE p109*

HUNTER, Anne (Mrs. John). née Home. b. 1742, Green-
    law, England. d. 1821, London. poetess. songs.
    EA*   HL (b. Scotland; d. Scotland)   IC*

HUNTER, Hortense Scott see SCOTT-HUNTER, Hortense

HUTCHINS, Helene Owen. fl. 20th cent., America. songs.
    SN

HYDE, Georgina Colvin. b. Fond du Lac, Wis., 20th cent.
    teacher, organist. songs.   WI p37*

HYE, Louise Geneviève la see LA HYE, Louise Geneviève

HYTREK, Sister M. Theophane, O.S.T. b. Feb. 28, 1915,
    Stuart, Neb. teacher, organist. chamber, choral,
    songs, piano, organ, orchestra.   AJ*   JA*   SN
    WI p73*

INVERARITY, Eliza. Mrs. Charles Martyn. b. March 23,
    1813, Edinburgh. d. Dec. 27, 1846, Newcastle-on-
    Tyne, England. soprano. songs.   EA   HL

IRWIN, Florence J. fl. 20th cent., America. songs.   SN

IRWIN, Lois. b. July 29, 1926, Westmont, Ill. author,
    pianist, singer. songs.   AN*   SN

ISABELLA, Leonarda. b. ca. 1620, Novara, Italy. d. ca.
    April 1700, Novara, Italy. songs, instrumental.
    BK p30   EA (b. 1641; Leonardo)   HL   JC*

IVEY, Jean Eichelberger. b. July 3, 1923, Washington,
    D.C. pianist, director Electronic Studio, writer.
    orchestra, choral, piano, electronic, chamber, mixed
    media, instrumental.   AJ*   CK*   JA*   PC* +biblio
    PE p337*   SD p5   SN   SR*

JACKSON, Mary. fl. 20th cent., Pennsylvania. songs, choral. SN

JACOB-LOEWENSON, Alice. German-Israeli. musicologist, pianist. ID

JACOBUS, Dale Asher. fl. 20th cent., America. songs, choral, operas. SN

JACQUES, Charlotte. fl. 19th cent., France. pianist. 1 operetta. EA* EG p189*

JAELL, Mme. Marie (Mrs. Alfred). née Trautermann. b. Aug. 17, 1846, Steinseltz, Alsace, France. d. Feb. 7, 1925, Paris. pianist, teacher. piano. EA* EG p191 HL

JAMBOR, Agi. b. Feb. 4, 1909, Budapest, Hungary. U.S. citizen 1954. pianist, teacher. piano. AJ*

JAMES, Dorothy. b. Dec. 1, 1901, Chicago. teacher. orchestra, piano, chamber, organ, songs, choral, 1 opera. AJ* HL ID MP* PJ* SN

JAPHA, Louise. Mrs. Langhans. b. Feb. 2, 1826, Hamburg. d. Oct. 13, 1910, Wiesbaden. pianist. opera, chamber, piano, songs, choral. EA EG p166 GF HL

JAQUE, Rhene, pseud. née Marguerite Cartier; Sister Jacques-René. b. Feb. 4, 1918, Beauharnois, Quebec, Can. teacher. songs, chamber, violin, piano. HL MA*

JENKINS, Ella. b. Aug. 6, 1924, St. Louis, Mo. author, singer. songs. AN* SN

JENKINS, Lora W. b. ca. 1870, America. d. 1947. teacher. ID

JENKS, Maud E. fl. 19th cent., America? songs, piano. EA

JENNINGS, Marie. fl. 20th cent., America. violin, songs, choral. SN

JESSYE, Eva. b. Jan. 20, 1895, Coffeyville, Kan. teacher,

conductor, arranger. choral.   AJ*   AN*   NE
WE p109-10*

JEWELL, Althea Grant.   fl. 19th cent., America.   songs.
EA*

JEWELL, Lucina.   b. 1874, Chelsea, Mass.   songs.   BE
p11*   EA*   EG p207

JEWITT, Jesse Mae.   b. Oberlin, Ohio, 20th cent.   organist, pianist.   songs.   EK Dec 1934 p698* +pict   ID

JOHNSON, Clair W.   saxophone.   LH*

JOLAS, Betsy.   b. Aug. 5, 1926, Paris.   editor, writer.
choral, chamber.   AO p111, 114*   BQ p65*   CG
HL   MM   RO*

JOLLEY, Florence Werner.   b. July 11, 1917, Kingsburg,
Cal.   teacher, author.   choral, chamber.   AJ*   AN*
JA (b. 1927)   SN

JONES, Abbie Gerrish.   b. 1863, Vallejo, Cal.   d. 1929.
writer, critic.   7 operas, piano.   BE p9-10* (under
G)   EG p257   EK Oct 1933 p640 +pict   HJ p242-7
ID   JD

JONES, Dovie Osborn.   b. near Corydon, Ind., 20th cent.
songs, piano.   IA p22*

JONES, Hart see HIGGINBOTHAM, Irene

JONES, Sister Ida, O.S.U.   b. Aug. 9, 1898, Louisville.
teacher, chairman music department.   choral.   AJ*

JONES, Martha K.   fl. 20th cent., America.   choral.   SN

JORDAN, Mrs. (pseud.).   Dora or Dorothea Bland.   b.
1762, near Waterford, England.   d. July 3, 1816, St.
Cloud, near Paris.   actress, singer.   songs.   EA*
EG p136*   HL (Jordan, Dora, née Bland)   IC*   WJ*

JORDAN, Alice (Mrs. Frank B.).   b. Dec. 31, 1916,
Davenport, Iowa.   choral.   AJ*   SN

JORGENSON, Nora.   fl. 20th cent., America.   songs,
chamber.   SN

JOY, Margaret E. fl. 20th cent., America. 1 opera. SN

JOYCE, Florence Buckingham. fl. 19th cent., America. songs. EA*

KAINERSTORFER, Clotilde. fl. 19th cent., Germany. organ, choral. EA* EG p172

KALKHÖF, Laura von. fl. 19th cent., Germany. piano. EA

KAMIEN, Anna. b. Jan. 29, 1912, New York, N.Y. choral conductor. choral, songs, chamber, 1 opera. AJ* SN

KANZLER, Josephine. b. 1780, Tolz, Germany. d. ? pianist. chamber, piano, songs. EA EG p165-6

KATWIJK, Viola Edna Beck Van (Mrs. Paul). b. Feb. 26, 1894, Denison, Texas. pianist, teacher. piano, songs. AJ p449* SN (under V)

KAUTH, Maria Magdalena. née Graeff. b. Berlin, 18th cent. pianist. songs, piano. EA FG* IC*

KAVASCH, Deborah. b. July 15, 1949, Washington, D.C. lecturer. 1 opera, 2 chamber, 2 choral. AJ*

KAYDEN, Mildred. b. New York City, 20th cent. teacher, radio programmer. songs, piano, chamber, choral, incidental. AJ* AN* SN

KECK, Pearl. fl. 20th cent., Pennsylvania. choral. SN

KEETMAN, Gunild. b. June 5, 1904, Elberfeld, Prussia. German teacher. songs, flute. HL

KEIG, Betty. fl. 20th cent., America. songs, piano. SN

KELLER, Ginette. b. May 16, 1925, Asnières, France. chamber, orchestra. HL RO*

KELLEY, Florence Bettray. b. Racine, Wis., 20th cent. teacher. piano. WI p39-40*

KEMBLE, Adelaide. Mrs. Sartoris. b. 1814, England.
    d. 1879. songs. EA

KENDRICK, Virginia (Mrs. W. Dudley). b. April 8, 1910,
    Minneapolis, Minn. pianist, organist, organ music
    consultant. choral, songs. AJ* SN

KENT, Ada Twohy (Mrs. W. G.). b. Feb. 8, 1888, Denver.
    pianist, organist. songs. HL KA*

KERCADO, Mlle. Le Senechal de. fl. 18th cent., France.
    1 opera. EA* EG p187*

KERN, Louise. fl. 19th cent., Germany. chamber. EA*
    EG p166

KERR, Mrs. Alexander. Louisa Hay. fl. 19th cent., Eng-
    land. author. songs. EK HL

KERR, Bessie Maude. b. June 4, 1888, Toronto. pianist,
    teacher. piano. HL KA*

KESSLER, Minuetta. U.S. citizen 1940. pianist. 1 opera,
    piano, choral, orchestra, chamber. AJ* SN

KETTERER, Laura. fl. 20th cent., America. songs,
    choral. SN

KETTERING, Eunice Lea. b. April 4, 1906, Savannah,
    Ohio. teacher. chamber, choral, organ, songs, pi-
    ano, orchestra. AJ* GH p7 SN

KILBY, Muriel Laura. b. Nov. 5, 1929, Toronto, Can.
    pianist, marimbist. songs, piano. HL KA*

KING, Betty Lou (née Jackson?). fl. 20th cent., America.
    pianist. 1 opera, piano, songs. WE p110-1*

KING, Julie Rive see RIVE-KING, Julie

KING, Mabel Shoup. fl. 20th cent., America. piano,
    choral. SN

KING, Pearl. b. Spring Green, Wis., 20th cent. 1 piano,
    1 band. WI p40*

KINGSTON, Marie Antoinette. Baroness von Zedlitz. fl.

19th cent., England. songs. HL

KINKEL, Johanna Matthieux (Mrs. Gottfried). née Mackel.
b. July 8, 1810, Bonn. d. Nov. 15, 1858, London.
pianist. 1 opera, songs, choral, piano. EA   EG
p167*   GF*   HL

KINSCELLA, Hazel Gertrude. b. April 27, 1895, Nora
Springs, Iowa. d. July 15, 1960, Seattle. teacher,
musician. choral, piano. AJ*   AN*   BE p25*
EG p269   EK Feb 1935 p66 +pict   HL   ID   SN

KIRBY, Suzanne. fl. 20th cent., America. chamber, songs,
piano, organ, instrumental. SN

KIRKMAN-JONES, Merle. b. Kokomo, Ind., 20th cent.
violinist. songs, violin. IA p23*

KIRKPATRICK, Edith K. b. Lisbon, La., 20th cent.
teacher, choir director. songs. PC* +pict

KLEIN, Ivy Frances (Mrs. Daryl). née Salaman. b. Dec.
23, 1895, London. singer, teacher. songs. HL

KLENZE, Irene von. fl. 19th cent., Germany. songs.
EA

KLIMISCH, Sister Mary Jane. b. Aug. 22, 1920, Utica,
S.D. teacher, chairman music dept. choral. AJ*
JA   SN

KLOSE, Hyacinthe Eléonore. b. 1808, Corfou. d. 1880,
Paris. clarinettest. saxophone. LH*

KLOTZMAN, Dorothy Hill. fl. 20th cent., America. songs,
choral, orchestra, chamber, piano. SN

KNAPP, Phoebe Palmer (Mrs. Joseph F.). b. 1839, New
York City. d. July 10, 1908, Poland Springs, Me.
songs. EA*   HL   SN

KNOUSS, Isabelle G. b. Arendtsville, Pa., 20th cent.
pianist, teacher. piano, violin, songs, choral. EK
April 1935 p194 +pict   ID

KNOWLTON, Fanny Snow. b. 1859, Cleveland. d. 1926.
songs. BE p7*   EA*   EK March 1935 p132* +pict

(b. Brecksville, Ohio)   HT p572   ID

KOELLING, Eloise.   fl. 20th cent., America.   chamber,
     songs.   SN

KÖNIG, Marie.   b. 19th cent., Loban, Saxony.   d. Dresden.
     songs, piano.   EA

KÖNNERITZ, Minna von.   fl. 19th cent., Germany.   songs,
     instrumental.   EA

KOHLER, Donna Jeanne.   b. 1937, America.   songs.   AN*
     SN p21

KOLB, Barbara.   b. Feb. 10, 1939, Hartford, Conn.   clari-
     netist, teacher.   songs, chamber, electronic.   AJ*
     CK*   CL*   HF*   HL   ML*   SD p6   SN   WN
     p7*

KORN, Clara Ann (Mrs.).   née Gerlack.   b. Jan. 30, 1866,
     Berlin.   d. July 14, 1940, New York, N.Y.   pianist,
     teacher.   orchestra, 1 opera, piano, songs, chamber.
     BE p7*   EA*   EG p204   EH p397*   EK April 1935
     p194 +pict   GF   HL (nee Gerlack)   HT p441   HX
     p779   ID   JD   LF   PL

KRALIKE, Mathilde von.   fl. 19th cent., Germany.   piano.
     EA*   EG p166   SF p27-8

KRÄMER, Caroline.   née Schleicher.   b. 1794, Stokesh,
     Germany.   d. ?   clarinetist.   chamber.   EA (Kraeh-
     mer)   EG p173

KRAUSE, Anna.   fl. 19th cent., Germany.   songs.   EA*

KREISS, Hulda E.   b. Dec. 15, 1924, Strasbourg, France.
     U.S. citizen 1933.   poetess, harpist, teacher, author.
     songs.   AJ*

KROGMAN, Carrie William (Mrs.).   pseud. Paul Ducelle.
     b. ?, Danvers, Mass.   d. 1943.   piano, songs.   BC
     EG p267   EK May 1935 p299 +pict   FD Dec 1933
     p858* +pict   ID   LF*

KRUGER, Lilly Canfield.   b. April 13, 1892, Portage, Ohio.
     d. 1969.   songs, piano.   AJ*   SN

KRZYZANOWSKA, Halina. b. 1860, Paris. pianist. piano.
    HL

KUKUK, Felicitas. née Kestner. b. Nov. 2, 1914, Ham-
    burg. songs, choral. HL

KUMMER, Clare. Clare Rodman Beecher. b. 1888, Brook-
    lyn. author, playwright. songs. AN* ID

KURZBÖCK, Magdalene von. fl. 19th cent., Germany.
    pianist. piano, songs. EA

KUYPER, Elizabeth. b. Sept. 13, 1877, Amsterdam. d.
    Feb. 26, 1953, Lugano. conductor, violinist, teacher.
    2 orchestra, 1 violin, 1 cello.   EK June 1935 p322
    +pict   HL   ID   RH* +biblio

LABEY, Charlotte. Mrs. Sohy. b. July 12, 1887, Paris.
    d. Dec. 19, 1956, Paris. piano, songs, chamber,
    choral. HL

LABRECQUE, Albertine see MORIN-LABRECQUE, Alber-
    tine

LAFFAILLE, Anne Terrier see TERRIER-LAFFAILLE,
    Anne

LAFLEUR, Lucienne. Soeur M. Thérèse de la Sainte Face.
    b. Feb. 8, 1904, Ste. Agathe-des-Monts, Quebec, Can.
    pianist, organist, teacher. choral, piano, songs.
    HL

LA GUERRE, Elisabeth de. née Jacquet. b. 1659, Paris.
    d. June 27, 1729, Paris. organist, harpsichordist,
    court musician, clavecinist. 1 opera, songs, harpsi-
    chord, choral.   BJ +biblio   BK p30, 31   EA*
    (under L and G)   EG p186-7*   FG* (b. 1669)   FP
    p25   GH p5   HC p5-6, 28-29*   HL (b. 1664?)   IC*
    (under Jacquet)   RH* +biblio (b. "probably 1664")
    RM p51

LA HYE, Louise Geneviève. née Rousseau. b. March 8,
    1810, Charenton, France. d. Nov. 17, 1838, Paris.
    teacher, pianist. organ, piano, choral.   BF Jan

1930 p12   EA*   EG p193, 195   HL   LF

LAIGHTON, Ruth.   fl. 19th cent., America.   chamber.
    EG p264

LAJEUNESSE, Marie Louise Cecilia Emma.   Mme. Albani.
    b. Nov. 1, 1847, Chambly, P.Q.   d. April 3, 1930,
    London.   singer, pianist.   piano.   HL (not as compos-
    er)   KA*

LAKE, Bonnie.   b. Waterloo, Iowa, 20th cent.   incidental.
    AN*   SN

LAMBERT, Cecily.   fl. 20th cent., America.   piano, cham-
    ber, songs.   AJ*   SN

LAMSON, Georgia.   fl. 19th cent., America.   songs.   BE
    p35*   EA*

LANG, Edith.   fl. 20th cent., America.   organist, teacher.
    choral, songs, organ, piano.   EG p268   EK June
    1935 p332 +pict   ID   SN

LANG, Josephine.   Mrs. Christian Kostlin.   b. March 14,
    1815, Munich.   d. Dec. 2, 1880, Tübingen, Germany.
    singer.   songs, piano.   EA*   EG p169-71*   FG
    GF*   HC p15-8, 32*   HL

LANG, Margaret Ruthven.   b. Nov. 27, 1867, Boston.
    d. May 30, 1972, Jamaica Plain, Mass.   songs, choral,
    chamber, piano, orchestra.   AL p152*   BC   BE
    p10*   EA*   EG p201-2*, 243, 244   EH p296, 305-6,
    397, 398*   EK Sept 1901 p312; June 1935 p322 +pict
    GF*   GG p10   HA p216*   HU p424, 432-9*   HV
    HW   HX p775, 778* +pict   ID   LF   SN   TE p112,
    113, 122, 123-4*

LANGHANS, Louise see JAPHA, Louise

LANNOY, Countess de.   nee Looz-Corswarem.   b. 1764,
    Belgium.   d. 1820, Liege.   songs, instrumentals.
    EA   EG p218, 219   FG*

LARA, Adelina De see DE LARA, Adelina

LA ROCHE, Rosa.   fl. 18th cent., France.   pianist.   piano.
    EA   EG p191

LARSEN, Libby. b. Dec. 24, 1950, Wilmington, Del.
teaching assistant. 2 operas, 2 guitar, 1 choral.
AJ*

LASANSKY, Julia Stilman see STILMAN-LASANSKY, Julia

LASZLO, Anna von. fl. 19th cent., Germany. chamber.
EA*

LATHROP, Gayle Posselt. b. Feb. 7, 1942, Chicago.
music director, teacher. chamber. AJ*

LATIOLAIS, Jayne. b. Oct. 20, 1928, Natchitoches, La.
faculty member. songs, chamber. AJ*

LAUFER, Beatrice. b. April 27, 1923, New York City.
1 opera, orchestra, songs, chamber, choral. AJ*
HL ID SN

LAURENT, Ruth Carew. fl. 20th cent., America. choral,
songs. SN

LAVAL, Mme. De see DELAVAL, Mme.

LAWRENCE, Elizabeth S. (Mrs.). fl. 19th cent., England.
organist. hymn. HL (not as composer, although its
source says is composer)

LAWRENCE, Emily M. b. 1854, Rugby, England. d. ?
pianist. choral, piano, songs. EA* EG p143*
HL

LEAF, Ann. Audrey Lynn. b. Nebraska, 20th cent. pianist, organist. piano, organ, songs. AN* SN

LEAHY, Mary Weldon. b. Aug. 20, 1926, St. Louis, Mo.
chamber, choral, songs. AJ*

LEATH, Vaughn De see DE LEATH, Vaughn

LEAVITT, Josephina. fl. 19th cent., Germany. piano,
songs. EA

LE BEAU, Louisa Adolpha. b. April 25, 1850, Rastatt,
Baden, Germany. d. July 2, 1927, Baden-Baden,
Germany. pianist, teacher. 1 opera, piano, choral,
chamber, violin, songs. EA* (Lebeau) EG p164-5,

236, 238*   GF*   HL   ID

LEBRUN, Francesca (Frau Ludwig August).   née Danzi.
    b. March 24, 1756, Mannheim.   d. May 14, 1791,
    Berlin.   soprano, pianist.   chamber.   EA   EG p168
    GF   HL   RH (under Ludwig Lebrun) + biblio

LEBRUN, Sophie.   Mme. Dulcken.   b. June 20, 1781, Lon-
    don.   d. ?   pianist.   piano.   EA   HL (under D)

LECHANTRE, Elisabeth.   fl. 18th cent. , France.   1 orches-
    tra.   EA   EG p191

LEECH, Lida Shivers.   b. July 12, 1873, Mayville, N. J.
    d. March 4, 1962, Long Beach, Cal.   author, pianist.
    songs.   AN*   SN

LEFEVER, Maxine Lane.   b. May 30, 1931, Elmhurst, Ill.
    editor, secretary-treasurer.   percussion.   AJ*

LEGINSKA, Ethel.   pseud. for Ethel Liggins.   b. April 13,
    1886, Hull, England.   d. Feb. 26, 1970, Los Angeles.
    pianist, teacher, conductor.   2 operas, choral, cham-
    ber.   AJ   BC   BE p21*   BT p33   EG p244-6
    + pict   EK Aug 1935 p441 + pict   GG p11   HL   ID
    LF   RH* + biblio   SN

LEHMAN, Evangeline.   b. Detroit, 20th cent.   singer.
    piano, songs, choral.   AJ p119 (under E. L. Dumes-
    nil) (married name)   BE p32*   BN* + pict   EK Aug
    1935 p441 + pict   FD Feb 1938 p131* + pict   ID   SN

LEHMANN, Amelia (Mrs. Rudolph).   (works published under
    "A. L. ").   fl. 19th cent.   arranger.   songs.   EA
    EG p147   LF

LEHMANN, Liza.   Elizabeth Nina Mary Frederika.   Mrs.
    Herbert Bedford.   b. July 11, 1862, London.   d. Sept.
    19, 1918, Pinner, Middlesex, England.   soprano.
    songs, 1 opera, choral, piano, incidental.   BC   EA*
    EG p146-8*, 236, 237   EJ Feb 1910 p87-8* + pict
    EK Aug 1935 p441 + pict   FA p238 + pict   GF*   HL
    ID   LF*   RH* + biblio   SN

LELEU, Jeanne.   b. Dec. 29, 1898, Saint-Michel, Meuse,
    France.   pianist, teacher.   saxophone, orchestra,
    songs.   HL   LH*   PJ*   RO*

LEMCKE, Anna. b. 1862, Elbing, Germany. piano, songs.
EA*

LEMMEL, Helen Howarth. fl. 19th cent. , America. songs.
EA*

LEMMENS, Helena see SHERRINGTON, Helena L.

LEMON, Laura. b. Guelph, Ontario, 20th cent. piano,
songs. KA p251

LEONARD, Grace (Mrs. Lloyd L.) b. Jan. 13, 1909, Dallas. choral, songs, piano, chamber. AJ* SN

LEONARDA, Isabella see ISABELLA, Leonarda

LEPKE, Charma Davies. fl. 20th cent. , America. piano,
songs. SN

LEUTNER, Minna Peschka see PESCHKA, Minna

LEVEY, Lauren. b. June 20, 1947, New York City. professor. 2 tape, 1 choral, 1 chamber. AJ*

LEWING, Adele. b. Aug. 6, 1866, Hanover, Germany.
d. Feb. 16, 1943, New York. pianist, teacher.
songs, piano. BE p7* EA* EG p171 EK Oct
1935 p567 + pict HL ID LF

LEWIS, Carrie Bullard see BULLARD, Carrie

LIBBEY, Dee. fl. 20th cent. , Florida. orchestra, songs,
band, piano. SN

LIEBMANN, Helen. née Riese. b. ca. 1796, Berlin.
d. ? piano, chamber, songs. EA*

LILIEN, Antoinette de (Baroness). fl. 18th cent. pianist.
piano. EA* FG IC*

LILIEN, Josephine de (Baroness). fl. 19th cent. , ? piano.
FG* IC*

LILLENAS, Bertha Mae. b. March 1, 1889, Hanson, Ky.
d. March 13, 1945, Tuscumbia, Mo. author, minister.
songs. AN* SN

LINDSAY, Miss M.   Mrs. J. Worthington Bliss.   b. Wim-
     bledon, England, 19th cent.   songs.   EA*   GF*
     HL (under Bliss)

LINEBARGER, Iva B.   b. Feb. 8, 1882, Montezuma, Ind.
     songs.   IA p26-7*

LINWOOD, Mary.   b. 1755, Birmingham, England.   d. March
     2, 1845, Leicester, England.   needlework artist.
     songs, 2 operas.   EA*   EG p132-3*   HL   ID

LIPPA, Kate Ockleston   see   OCKLESTON-LIPPA, Kate

LIPSCOMP, Helen.   b. April 20, 1921, Georgetown, Ky.
     d. Jan. 4, 1974, Lexington, Ky.   pianist, teacher.
     choral, piano, chamber.   AJ*   AN*   SN

LISZNIEWSKA, Marguerite   see   MELVILLE-LISZNIEWSKA,
     Marguerite

LITTLE, Anita Gray.   b. 1885, America.   d. 1966, Ameri-
     ca.   songs.   SN

LLOYD, Caroline Parkhurst.   b. April 12, 1924.   choral di-
     rector, teacher, organist.   songs, piano, 1 opera.   AJ*

LOCKSHIN, Florence Levin.   b. March 24, 1910, Columbus,
     Ohio.   pianist, teacher.   orchestra, choral, piano,
     chamber.   AJ*   SN

LODER, Kate Fanny.   Lady Henry Thompson.   b. Aug. 21,
     1825, Bath.   d. Aug. 30, 1904, Headley, Surrey.
     pianist, teacher.   1 opera, chamber, piano, songs,
     organ.   EA*   EG p136*   GF*   HL

LOEB-EVANS, Matilee.   Mrs. M. L. Preston.   b. Toledo,
     Ohio, 20th cent.   pianist.   piano.   EK April 1937
     p216   FD May 1937 p353* +pict   ID (cornetist)
     LF (Mathilde; b. Calif.)

LOEWE, Augusta.   b. 1822, Berlin.   singer.   songs.   EA

LOGAN, Virginia Knight.   b. 1850, Washington County, Pa.
     d. 1940.   author.   songs, choral.   AN*   SN

LOHOEFER, Evelyn (pseud.).   b. Dec. 28, 1921, Clinton,
     N. C.   teacher, accompanist.   orchestra.   AJ p503*

LOHR, Ina. b. 1903, Amsterdam. choral. SK*

LONG, Grayce E. fl. 20th cent., America. songs. SN

LORD, Helen Cooper. b. 1892, America. d. 1957. songs, choral. SN

LORENZ, Ellen Jane. Mrs. James B. Porter. b. May 3, 1907, Dayton. editor, educator, choirmaster. choral, organ, operas, orchestra, chamber. AJ* AN* SN

LORIOD, Yvonne. Mme. Olivier Messaien. b. Jan. 20, 1924, Houilles, Seine-et-Oise, France. pianist. orchestra, chamber. HL PJ*

LOUD, Annie Frances. b. Nov. 16, 1856, Weymouth, Mass. organist. songs, organ, piano, choral. HI LF

LOUIS, Mme. fl. 18th cent., France. piano, songs, 1 opera. EA* EG p187* FG*

LOVAN, Lydia. fl. 20th cent., America. piano, organ, harpsichord. SN

LOWELL, Dorothy Dawson. fl. 20th cent., America. choral. SN

LOWTHIAN, Caroline. Mrs. Cyril A. Prescott. fl. 19th cent., England. songs, piano. EA* HL

LU, Yen. b. Sept. 7, 1930, Nanking, China. (to U.S. 1963). editor. chamber. AJ*

LUCAS, Mary Anderson. b. May 24, 1882, London. d. Jan. 14, 1952, London. chamber, songs. HL

LUCK, Maude Haben. b. ?, Milwaukee. d. Nov. 27, 1944, Milwaukee. songs, choral. SN WI p47*

LUCKE, Katherine E. b. March 22, 1875, Baltimore. d. May 21, 1962, Baltimore. teacher. songs, choral. AJ* SN

LUCKMAN, Phyllis. b. Sept. 13, 1927, New York, N.Y. cellist, teacher. chamber. AJ*

LUDWIG, Rosa. fl. 19th cent. , Germany. piano.   EA*

LUND, Agnes van der (Baroness). fl. 19th cent. , Netherlands. piano.   EA*   EG p217

LUNDQUIST, Christie. fl. 20th cent. , America. 1 chamber.   AJ*

LUTYENS, Elisabeth. b. July 9, 1906, London. chamber,
orchestra, saxophone, songs, piano, wind, incidental.
AC*   BM   FJ p52   HF   HG   HL   HS*   LH*
PJ*   PM*   RO*   SE p103-12* +pict   SM p90-2*
+pict p120

LUTYENS, Sally Speare. b. Oct. 31, 1927, Syracuse, N. Y.
head music department. chamber.   AJ*

MAAS, Marguerite Wilson. b. 1888, Baltimore. pianist,
teacher. piano, songs.   BE p36   HL

MacARTHUR, Helen. b. 1879, La Crosse, Wis. d. 1936.
pianist, teacher. songs.   WI p49*

McCARTHY, Charlotte. fl. 20th cent. , America. songs,
choral.   SN

McCLEARY, Fiona. b. Jan. 29, 1900, Sanderstead, Surrey,
England. U. S. citizen 1932. pianist. piano, cello.
AJ p504*   AN*

McCOLLIN, Frances. b. Oct. 21, 1892, Philadelphia.
d. Feb. 26, 1960, Philadelphia. lecturer, teacher,
choral conductor (blind). songs, choral, organ, 1
opera, chamber.   AJ*   AL p154*   BE p29*   EG
p261*   EK March 1936 p182 +pict   HL   ID   SN

MacDONALD, Catherine. b. Oct. 22, 1940, New York, N. Y.
conductor, teacher. incidental.   AJ*

MacFARREN, Emma Marie (Mrs. John). nee Bennett.
pseud. Jules Brissac. b. June 19, 1824, London.
d. Nov. 9, 1895, London. pianist, lecturer, teacher,
writer. piano.   EA*   HL

McGILL, Josephine. b. Oct. 20, 1877, Louisville, Ky.
    d. Feb. 24, 1919, Louisville, Ky. writer, folksong
    collector. songs. EG p265 HL ID

McGOWAN SCOTT, Beatrice. fl. 20th cent. , Wisconsin.
    piano, songs. EG p265 WI p81* (McGowen)

MacGREGOR, Helen. fl. 20th cent. , America. piano.
    SN

McILWRAITH, Ilsa Roberta. b. May 17, 1909, Paterson,
    N. J. organist, teacher. choral, organ. AJ*

MacINTOSH, G. A. Claire Harris Macintosh, pen-name.
    b. 1882, Londonderry, Nova Scotia, Can. nurse,
    writer. songs. HL KA*

McINTYRE, Margaret. b. 1905, England. violinist. or-
    chestra, vocal. HL KA*

MACIRONE, Clara Angela. b. Jan. 20, 1821, London.
    d. 1895. teacher, pianist. choral, songs, piano.
    EA* EG p151-2 (Macironi) EK Dec 1935 p697 +pict
    HL ID

McKEE, Jeanellen. fl. 20th cent. , America. songs, piano.
    SN

McKEEL, Joyce. fl. 20th cent. , America. choral, vocal,
    instrumental. AO p114 SD p7*

MACKEN, Jane Virginia. b. Jan. 14, 1912, St. Louis, Mo.
    author. songs. AN* SN

MacKENZIE, Grace. fl. 20th cent. , America. songs.
    EA*

MACKIE, Shirley. b. Rockdale, Texas, fl. 20th cent. band di-
    rector. piano, chamber, orchestra, choral, operas,
    songs. PC* +pict SN

MacKINLAY, Mrs. fl. 19th cent. , England. songs. EA*

McKINNEY, Ida Scott Taylor. b. Springfield, Ill. , 19th
    cent. author. songs. HI

McKINNEY, Mathilde. b. Jan. 31, 1904, South Bend, Ind.

pianist, teacher. piano, chamber, choral. AJ*
HD p67   SN

McLAIN, Margaret Starr. b. Chicago, 20th cent. teacher.
choral, songs. AJ

McLAUGHLIN, Erna. fl. 20th cent., Wisconsin. piano.
WI p80*

McLAUGHLIN, Marian. b. Nov. 26, 1923, Evanston, Ill.
teacher. choral, organ, piano, chamber. AJ   SN

McLEAN, Priscilla. b. May 27, 1942, Fitchburg, Mass.
lecturer. chamber, electronic. AJ*

McLEOD, Evelyn Lundgren. fl. 20th cent., America. piano, violin, cello, chamber. SN

McLIN, Lena. nee Johnson. fl. 20th cent., America.
teacher, singer, musician. choral, piano, songs, orchestra, organ, operas. WE p111*   WG* +pict

McMASTER, Nelle. Nelle McMaster Sprott. fl. 20th cent.,
America. songs. SN (under M and S)

McMILLAN, Ann. b. March 23, 1923, New York, N.Y.
music editor, music director, writer, library director,
lecturer. electronic, chamber, harpsichord, incidental.
AJ*   SN

McNEIL, Jan Pfischner. b. March 20, 1945, Pittsburgh.
professor, assistant director Fine Arts Center. chamber, multi-media, incidental. AJ*

MACONCHY, Elizabeth. b. March 19, 1907, Broxbourne,
England. chamber, orchestra, songs, piano, operas.
AC*   BB*   FJ p52   HL   MB   MC   MH   PJ*
SM p86-7

McPHERSON, Frances Marie. b. 1912, Tarkio, Mo.
teacher. 1 opera, piano, songs, choral. AJ*

MADSEN, Florence J. fl. 20th cent., America. choral,
songs, instrumental. AJ*   SN

MAEDER, Emily P. fl. 19th cent., America. songs.
BE p36*   EA*

MAGEAU, Sister Mary Magdalen. b. Sept. 4, 1934, Milwaukee, Wis. teacher, lecturer. organ, orchestra. AJ*   JA*   SN

MAGNEY, Ruth Taylor. fl. 20th cent., America. choral, 1 opera, piano, instrumental. SN

MAHLER, Alma Maria see SCHINDLER-MAHLER, Alma Maria

MAISTRE, Baroness de. b. ? d. 1875, Cannes, France. 3 operas, songs. EA*   EG p189*

MALEY, Florence Turner. b. Aug. 23, 1871, Jersey City, N.J. d. Jan. 3, 1962, Point Pleasant, N.J. singer, teacher. songs, choral, piano. AN*   BE p24* EK May 1939 p320 + pict   ID   LF

MALIBRAN, Maria Felicitas. née Garcia; Mme. de Beriot. b. March 24, 1808, Paris. d. Sept. 23, 1836, Manchester, England. soprano, pianist. songs. BC (not as composer)   EA*   EG p184-5   FB p162-75 FG*   FI (see index--many pages)   HC p14-5, 31-2 + pict   HL   HO p129-41   KF p143-200, 319 + pict LF   RH* + biblio

MALLEVILLE, Charlotte Tardieu de. fl. 19th cent., France. pianist. piano. EA (under T)   EG p193

MAMLOK, Ursula. née Lewis. b. Feb. 2, 1928, Berlin. U.S. citizen 1945. teacher. chamber, choral. AJ* JA* (b. Feb. 1)   NC   SD p7*   SN

MAMPE-BABNIGG, Emma. fl. 19th cent., Germany. singer. songs. EA*

MANA-ZUCCA. née Augusta Zuckermann; Mrs. Irwin Cassel. b. Dec. 25, 1887, New York City. actress, pianist, singer. songs, violin, cello, piano, choral, saxophone, 2 operas, orchestra. AJ*   AL p153-4*   AN*   BB BE p16-17*   CJ   EK Dec 1935 p697 + pict   FD Feb 1933 p140* + pict   GE   HL   HP p104*   ID   LF (under Z)   LH*   OA + pict   PI + pict   PJ*   SD p4 SN

MANNING, Kathleen Lockhart. b. Oct. 24, 1890, Hollywood, Cal. d. March 20, 1951, Los Angeles. pianist,

singer. 5 operas, choral, orchestra, songs, piano.
AJ*   AN*   BE p29*   EK Jan 1936 p2 + pict   HJ
p310*   HK p246   HL   ID   SN

MANNKOPF, Adolphine. fl. 19th cent. , Germany. songs,
choral.   EA

MANZIARLY, Marcelle de. b. Oct. 13, 1900, Kharkov,
Russia. pianist. orchestra, songs, piano.   HL
LH*   RO   TB (not in HL)

MARA, Gertrude Elisabeth. née Schmeling. b. 1749.
d. 1833. songs.   WJ*

MARCELL, Florence. b. May 1885, Minneapolis. organist.
1 orchestra.   WI p80*

MARCELLI, Anais see PERRIERE-PILTE, Comtesse Anais
de

MARCHAND, Margarethe see DANZI, Margarete

MARCHESI, Mathilde de Castrone. née Graumann.
b. March 24, 1821, Frankfort am Main. d. Nov. 17,
1913, London. soprano, teacher, writer. songs.
BC   EA* (b. March 26, 1826)   EG p193-4   HL
LF

MARCKWALD, Grace. fl. 19th cent. , America. orchestra,
songs, piano.   BE p36   EA   EG p204-5

MARCUS, Adabelle Gross. b. July 8, 1929, Chicago. pianist, teacher, vocal coach. piano, songs, chamber,
1 opera, orchestra, choral.   AJ*   SN

MARI, Pierrette. b. Aug. 1, 1929, Nice. critic, musicologist. saxophone.   LH*

MARIA Antonia, Princess of Saxony see WALPURGIS,
Maria Antonia

MARIA Charlotte Amalia. Duchess of Saxe-Gotha. b. 1751.
d. ? songs.   EA   EG p155

MARIA Paulowna. Grand Duchess of Weimar. b. 1786.
d. 1859. musician. piano.   EA

MARIANI, Virginia. Virginia Mariani Campolieti. fl. 19th
cent., Italy. 1 opera, songs, piano. EA* EG
p215*

MARIE Amalie Friedericke Auguste of Saxony see AMALIE
Friedericke

MARIE Cecile (Sister). b. Stratford, Ont., 20th cent.
pseud. Gerald Rean. teacher, organist, choir director.
choral, songs. IA p28*

MARIE de France. fl. 13th cent., England. songs. BK
p28 EG p58-9

MARIE Elizabeth. fl. 19th cent., Saxe-Meiningen. piano,
chamber. EA* EG p156*

MARIE-ANTOINETTE-Amalie. b. Sept. 17, 1752. Duchess
of Saxe-Gotha. harpsichord, songs. FG*

MARSCHAL-LOEPKE, Grace (pseud.). Grace Cotton-
Marshall. Mrs. H. Clough-Leighter. b. 1885, Nine-
vah, Ind. pianist. songs, piano, choral. EK Sept.
1932 p608 +pict EK Jan 1936 p2 +pict IA p29-30*
ID LF (under C)

MARSH, Gwendolyn. fl. 20th cent., America. piano, songs.
SN

MARSH, Lucille Crews see CREWS, Lucille

MARSHALL, Florence A. (Mrs. Julian). née Thomas.
b. March 30, 1843, Rome. d. ? musician, writer,
conductor. orchestra, choral, 1 opera, songs. EA*
EG p138 HL

MARSHALL, Jane M. b. Dec. 5, 1924, Dallas. organist,
teacher. choral. AJ* SN

MARSHALL, Mrs. William. fl. 19th cent., England.
songs. HL

MARSTON, Agnes L. fl. 20th cent., Maine. songs. BE
p36* EG p266-7

MARTH, Helen Jun. b. May 24, 1903, Alton, Ill. author,
pianist, teacher, drama coach, choral director, radio

director. choral. AJ* AN SN

MARTIN, Angelica (Mrs.). fl. 19th cent., America. teacher. songs. WJ

MARTIN, Judith. Sister Mary Norbert, F.D.C. b. Oct.
15, 1914, Ashville, Pa. author, teacher. songs.
AN SN

MARTINEZ [Martines], Marianne di. Anna Katharina (born).
b. May 4, 1744, Vienna. d. Dec. 13, 1812, Vienna.
pianist, singer. choral, orchestra. BK p31 EA*
EG p158-9 GF* HL ID

MARX, Berthe. Mme. Otto Goldschmidt. b. 1859, Paris.
d. ? pianist. piano. EA EG p192-3 LF

MARY, Queen of Scots. b. 1545, Scotland. d. 1587, Scotland. songs. EA* EG p67

MASON, Margaret C.M. fl. 20th cent., America. piano.
SN

MASONER, E. L. (Betty). b. May 22, 1927, Bemidji,
Minn. teacher. percussion. AJ*

MASSART, Louise Aglae. née Masson. b. June 10, 1827,
Paris. d. July 26, 1887, Paris. pianist, teacher.
piano. EA EG p192 HL (not as composer)

MASSON, Elizabeth. b. 1806, Scotland. d. Jan. 9, 1865,
London. editor, contralto. songs. EA* GF*
HL

MASTERS, Juan (pseud.). Mrs. Juanita Masters. b. Chicago, 20th cent. teacher. piano. BE p32-3* SN

MATTHEWS, Blanche Moore. fl. 20th cent., America.
teacher. songs, piano. LF (B. Dingley M.) SN

MAUD DE BAUR, Constance. b. 1776, Stuttgart. d. ?
songs. same as Constance M. Maud? EA* HT
p441

MAURICE, Paule. b. Sept. 29, 1910, Paris. d. Aug. 18,
1967, Paris. teacher. saxophone. HL LH*

MAURICE-JACQUET, H. b. March 18, 1886, St. Mande, France. d. June 29, 1954, New York City. pianist, conductor, teacher. 4 operas, orchestra. AJ* p504

MAURY, Mme. Renaud. fl. 19th cent., France. orchestra. EA* EG p185-6*

MAXWELL, Elsie. fl. 19th cent., America. violin, piano, songs, 1 opera. BE p36* EG p264

MAXWELL, Helen Purcell. b. Dec. 20, 1901, Vincennes, Ind. choral, songs. AN* SN

MAXWELL, Jacqueline Perkinson. b. Sept. 16, 1932, Denver. piano. AJ*

MAY, Florence. b. Feb. 6, 1845, London. d. June 29, 1923, London. pianist, writer. piano, choral, songs. EA* HL

MAYER, Anne Wolbrette. pseud. Anne Brett. b. New Orleans, La., fl. 20th cent. business executive, singer. songs. PC* +pict

MAYER, Emilie. b. 1812, Friedland, Germany. d. 1883, Berlin. pianist. orchestra, chamber, piano, 1 opera. EA* EG p161-2*, 236, 238 (Emelie) GF* (b. Mecklenburg) ID LF

MAYFIELD, Alpha C. fl. 20th cent., America. choral. SN

MAYHEW, Grace. fl. 19th cent., America. same as Grace Mayhew Stults? songs. EA*

MAZEL, Helen Roberts. fl. 19th cent., France. songs. EA*

MAZZUCATO, Elisa. fl. 19th cent., Italy. operas. HL HX p779*

MEAD, Catherine Pannill. b. 1868, Norfolk, Va. d. 1936, Milwaukee. singer, critic. songs. BE p10* WI p51* (d. 1940)

MEADER, Emily Peace. b. 1858, America. d. 1914, America. songs. SN

MEDA, Bianca Maria. fl. 17th cent. motets.   FG*
(Blanche)   IC*

MEDICI, Isabella de. b. ca. 1540. d. 1576.   RD*

MEEK, Ethel. b. Stamps, Ark., fl. 20th cent. teacher, organist. 1 piano, 1 orchestra.   PC* + pict

MEKEEL, Joyce H. b. July 6, 1931, New Haven. teacher,
sculptist. incidental, chamber, piano, choral.   AJ*
HF*   SN

MELOY, Elizabeth. b. Aug. 7, 1904, Hoopeston, Ill.
teacher. songs, piano, organ, chamber.   AJ*   IA
p49   SN

MELVILLE-LISZNIEWSKA, Marguerite. b. 1884, Brooklyn.
d. March 7, 1935, Cincinnati. pianist, teacher.
chamber, songs.   AL p154 (Meville)   BE p36*   EA
EG p206   EH p398   EK Oct 1935 p567 + pict   HT
p566   LF

MENDELSSOHN, Fanny. F. Cecile Hensel (Mrs.). b. Nov.
14, 1805, Hamburg. d. May 14, 1847, Berlin. pianist. songs, choral.   BT p32*   CH p41-2*   EA
(under H)   EG p125-8*   EH p293   EL   EK June
1934 p332 + pict (under H)   EK March 1936 p182 + pict
(under M)   FG* (under H)   GF* (under H)   GH p6
HC p10-3, 30-1*   HL   HT p425   ID   KG   LF
(under H)   RH* (under H)   SF p24*

MENEELY, Sarah Suderley. b. Feb. 18, 1945, Albany,
N. Y. chamber.   AJ*

MENTER, Sophie. Mrs. David Popper. b. July 29, 1846,
Munich. d. Feb. 23, 1918, Stackdorf, Germany. pianist, teacher. piano.   HL

MERRICK, Mrs. C. pseud. Edgar Thorn. fl. 20th cent.,
America. choral, piano.   EG p208-9*   HT p560
ID

MERRIMAN, Margarita. b. Nov. 29, 1927, Barcelona,
Spain. music director, teacher. 1 song, 1 choral,
1 orchestra, 1 chamber.   AJ*   JA*   SN

METZLER, Bertha. fl. 19th cent., America. piano, songs.

EA   LF

MEYSENBURG, Sister Agnes. b. March 3, 1922, David
    City, Neb. orchestra.   JA*

MEZARI, Maddalena Casulana de see CASULANA DE
    MEZARI, Maddalena

MIER, Anna von (Countess). fl. 19th cent., Austria?
    songs. EA

MIKULAK, Marcia Lee. b. Oct. 9, 1948, Winston-Salem,
    N. C. pianist. 1 electronic. AJ*

MIKUSCH, Margarete von. b. 1884, Baydorf, Austria.
    chamber, piano, songs. HL

MILANOLLO, Teresa. Domenica-Maria-Teresa Milanollo.
    b. Aug. 28, 1827, Savigliano, Italy. d. Oct. 25, 1904,
    Paris. violinist. violin, piano.   EA*   EG p215
    EK April 1936 p198 +pict   FG*   GF*   HL   ID
    RH +biblio   SF p34

MILETTE, Juliette. Sister M. Henri de la Croix. b. June
    17, 1900, Montreal. organist, teacher. organ, choral,
    songs. HL

MILLAR, Marian. fl. 19th cent., England. pianist, writer.
    songs, orchestra, choral.   EA*   EG p134   HL

MILLARD, Mrs. Philip. b. ?, England. d. ca. 1840.
    songs. EA* HL

MILLER, Joan. fl. 20th cent., America. 1 choral.   AJ*

MILLER, Lillian Anne. b. May 31, 1916, North Hadden-
    field, N. J. author, pianist, teacher. songs, piano,
    instrumental.   AN*   SN

MILLS, Joan Geilfuss. fl. 20th cent., America. piano,
    chamber. SN

MIRANDA, Erma Hoag. b. Plainfield, Ill., 20th cent.
    teacher. songs, choral, piano, 1 opera.   SN   WI
    p52*

MISHELL, Kathryn Lee. b. June 5, 1940, Los Angeles.

pianist, teacher, lecturer, opera coach. 1 chamber.
AJ*

MITCHELL, Izah Pike. b. 1888, America. d. 1967. piano, songs. SN

MIZANGERE, Marquise. b. 1693, France. clavecinist.
clavecin. EA   EG p192

MOLINOS-LAFITTE, Mlle A. b. 1798, France. d. ?
songs, piano. EA   EG p193   FG*

MOLIQUE, Caroline. fl. 19th cent., Germany. songs, violin. EA

MOLITOR, Fredericke. fl. 19th cent., Germany. songs.
EA*

MOMY, Valerie. fl. 19th cent., Germany. piano.   EA*

MONCRIEFF, Mrs. L. fl. 19th cent., England. songs.
EA*   LF*

MONGEROULT, Hélène de Nervode. Comtesse de Charnay.
b. March 2, 1764, Lyons. d. May 20, 1836, Florence. teacher, pianist. piano. EA   EG p192   FG*
HL (d. June 20)

MONK, Meredith. b. Nov. 20, 1944, Lima, Peru. U.S.
citizen 1945. lecturer, teacher. songs. AJ*

MONTE-VARCHI, Anna von Cerrini de see CERRINI DE
MONTE-VARCHI, Anna von

MONTGOMERY, Merle. pseud. Aline Campbell. b. May
15, 1904, Davidson, Okla. pianist, editor, teacher,
lecturer, musicologist, author. piano, songs, choral.
AJ*   AN*   HD p53   SN

MOODY, Marie. fl. 19th cent., England. orchestra, piano,
instrumental. EA*   HL

MOORE, Dorothy Rudd (Mrs. Kermit). b. June 4, 1940,
Wilmington, Del. poet. chamber, songs.   IB   WE
p111-2*

MOORE, Luella Lockwood. fl. 20th cent., America.

pianist, teacher. songs, piano. EK June 1936 p340
+pict ID

MOORE, Mary Carr. b. Aug. 6, 1873, Memphis. d. Jan.
11, 1957, Ingleside, Cal. singer, teacher. 10 operas,
orchestra, songs, chamber. AJ* (M. Carter Moore)
AL p152* AN* BE p12* EH p397* EK May
1936 p328 +pict GG p11 HJ p287-91* HL HP
p73* HT p570 ID JD PL SN

MOORE, Maurine Ricks. b. Nov. 1, 1908, Vermillion, Kan.
pianist, teacher. piano. AJ*

MOORE, Undine. née Smith. b. Aug. 25, 1904, Jarrat,
Va. teacher. chamber, choral, songs, piano. RF*
+pict WE p112-3*

MORE, Isabella Theaker. fl. 18th cent., England. song.
HK p360

MORE, Margaret (Elizabeth). b. June 26, 1903, Harlech,
England. orchestra, chamber, 1 opera, songs.
HL

MOREA, Vincenza Garelli della see GARELLI DELLA
MOREA, Vincenza

MOREL DU VERGER, Virginie see VERGER, Virginie
Morel du

MORGAN, Lady. née Sydney Owenson. b. ca. 1783, Dublin. d. April 14, 1859, London. author. songs, 1
opera. EA* EG p152-3*

MORGAN, Maud. b. Nov. 22, 1860, New York City.
d. Dec. 2, 1941, Prince's Bay, N.Y. harpist, teacher. harp. HL

MORGAN, Patria. b. 1915, England. songs. FJ p53*

MORIN-LABRECQUE, Albertine (Dr.). b. June 8, 1896,
Montreal. pianist, teacher. 3 operas, orchestra,
band, piano, choral, songs. HL KA*

MORISON, Christina W. née Bogue. b. 1840, Dublin.
d. ? songs, piano, 1 opera. EA* EG p152* HL

MORREY, Marion see RICHTER, Marion Morrey

MORRIS, Mrs. C. H. b. 1862, (American). d. 1929.
    songs. SN

MORRISON, Julia. fl. 20th cent., America. songs, choral,
    percussion, operas, chamber, orchestra, electronic,
    organ. GH p7 SN

MOSCOVITZ, Julianne. b. Jan. 18, 1951, Oakland, Cal.
    guitarist, assistant music director. guitar. AJ*

MOSELEY, Caroline Carr. fl. 19th cent., England. cham-
    ber, choral. EA EG p144 HL

MOSEMILLER, Ruby Lane (Mrs. Charles). b. Indianapolis,
    20th cent. teacher. piano. IA p33, 49*

MOSHER, Frances Elizabeth. née Jordan. b. Oct. 23,
    1911, St. John, New Brunswick. piano. HL KA*

MOULTON, Mrs. Charles. née Lilly Greenough. fl. 19th
    cent., America. songs. EA* LF*

MOUNSEY, Ann Shepard. Mrs. Bartholomew. b. April 17,
    1811, London. d. June 24, 1891, London. pianist,
    organist, teacher. songs, piano, organ. EA* (under
    B) EG p134-5* HL ID

MOUNSEY, Elizabeth. b. Oct. 8, 1819, London. d. Oct.
    3, 1905, London. organist. songs, piano, organ,
    guitar. EA EG p134 HL

MOZART, Marianne (Nannerl). b. July 30, 1751, Salzburg.
    d. Oct. 29, 1829, Salzburg. clavecinist. CH p38-
    44 +pict HL (Maria Anna Walpurga Ignatia; not as
    composer) MU RH

MUG, Sister Mary Theodosia. H. Maery, pseud. b. Attica,
    Ind., 20th cent. organist. vocal. IA p33*

MUKLE, May Henrietta. b. May 14, 1880, London. cell-
    ist. cello. BF Feb 1930 p92 HL LF (Muckle)

MÜLLER, Elise. b. 1782, Brême, Germany. d. ? songs.
    EA* FG* SF p37*

MÜLLER-GALLENHOFER, Josepha. b. 1770, Vienna.
    d. ? harpist. harp, 1 opera.   EA*   EG p167*

MÜLLER HERMANN, Johanna. b. Jan. 15, 1878, Vienna. d.
    April 19, 1941, Vienna. teacher. chamber, songs.   HL

MUNDELLA, Emma. b. 1858, Nottingham, England. d.
    Feb. 20, 1896, England. pianist, teacher. piano, choral.
    EA*   EG p135*   HL

MUNGER, Millicent Christner. b. Sept. 15, 1905, Rosa-
    mond, Ill. organist, choir director, piano teacher.
    organ, piano, songs.   AJ*

MUNGER, Shirley. b. Everett, Wash., 20th cent. pianist,
    teacher. organ, chamber, piano.   AJ*   JA*   SN

MURI-COLLI, Adelina. fl. 19th cent., America? singer,
    teacher. piano, songs.   EA*

MURRAY, Grace Mel. fl. 20th cent., Louisiana. poet.
    songs.   PC*

MUSGRAVE, Thea. Mrs. Peter Mark. b. May 27, 1928,
    near Edinburgh, Scotland (to U.S. 1972) English.
    teacher, lecturer. 3 operas, chamber, orchestra,
    choral.   AJ*   AO p114*   BB   CA*   HL   KC
    p92-3* +pict   RI p11*   SA p83*   WN p7*

MUSSER, Clare. fl. 20th cent., America. marimba.   AJ

MUSSINI, Adele Branca. fl. 19th cent., Italy. pianist.
    piano.   EA   EG p216

MUSTILLO, Lina. b. Oct. 13, 1905, Newport, R.I. or-
    ganist, choir director, music school director. piano.
    AJ*   SN

NAESER, Martha. b. 1860, Luckenwalde, Germany. d. ?
    songs, piano.   EA*

NASCIMBENI, Maria Francesca. b. 1658, Ancona, Italy.
    d. ? songs.   HL

NASH, Grace Helen. b. 1882, Clinton, Iowa. teacher. piano.   BE p30*

NATHUSIUS, Marie. b. 1817, Magdeburg, Germany.
    d. 1857, ? writer. songs.   EA

NAUMANN, Ida. b. ? d. 1897, Berlin. singer. songs.   HL

NEAS, Margaret. fl. 20th cent., America. vocal.   SN

NEEDHAM, Alicia Adelaide. b. 19th cent., near Dublin
    County Meath. songs, piano.   BF Feb 1930 p92
    EA*   EG p152   LF

NEUMANN, Elizabeth. b. 19th cent., Capetown. piano.   EA

NEUVILLE, Mme. Alphonse de. fl. 19th cent., France.
    songs, violin.   EA*   EG p190-1

NEWCOMBE, Georgeanne Hubi. b. Dec. 18, 1843, London.
    d. ? soprano, author, organist. songs, piano.   EA*
    EG p248   HL

NEWELL, Mrs. Laura E. b. Feb. 5, 1854, New Marl-
    borough, Mass. poet. songs.   HB p314-17 + pict

NEWLIN, Dika. b. Nov. 22, 1923, Portland, Ore. writer,
    musicologist, teacher, administrator, chairman music
    dept. piano, chamber, orchestra.   AJ*   HL   JA*
    PJ*   SD p4   SN   WK

NEWTON, Adelaide (or Emily) (Mrs. Alexander). née Ward.
    b. 1821, London. d. Dec. 22, 1881, London. singer.
    songs, piano.   EA   HL

NICHOLS, Alberta. b. Dec. 3, 1898, Lincoln, Ill. d. Feb.
    4, 1957, Hollywood, Cal. songs, incidental.   AJ*
    AN*   SN

NICKERSON, Camille Lucie. b. New Orleans, La., fl. 20th
    cent. teacher. songs, choral.   AJ*   PC* + pict
    WE p113*

NIEDERSTETTER, Emilie. fl. 19th cent., Germany. pi-
    ano.   EA*

NIEMACK, Ilza. b. Charles City, Iowa, 20th cent. violin-
    ist, teacher. violin, songs.   AJ*   EK Aug 1936
    p468 + pict   ID   SN

NIGHTINGALE, Mae Wheeler. b. Dec. 30, 1898, Blencoe, Iowa. author, teacher. choral, operas. AJ* AN* SN

NOBLITT, Katheryn McCall. b. Feb. 10, 1909, Marion, N.C. author, teacher. songs, piano. AN* SN

NOHE, Beverly. b. Sept. 24, 1935, East Rochester, N.Y. choir director, organist, teacher. choral, chamber. AJ*

NORBURY, F. Ethel. née Fall. b. April 20, 1872, Liverpool, England. music teacher. songs, choral, operas. HL KA*

NORDENSTROM, Gladys. Mrs. Ernst Krenek. b. May 23, 1924, Pokegama, Minn. 2 electronic, 2 orchestra, 1 chamber, 1 piano. AJ*

NORTHEY, Carrie see ROMA, Caro

NORTON, Caroline Elizabeth Sarah. née Sheridan. b. 1808, Huddersfield, England. d. June 15, 1877, London. author, poetess, singer, musician. songs. EA* FQ p325* HD p69* HL LF

NOVELLO-DAVIES, Clara. b. April 7, 1861, Cardiff, Wales. d. March 1, 1943, London. teacher, choral conductor, author. songs. HL

NOWAK, Alison. b. April 7, 1948, Syracuse, N.Y. 2 chamber, 1 opera, 1 orchestra. AJ*

NUGENT, Maude. Mrs. William Jerome. b. 1877, America? d. 1958, New York City. author, actress. songs, instrumentals. AN* FQ p543-4*

NUNLIST, Juli. b. Dec. 6, 1916, Montclair, N.J. teacher, music director. 2 piano, 2 songs. AJ*

NUNN, Elizabeth Annie. b. 1861, ? d. Jan. 7, 1894, Fallowfield, Manchester, England. songs. EA EG p135* HL

NYMAN, Amy Utting. fl. 20th cent., America? chamber. SD p6*

NYQUIST, Morine A. fl. 20th cent., America. band, choral. SN

OBENCHAIN, Virginia. Mrs. Daunch. b. April 26, 1919,
    Ohio. author, teacher. 1 opera, organ, piano. AN*
    SN

O'BRIEN, Drena. fl. 20th cent. , America. piano, organ,
    songs. SN

O'BRIEN, Katherine. b. April 10, 1901, Amesbury, Mass.
    math lecturer, writer. choral. AJ*   SN

OCKLESTON-LIPPA, Kate. fl. 19th cent. , England. piano,
    choral. EA*

ODDONE, Elisabetta Sulli-Rao. b. Aug. 13, 1878, Milan.
    singer. chamber, songs, operas. HL

O'HARA, Mary (penname). Mary O'Hara Alsop Sture-Vasa.
    b. 1885, Cape May Point, N.J. author. 1 song.
    ID

OHE, Adele Aus der. b. Dec. 11, 1864, Hanover, Germany.
    d. Dec. 7, 1937, Berlin. pianist. songs, piano.
    BC (under A) EA* (under A) EG p171 + pict EK
    Feb 1932 p84 + pict GF (under A) HL HX p772,
    776-7* ID MW RH + biblio

OHLSON, Marion. b. Jersey City, N.J. 20th cent. piano,
    songs, 1 opera, choral. AJ*   SN

OKEY, Maggie (Marguerite) (Oakey). Mrs. Labori, Mrs.
    Vladimir de Pachman. b. 1864, Sydney. d. July 3,
    1952, Paris. pianist. piano, violin. EA   EG p144
    + pict HL   ID

OLAGNIER, Marguerite. fl. 19th cent. , France. 2 operas.
    EA*   EG p189*

OLCOTT, Grace. fl. 19th cent. , America. songs. EA*

OLDENBURG, Elizabeth. fl. 20th cent. , Ohio. piano,
    songs. SN

OLDHAM, S. Emily. fl. 19th cent. , England. songs. EA*
    HL

O'LEARY, Rosetta (Mrs. Arthur). nee Vinning. b. ?
    d. June 17, 1909, London. choral conductor, teacher.

songs. EA* GJ (under Arthur O'Leary) HL (doesn't include Grove)

OLIVER, Kate. fl. 19th cent., England. violin. EG p144

OLIVER, Madra Emagene. b. Oct. 28, 1905, Three Rivers, Mich. author, pianist, singer, teacher, organist. songs, choral, piano, organ. AJ AN*

OLIVER, Mary. fl. 19th cent., England. piano, chamber. EA

OLIVEROS, Pauline. b. May 30, 1932, Houston. teacher. chamber, electronic, multi-media. AJ* GH p7 HL JA KB RM p52 SN

OLIVIER, Blanche (Mrs. Harry). fl. 20th cent., Louisiana. 1 piano. PC*

OLIVIER, Charlotte. fl. 19th cent., Germany. piano. EA

OPIE, Mary Pickens. fl. 20th cent., America. choral. SN

ORGER, Caroline see REINAGLE, Caroline

ORTH, Lizette Emma (Mrs. John). née Blood. b. 1858, Milford, N.H. d. Sept. 14, 1913, Boston. pianist. songs, piano, choral, opera. AL p154 (wrong initials) BA (under John Orth) BE p36 EA EG p206, 207 EK Oct 1936 p606 +pict HI* HT p561 ID LF PL TB (under John Orth)

OSGOOD, Marion G. b. Chelsea, Mass., 20th cent. violinist, conductor. piano, songs, violin. BE p36* EA EG p263 EK Oct 1936 p606 +pict ID

OSTLERE, May. fl. 19th cent., England. songs, orchestra. EA* HL LF*

OSTRANDER, Linda Woodaman. b. Feb. 17, 1937, New York City. lecturer, teacher, music consultant. chamber, multi-media. AJ* SN

OTIS, Edna Cogswell. b. Nov. 24, 1886, Scranton, Pa. teacher. choral, piano. IA p34* SN

OURY, Anna Caroline see BELLEVILLE, Emilie

OWEN, Anita. fl. 20th cent., America. piano, songs, 1
    opera.   BE p36*   EA*   EG p259

OWEN, Dr. Blythe. b. Dec. 26, 1898, Bruce, Minn.
    teacher. choral, piano, organ, chamber, woodwind,
    brass.   AJ*   CK* (1975)   JA   MP*   SN

OWEN, Julia D. fl. 20th cent., America. singer, teacher.
    songs.   EK Oct 1936 p606 + pict   ID

PACK, Beaulah Frances. fl. 20th cent., America. piano,
    songs, chamber.   SN

PAGE, Florence Du see DU PAGE, Florence

PANETTI, Joan. fl. 20th cent., America. teacher, pian-
    ist. songs.   AJ*   SN

PAQUIN, Anna. b. 1878, Saint Cuthbert, Prov. Quebec.
    d. 1923, Saint-David d'Yamaska, Can. organist,
    teacher. "religious works."   KA p252

PAQUIN, Dr. Louisa. Rev. Soeur Marie-Valentine.
    b. 1865, Prov. Quebec. d. 1950. music teacher.
    "church music."   KA p253

PARADIS, Maria Theresa von. b. May 15, 1759, Vienna.
    d. Feb. 1, 1824, Vienna. pianist, singer, teacher,
    organist. 2 operas, piano, songs, choral.   BK p31*
    BT p17, 32   EA*   EG p156-8*   FG*   GF*   GH
    p6   HC p8-9*   HL*   MX*   RM p51   UA

PARCELLO, Marie. fl. 19th cent., America. songs.
    BE p36*   EA*

PARK, Edna Rosalind. b. Boston, 19th century. songs.
    BE p36*   EA*   EG p205   HT p566   LF

PARKE, Maria Hester. Mrs. Beardmore. b. 1775, Lon-
    don. d. Aug. 15, 1822, London. pianist, singer.
    piano, songs, violin, chamber.   EA*   EG p132-3
    (b. 1755)   HL (singer only)

PARKER, Alice. b. Dec. 16, 1925, Boston. arranger, teacher. choral, 1 opera, songs, chamber. AJ* AN* SN

PARKYNS, Mrs. Beatrice. née Crawford. b. Bombay, India, 19th cent. songs, piano, violin. EA EG p144 HL

PARR, Patricia. b. 1937, Toronto. pianist. piano. KA

PARR-GERE, Florence. fl. 20th cent., America. pianist. songs, piano, chamber, orchestra. EK Sept 1933 p560 +pict ID

PATERSON, Wilma. fl. 20th cent., Scotland. chamber, RI p13*

PATTERSON, Annie Wilson. b. Oct. 27, 1868, Lurgan County Armagh, Ireland. d. Jan. 13, 1934, Cork. folklorist, organist, pianist, author, lecturer. choral, songs, 2 operas, orchestra. EA* HL (d. Jan. 16) LF

PATTI, Adelina (Adela Juana Maria). b. Feb. 10, 1843, Madrid. d. Sept. 27, 1919, Craig-y-Nos Castle, Wales. soprano. songs. EA* EG p152 HL (b. Feb. 19; not as composer) MI p188-90 +pict

PAUL, Barbarie. b. July 27, 1945, New York City. director musical theater. chamber, electronic, songs. AJ* GG p11

PAUL, Doris A. b. Aug. 16, 1903, Upland, Ind. author, conductor, teacher. songs, choral. AJ* AN*

PAULOWNA, Maria see MARIA Paulowna

PEASE, Jessie L. fl. 20th cent., America. pianist, teacher. songs, "musical readings." EA* EK Dec 1936 p749 +pict ID

PEEK, Betty. fl. 20th cent., America. anthems. SN

PENGILLY, Sylvia. b. March 23, 1935, London. (to U.S. 1957). teacher. 2 songs, 1 electronic, 1 wind, 1 chamber. AJ*

PENNA, Catherine.   Mrs. M. Hooper.   b.   ?, England?
     d. June 6, 1894, England.   soprano.   songs, organ.
     HL

PENTLAND, Barbara.   née Lally.   b. Jan. 2, 1912, British
     Columbia.   teacher, lecturer, pianist.   songs, orches-
     tra, chamber, piano, opera.   AL p163-4*   BB*
     CB* +pict   GH p6-7   HL   KA*   MA* +biblio   PB
     v6 1960 p88-94* +pict (b. Winnipeg)

PERISSAS, Madeleine.   fl. Paris.   choral, orchestra, cham-
     ber.   PJ*

PERRIERE-PILTE, Anaïs (Comtesse).   née Marcelli.   b. ?,
     France.   d. 1878, Paris.   operas (at least 3)   EA*
     EG p188-9*

PERRONET, Mme. Amelie.   fl. 19th cent.   operas, songs.
     EG p189

PERRY, Julia.   b. March 25, 1924, Akron, Ohio.   choral,
     3 operas, percussion, chamber, orchestra.   AJ*
     GG p12*   HD p70*   HL   SN p28, 46   SS p464,
     472*   WE p98, 113-5* +biblio +recordings

PESADORE, Antoinette de.   b. March 6, 1799, Dresde,
     France.   d. ? pianist.   piano.   EA   FG*

PESCHKA, Minna.   nee Leutner.   b. Oct. 25, 1839, Vienna.
     d. Jan. 12, 1890, Wiesbaden.   singer (soprano).   songs.
     EA (Peschka-Leutner)   HL (not as composer; M.
     Peschka Leutner)

PESSIAK-SCHMERLING, Anna.   b. 1834, Vienna.   d. 1896,
     Vienna.   teacher.   choral, piano, songs.   EA   EG
     p167

PETER, Lily.   fl. 20th cent. , America.   songs.   SN

PETERSEN, Marian F.   b. July 4, 1926, Salt Lake City,
     Utah.   teacher.   1 opera, 1 choral.   AJ*

PETERSON, Melody.   b. Feb. 5, 1942, Oak Park, Ill.
     teacher, music journalist.   1 piano, 1 organ, 1 cham-
     ber, 1 song.   AJ*

PETRELLI.   stage name of Eleanora Louise Marianne

Petrov, née Wigström. b. April 9, 1835, Siemtuna, Sweden. d. Feb. 21, 1904, Chicago. soprano, administrator. songs. HL

PEYCKE, Frieda. b. Omaha, 20th cent. pianist, music teacher. "musical readings." ID

PFEIFFER, Clara Virginie. b. 1816, Versailles. d. ? pianist. piano. FG*

PFEILSCHIFTER, Julie von. b. 1840, Mannheim, Germany. d. ? pianist. piano, songs. EA* EG p168*

PFOLH, Bessie Whittington. fl. 20th cent., America. songs, choral. SN

PFUND, Leonore. née Thiele. b. May 21, 1877, Glauchau, Germany. songs. HL

PHILIBA, Nicole. b. Aug. 30, 1937, Paris. saxophone. LH*

PHILLIPS, Vivian D. b. March 9, 1917, Colby, Kan. chamber, songs. AJ*

PHILP, Elizabeth. b. 1827, Falmouth, England. d. Nov. 26, 1885, London. singer. songs. EA EK Jan 1937 p3 GF* HL

PHIPPEN, Laud German. b. Whitewright, Tex., 20th cent. music teacher, pianist. piano. EK Jan 1937 p3 ID

PICCOLOMINI, Marietta. b. 1834. d. 1899. saxophone. LH*

PICHE, Eudore. b. Feb. 9, 1906, Montreal. choral conductor. choral. HL

PICKEN, Emele M. fl. 20th cent., America. songs, piano. SN

PICKHARDT, Ione. b. May 27, 1900, Hempstead, L. I., N. Y. pianist. piano, 1 opera. HJ p360*

PIERCE, Seneca. fl. 20th cent., America. songs, choral. SN

PIERPONT, Marie de. b. ?, France. d. 1896, France.
    organist. organ, piano, songs, 1 opera.   EA*   EG
    p189*

PIETSCH, Edna Frida. b. May 7, 1894, Milwaukee. teach-
    er. songs, chamber, orchestra, choral.   AJ*   EK
    May 1936 p312*   SN   WI p60, 83*

PITCHER, Gladys. b. 1890, Belfast, Me. songs, choral,
    piano, 1 operetta.   BE p30*   SN

PITOT, Genevieve. b. May 20, 1901, New Orleans, La.
    pianist, arranger. incidental, songs.   PC* +biblio

PITT, Emma. fl. 19th cent., America. musician, author.
    songs.   BE p36*   EA*

PITTMAN, Alice Locke (Mrs. Wesley). fl. 19th cent.,
    America. violin, songs, chamber.   EA*   EG p206
    (Pitman)

PITTMAN, Evelyn LaRue. b. ca. 1905, McAlester, Okla.
    writer. choral, songs, operas.   WE p115*

PITTS, Carol Marhoff. b. 1888, America. conductor,
    teacher.   ID

PLANICK, Annette Meyers. fl. 20th cent., America. songs,
    chamber, orchestra.   SN

PLEYEL, Marie (Felicite Denise) (Mrs. Camille). née
    Mocke or Mooke. b. July 4, 1811, Paris. d. March
    30, 1875, Brussels. pianist, teacher. piano.   EA
    (b. Sept. 4)   EG p192 (Camille Marie) (b. Sept. 4)
    FG   HL (d. St. Joose-ten-Noode, near Brussels; not
    as composer)

PLITT, Agathe. b. 1831, Thorn, Germany. d. ? pianist.
    choral, songs.   EA   EG p167

POLDOWSKI (pseud.) see WIENIOWSKI, Lady Dean Paul

POLIGNAC, Armande de. b. Jan. 8, 1876, Paris. d. ?
    orchestra, operas (no number given).   HL

POLIN, Claire. b. Jan. 1, 1926, Philadelphia. teacher.
    flute, harp, chamber, choral, orchestra.   AJ*   CK

1974*   JA*   SN

POLK, Grace Porterfield. b. Richmond, Ind. , 20th cent.
    soprano. songs, 3 operas.   BE p36*   EK Feb 1937
    p72 (b. Ohio)   IA p35*   ID

POLKO, Elise. née Vogel. b. 1822, Leipzig. d. 1899,
    Munster, Westphalia, Germany. singer, author.
    songs.   EA (b. 1834)   EG p240   HL (not as com-
    poser)

POLLET, Marie-Nicole Simonin. b. May 4, 1787, Paris.
    d. ? harpist. harp.   EA   EG p194   FG

POLLOCK, Muriel. Molly Donaldson. b. Jan. 21, 1904,
    Kingsbridge, N.Y. pianist, organist. orchestra,
    songs, piano, incidental.   AN*   BE p30-1*

POND, Ada L. b. Nov. 14, 1859, Janesville, Wis. d.
    March 1925. teacher. songs.   WI p60-1*

POOLER, Marie. b. April 22, 1928, Wisconsin. choral.
    AJ   SN

PORTER, Edith Rowena (Mrs. David). nee Noyes. Mrs.
    Roy G. Greene. b. March 26, 1875, Cambridge,
    Mass. d. ? pianist, teacher. choral, piano, cham-
    ber, songs, operas.   AL p154, 155 (under Porter
    and Greene, as different people)   BE p11*   EA (un-
    der Porter and Noyes)   EG p205   EH p307, 397
    EK Sept 1936 p534 + pict   HJ p220-1*   HL   ID   PL
    SN

POSTON, Elizabeth. b. Oct. 24, 1905, Highfield, Hertford-
    shire, England. author, pianist, administrator. songs,
    choral, chamber, incidental.   HL   LG* + pict

POTT, Aloyse. b. April 23, 1815, Vienna. d. ? pianist.
    songs.   FG*

POUILLAN, Mlle. fl. 18th cent. , France. pianist. piano.
    EA (Pouillau)   FG*

POWELL, Mrs. Watkins. fl. 19th cent. , America. songs.
    EA*

POWERS, Ada Weigel. b. Watertown, N.Y. , 20th cent.

pianist. songs, violin, piano.   EK March 1937 p144
ID

POWNALL, Mary Ann. née Wrighten. b. Feb. 1751, England. d. Aug. 11, 1796, Charleston, S.C. actress,
singer. songs. GG p10   HK p153-4, 368-9, 452,
527, 529, 568, 572   HL   ID

PRATTEN, Mrs. Sidney. b. 1840, England. d. ? guitarist. guitar.   EA   HL

PRAY, Ada Jordan. b. California, 20th cent. pianist,
teacher, lecturer. songs, piano.   EK March 1937
p144   ID

PRENTICE, Marion. b. Philadelphia, 20th cent. director,
music teacher.   EK March 1937 p144   ID

PREOBRAJENSKA, Vera N. b. April 27, 1926, San Francisco. music editor, writer, arranger, teacher, pianist, chairman music dept. piano, chamber, orchestra, choral.   AJ*   JA*   SN

PRESCOTT, Oliveria Louisa. b. Sept. 3, 1842, London.
d. 1919, London. writer, teacher. orchestra, songs,
choral.   EA*   EG p138   HL

PRESTI, Ida. b. May 31, 1924, Suresnes, France.
d. April 24, 1967, Rochester, N.Y. guitarist, teacher.   HL

PRESTON, Mrs. M. L. see LOEB-EVANS, Matilee

PRICE, Florence B. Smith. b. April 9, 1888, Little Rock,
Ark. d. June 3, 1953, Chicago. pianist, organist,
teacher. orchestra, choral, organ, songs, piano,
chamber.   AJ*   AN*   BE p22   EK April 1937
p216 +pict   GD p691* +pict   HD p70   HE p263-4,
261   ID   PD p192-3   SS p449*   WE p98, 115-9*
+biblio + recordings   YB p26*

PRIESING, Dorothy. née McLemore. b. July 31, 1910,
Nantucket, Mass. teacher. piano, choral, songs.
AJ*   JA   SN

PROCTOR, Alice McElroy. b. April 18, 1915, Albany, N.Y.
pianist. songs, choral, piano.   HD p70   SN

PUGET, Louise. Mme. Lemoine. b. Feb. 11, 1810, Paris.
    d. 1889, Paris. songs, 2 operas. EA* EG p188*
    HL   SF p44*

PUIG-ROGET, Henriette see ROGET, Henriette Puig

PYNE, Louisa. Mrs. Wilmore. fl. 19th cent., England.
    organist. HL

QUEEN, Virginia. b. Oct. 25, 1921, Dallas. teacher.
    piano, choral. AJ*   SN

QUESADA, Virginia. b. Feb. 11, 1951, Bayside, N. Y.
    electronic. AJ*

QUINAULT, Marie Anne. b. 1692, France. d. ? singer.
    motets. EA   EG p190   FG

QUINLAN, Agnes Clune. b. ? d. 1949, Limerick, Ireland.
    pianist, teacher, author, lecturer. songs, piano.
    EK April 1937 p216   ID   LF

RABINOF, Sylvia (Mrs. Benno). b. New York City, 20th
    cent. pianist. piano, orchestra, 1 opera. AJ*
    AN*   HL   SN

RADNOR, Countess of. formerly Viscountess Folkestone.
    fl. 19th cent., England. conductor, singer, editor.
    songs. HL

RAINIER, Priaulx. b. Feb. 3, 1903, Howick, Natal, South
    Africa (English). teacher, violinist. orchestra,
    chamber, wind, choral, songs, piano. BB   FJ p53
    HL   MH* +pict   MX*   PJ*   SM p85-6* +pict, p120

RALPH, Kate (Mrs. Francis). née Roberts. fl. 19th cent.,
    London. pianist. violin, chamber. EA   EG p144
    HL

RALSTON, Fanny Marion. b. 1875, St. Louis, Mo. d. ?
    pianist, music teacher. songs, piano. BE p36*

EA*   EK May 1937 p288   ID   LF   PL   SN

RAMSAY, Katharine (Lady). fl. 19th cent. , England. songs.
    EA*   EG p152, 238

RAMSEY, Ann. b. New Orleans, La. , 20th cent. songs.
    PC*

RAN, Shulamit. b. Oct. 21, 1949, Tel Aviv, Israel (in U.S.
    since 1966). teacher. piano, orchestra.   AJ* (b.
    1948)(Shalamit)   HF*   ML* (b. 1948)   SN (Shulamith)
    WN p7

RAPOPORT, Eda Ferdinand. b. 1900, Dvinsk, Latvia.
    d. May 9, 1969, New York City. pianist. piano,
    orchestra, opera, chamber.   AJ*   HL   ID   SN

[RAVENWALL, Mrs. : one of three pseudonyms for Robert
    A. Keiser, a male]

RAWLINSON, Angela. fl. 19th cent. ?, England. 1 operetta.
    EA*

RAYMOND, Emma Marcy. fl. 19th cent. , America. songs.
    piano.   BE p37*   EA*

RAYMOND, Madeleine. b. July 5, 1919, Donnaconna, Prov.
    Quebec. pianist. piano.   HL   KA*

REBE, Louise Christine. b. 1900, Philadelphia. pianist,
    teacher. piano.   BE p31*   FD April 1934 p268*
    +pict   ID   SN

RECLI, Giulia. b. Dec. 4, 1890, Milan. orchestra,
    choral, violin, songs.   HL

RED, Virginia Stroh. fl. 20th cent. , America. choral,
    chamber, orchestra.   SN

REED, Ida L. b. Nov. 30, 1865, Barbour County, W. V.
    choral.   HB p384-6* +pict

REES, Clara H. fl. 19th cent. , America. organist.
    organ, songs, piano.   BE p37   EA*   EG p207

REICHARD, Louise. b. April 11, 1779, Berlin. d. Nov.
    17, 1826, Hamburg. soprano, teacher. songs.   EA

(b. 1780)   EG p171-2   FG* (b. 1778)   HL (Luise)

REICHARDT, Julia see BENDA, Julia

REID, Lois C. fl. 20th cent., America. choral.   SN

REINAGLE, Caroline Orger. nee Orger. b. 1818, London.
    d. March 11, 1892, Tiverton, Devonshire, England.
    pianist, writer. piano, chamber.   EA* (under Orger)
    EG p136* (under Orger)   HL

REISER, Violet. b. July 3, 1915, New York City. organist,
    teacher. piano.   AN*   SN

REISET, Maria Felice Clemence de see GRANDVAL, Mme.
    la Vicomtesse de

REMICK, Bertha. fl. 20th cent., America. orchestra,
    piano, songs.   BE p37*   EK June 1937 p356   ID

RENE, Victor see HALE, Mrs. Philip

RENIE, Henriette. b. Sept. 18, 1875, Paris. d. March 1,
    1956, Paris. harpist, teacher. chamber, songs,
    harp.   HL   PJ*

RENNES, Catherine van. b. Aug. 2, 1858, Utrecht, Nether-
    lands. d. Nov. 23, 1940, Amsterdam. teacher, sing-
    er. songs.   EA*   EG p217 (d. 1858)   HL

RENSHAW, Dr. Rosette. b. May 4, 1920, Montreal.
    linguist, pianist, organist. 1 orchestra, 1 song, 3
    piano, 1 instrumental.   HL   KA*

RESPIGHI, Elsa Olivieri. b. March 24, 1894, Rome.
    singer. 1 opera, 2 orchestra, songs.   HL   ID

REYNOLDS, Erma. b. March 25, 1922, Laurel, Miss.
    teacher. chamber, orchestra.   AJ*

REYNOLDS, Florence. fl. 20th cent., America. choral.
    SN

RHEA, Lois (Mrs. Raymond). fl. 20th cent., America.
    choral.   SN

RHODES, Mrs. W. I. see HARDELOT, Guy d'

RICH, Gladys. b. April 26, 1892, Philadelphia. music director. songs, choral, operas. AJ AN   BE p17
SN

RICHARDS, Kathleen see DALE, Kathleen

RICHARDSON, Cornelia Heintzman. b. 1890, Waterloo,
Ontario. pianist. songs. HL KA*

RICHARDSON, Jennie V. fl. 19th cent., America. piano.
EA

RICHARDSON, Sharon. b. Aug. 3, 1948, Houston, Tex.
band, instrumental. AJ*

RICHER, Janine. b. June 6, 1924, Candebec-en-Eaux,
France. saxophone. LH*

RICHTER, Ada. b. Philadelphia, 20th cent. teacher,
lecturer, pianist. operas, choral, piano, songs.
AI Jan 1944 p11-2 + pict   AN*   EK July 1937 p479
ID SN

RICHTER, Marga. b. Oct. 21, 1926, Reedsburg, Wis.
teacher. piano, choral, chamber, orchestra. AJ*
HL JA* SN

RICHTER, Marion Morrey. b. Oct. 2, 1900, Columbus,
Ohio. teacher, pianist. 1 opera, 1 orchestra, 2 piano, 2 choral. AJ* SN (under M)

RICHTER, Pauline. fl. 19th cent., Germany. songs, piano. EA

RICOTTI, Onestina. fl. 19th cent., Italy. pianist, author.
songs, piano. EA EG p216

RIEGO, Teresa Clotilde Del see DEL RIEGO, Teresa
Clotilde

RIESE, Helen see LIEBMANN, Helen

RILEY, Sister Ann. Ann Marion Riley. b. April 28, 1928,
New Richmond, Wis. teacher. chamber, piano, organ, choral. AJ* SN p30

RING, Claire. fl. 19th cent., America. piano. EA*

RISHER, Anna Priscilla. b. 1875, Pittsburgh. d. ? or-
    ganist, conductor, music teacher. piano, songs,
    chamber.   BE p22-3*   EG p261-2   FD May 1933
    p356* +pict   ID   SN

RITTENHOUSE, Elizabeth Mae. b. July 23, 1915, Woodlawn,
    Ala. author, evangelist. songs. AN*   SN

RITTER, Fanny Raymond. b. 1840, Philadelphia. d. 1890,
    ?. author, translator. songs. BE p37   EA   EG
    p210, 240   HL (not as composer)

RIVE-KING, Julie (Mrs. Frank). b. Oct. 31, 1857, Cin-
    cinnati. d. July 24, 1937, Indianapolis. teacher, pi-
    anist. piano.   AL p154   BC   BE p4*   EA*   EG
    p203-4* +pict   EH p299, 308-9 +pict   EJ Oct 1910
    p449-50 +pict   EK Aug 1937 p544 +pict   GF   HL
    HT p441   HW   ID   JC +biblio   JG   LF   MI
    p122-6* +pict   PL   SN

ROBERT-MAZEL, Helene. fl. 18th cent. , France. pianist.
    songs.   EA*   EG p190*

ROBERTS, Gertrude Kuenzel. b. Aug. 23, 1906, Hastings,
    Minn. harpsichordist, pianist, teacher. harpsichord,
    songs.   AJ*   SD p6   SN

[ROBERTS, Kathleen A. : one of three pseudonyms for
    Robert A. Keiser, a male]

ROBERTS, Nellie Wilkinson. fl. 19th cent. , America.
    songs.   EA*

ROBERTS, Ruth Olive. b. Aug. 31, 1926, Portchester, N.Y.
    author. piano, songs. AN*   SN

ROBERTSON, Donna Nagey. b. Nov. 16, 1935, Indiana,
    Pa. teacher, organist, editor. songs, chamber,
    choral.   AJ*

ROBINSON, Fanny (Mrs. Joseph). née Arthur. b. Sept.
    1831, Southampton, England. d. Oct. 31, 1879,
    Dublin. songs, piano. EA*   HL   HW

ROCHAT, Andree. b. Jan. 12, 1900, Geneva. chamber,
    songs. HL   MH* +pict

ROCHE, Rosa La see LAROCHE, Rosa

ROCKWOOD, Marie Rich. b. Indianapolis, 20th cent. songs.
     IA p37*

RODGERS, Irene. fl. 20th cent. , Washington. pianist.
     piano, songs.   EK Aug 1937 p544   ID   SN

RODGERS, Mary. b. Jan. 11, 1931, New York City. songs.
     AJ*   AN   ID   SN

ROE, Gloria Ann. b. Jan. 5, 1935, Hollywood, Cal. au-
     thor, pianist. songs, choral.   AN*   SN

ROECKEL, Jane (Mrs. Joseph Leopold). née Jackson.
     pseud. Jules de Sivrai. fl. 19th cent. , England. pi-
     anist. piano.   EA*   HL   LF (pseud. Julie de Viv-
     rai)

ROELOFSON, Emily B. (Mrs.). fl. 19th cent. , ?. songs.
     EA*

ROESGEN-CHAMPION, Marguerite Sara. pseud. Jean
     Delysse. b. Jan. 25, 1894, Geneva. pianist, harpsi-
     chordist. songs, piano, orchestra, chamber, saxo-
     phone.   HL   LH*   MX*

ROESSING, Helen. fl. 20th cent. , Pennsylvania. piano.
     SN

ROGER, Denise. b. Jan. 21, 1924, Paris. chamber.
     LH*

ROGERS, Clara Kathleen. née Barnett. stage name Clara
     Doria. b. Jan. 14, 1844, Cheltenham, England.
     d. March 8, 1931, Boston. soprano, teacher, writer.
     chamber, piano, songs, violin, cello.   AL p58   BC
     BE p4*   EA   EG p202-3*   EH p307   EK Aug
     1937 p544 + pict   GF*   GG p10   HL   HW   HX
     p776, 778-9   ID   LF   PL   UB p102-3, 110-1

ROGERS, Cornelia P. fl. 20th cent. , America. songs,
     chamber.   SN

ROGERS, Emma Brady. fl. 20th cent. , America. piano,
     operas, orchestra.   SN

ROGERS, Ethel Tench. b. Feb. 21, 1914, Newark, N.J.
teacher, organist, pianist, music director. choral,
organ, piano. AJ* SN

ROGERS, Susan Whipple. b. Aug. 15, 1943, Dallas.
teacher, arranger. 2 chamber, 1 piano. AJ*

ROGET, Henriette Puig. b. Jan. 9, 1910, Bastia, Corsica.
organist, pianist. orchestra, organ, chamber. HL
PJ* RO*

ROHRER, Gertrude Martin. fl. 20th cent., America. club
leader. songs, 1 opera, choral. EK Aug 1937 p544
ID SN

ROKSETH, Yvonne. b. July 17, 1890, Maisons-Laffitte,
near Paris. d. Aug. 23, 1948, Strasbourg. musicologist, writer, organist, editor, teacher, music librarian.
1 choral, 1 chamber, 1 orchestra. HL

ROMA, Caro (pseud.). Carrie Northey. b. 1866, Oakland,
Calif. d. 1937. author, singer, prima donna. songs,
1 opera. AN* BE p12* EG p266 EK Aug 1937
p544 ID LF TB

RONALDS, Belle (Mrs.). fl. 19th cent., America. songs.
EA*

ROSENBERG, Fanny Gaschin de see GASCHIN DE ROSEN-
BERG, Fanny

ROSENBERGER, Margaret A. b. Micanopy, Fla., 20th
cent. author, teacher. songs. AN* SN

ROSS, Gertrude. b. Dayton, 20th cent. pianist. songs.
EG p266 EK Sept 1937 p556 ID

ROSSI, Camilla de see SONNTAG, Henriette

ROTHSCHILD, Baroness W. de. fl. 19th cent., Germany.
songs. EA p118-9*

ROWAN, Barbara. b. 1932, Colorado. choral, songs,
chamber. MH* +pict

RUDOW, Vivian Adelberg. b. April 1, 1936, Baltimore.
pianist, teacher. electronic. AJ*

RUEFF, Jeanine. b. Feb. 5, 1922, Paris. chamber, orchestra, 1 opera, saxophone.   HL   LH*   RO*

RUEGGER, Charlotte. b. ? d. 1959, America. choral,
chamber.   SN

RUNCIE, Constance Faunt le Roy (Mrs. James). b. 1836,
Indianapolis. d. 1911, ? pianist, club leader. songs,
organ, choral, 1 opera.   BE p1-2*   EA*   EG p258-
9 (b. Virginia)   EK Oct 1937 p628   GG p10   HJ
p321-2   ID (Constance Owen Runcie)   MI p103-6*
+ pict

RUSSELL, Olive Nelson. fl. 20th cent., America. choral.
SN

RUSSELL, Velma Armistead. fl. 20th cent., America.
piano.   SN

RUTA, Gilda (Countess). b. Oct. 13, 1853?, Naples.
d. Oct. 26, 1932, New York City. pianist, music
teacher. 1 opera, songs, orchestra, chamber.   EA
EG p211-2*, 238   HL   ID

RUTTENSTEIN, Constance (Baroness). fl. 19th cent.,
Germany. songs.   EA*

RYAN, Winifred. fl. 20th cent., Wisconsin. organist,
choir director. songs, piano.   WI p66*

RYBNER, Dagmar de Corval [Ryber]. b. Sept. 9, 1890,
Baden, Germany. d. July 22, 1965, Long Island,
N.Y. pianist. songs, chamber.   EK Oct 1937 p628
HL   ID

RYCKOFF, Lalla. b. 1891, Milwaukee. pianist. songs,
"musical readings."   BE p23*   EK Nov 1937 p700

RYDER, Theodora Sturkow. b. Philadelphia, 20th cent.
pianist. piano, clarinet, songs.   AN*   EK Nov
1938 p702   ID   LF (under Sturkow)

SABININ, Martha von. fl. 19th cent., Germany. songs,
piano.   EA*

SADOVNIKOFF, Mary Briggs. fl. 20th cent., America.
chamber, songs, choral. SN

SAFFERY, Eliza. Mrs. Henry Shelton. fl. 19th cent.,
England. songs. EA* HL

SAINT-DIDIER, Comtesse de. b. 1790, France. d. ?
1 choral. EA* EG p190*

ST. JOHN, Georgie Boyden. fl. 19th cent., America.
songs. EA* BE p37*

SAINT-MARCOUX, Micheline Coulombe see COULOMBE,
Micheline Saint-Marcoux

SAINTE-CROIX, Mlle. de. fl. 19th cent. 4 operas. EA*
EG p189

SAINTON-DOLBY, Charlotte Helen. (née Dolby.) b. May
17, 1821, London. d. Feb. 18, 1885, London. contralto, administrator. songs, choral. EA* EG
p136* EK Nov 1937 p700 (singer only) GF* HL
LF

SALAMAN, Ivy Frances see KLEIN, Ivy Frances

SALE, Sophia. b. ? d. 1869, Westminster, England. organist. hymns. EA

SALIGNY, Clara. fl. 19th cent., Germany. piano. EA

SALM-DYCK, Constance Marie de Theis see THEIS SALM-
DYCK, Constance Marie de

SALTER, Margaret. fl. 20th cent., America? songs.
TE p119-20*

SALTER, Mary Elizabeth (Mrs. Sumner). née Turner.
b. March 15, 1856, Peoria, Ill. d. Sept. 12, 1938,
Orangeburg, N.Y. soprano, teacher. songs. AL
p151* AN* BC BE p4* EA* EK Nov 1937
p700 GF GG p10 HL HT p563-5 HW ID
LF MI p713 (not as composer) PL SN TE*
p117-20

SAMSON, Valerie Brooks. b. Oct. 16, 1948, St. Louis,
Mo. music director, radio announcer. chamber.

AJ*

SAMUEL, Caroline. b. Nov. 1, 1822. teacher, pianist.
     piano, songs.   FG

SAMUEL, Mme. Marguerite. b. Paris; fl. 20th cent.,
     America. pianist, teacher. piano.   PC* + pict

SANDERS, Alma M. b. March 13, 1882, Chicago. d. Dec.
     15, 1956, New York City. pianist, teacher. piano,
     songs, chamber, incidental.   AJ*   AN*   EA*   EG
     p144   HL (English, 19th cent.)   SN

SANDIFUR, Ann E. b. May 14, 1949, Spokane, Wash.
     journalist. electronic.   AJ*

SANDRESKY, Margaret Vardell. b. April 28, 1921, Macon,
     Ga. teacher, organist. orchestra, piano, choral,
     chamber.   AJ*   JA*   SN

SANDY, Grace Linn. b. Greencastle, Ind., 20th cent.
     teacher, organist. piano, songs.   IA*

SANTA COLOMA-SOURGET, Helene. b. 1827, Bordeaux,
     France. d. ? pianist. songs, 1 opera.   EA*   EG
     p188*

SARGENT, Cora Decker. fl. 19th cent., America. songs.
     EA*

SAVAGE, Jane. fl. 18th cent., England. harpsichordist.
     harpsichord, piano.   HL

SAWATH, Caroline. fl. 19th cent., Germany. piano.   EA

SAWYER, Elizabeth (Betty). fl. 20th cent., America.
     chamber.   SN

SAWYER, Harriet P. (Hattie). fl. 19th cent., America.
     songs.   EA*   HT p441   LF

SCHADEN, Nanette von. b. Salzburg, Austria, 19th cent.
     d. Salzburg. pianist. piano.   EA   EG p163 (Schar-
     den)

SCHAEFER, Sister Mary see CHERUBIM, Sister Mary
     Schaefer

SCHAEFFER, Theresa. fl. 19th cent., Germany. piano, songs. EA* EG p163

SCHAFMEISTER, Helen. fl. 20th cent., America. songs. SN

SCHÄTZELL, Pauline von see DECKER, Pauline von

SCHAUROTH, Delphine von. b. 1814, Magdeburg, Germany. d. after 1881. pianist. piano. EA* EG p171 HL (Delphine [Adolphine])

SCHICK, Philippine. b. Feb. 9, 1893, Bonn. d. 1970. songs, chamber, choral, 1 opera, orchestra, piano. FL HL MH* +pict MW PJ*

SCHINDLER-MAHLER, Alma Maria. b. ? d. 1964. songs. GH p6 MD ME p13-7 SF p32 (Alma Mahler Werfel) SO p74-8

SCHIRMACHER, Dora. b. Sept. 1, 1857, Liverpool, England. pianist. piano, songs. EA EG p146 (b. 1862) GF* HL ID

SCHLICK, Elise (Countess of). fl. 19th cent., Germany. songs. EA*

SCHMEZER, Elise. fl. 19th cent., Germany. songs, 1 opera. EA* EG p168* (Schnezer) SF p45*

SCHMIDT, Diane Louise. b. Nov. 23, 1948, Seattle, Wash. accordionist. accordion. AJ*

SCHMIDT, Mrs. Louis Bernard. fl. 20th cent., America. songs. SN

SCHNORR VON CAROLSFELD, Malvina. fl. 19th cent., Germany. songs. EA*

SCHOLL, Amalie. b. 1823, Dresden. d. 1879, Dresden. songs. EA*

SCHONTHAL-SECKEL, Ruth. b. June 27, 1924, Hamburg (U.S. citizen 1956). teacher. chamber, piano, songs. AJ* SN

SCHORR-WEILER, Eva. b. 1927, Crailsheim/Württ.

chamber, choral, piano, organ, songs.   MH* +pict

SCHREINZER, Mlle. F. M.   b. 1812, Danzig, Prussia.
    d. 1873. pianist, singer. songs, piano.   EA   FG*

SCHRÖTER, Corona Elizabeth Wilhelmina von. b. Jan. 14,
    1751, Guben, Germany. d. Aug. 23, 1802, Ilmenau,
    Germany. soprano, actress, court musician. songs.
    EA   EK March 1938 p138 +pict   FG   GF   HL   ID

SCHUBERT, Georgine. b. 1840, Dresden. d. 1878, Pots-
    dam. soprano. songs. EA

SCHUMAKER, Grace L. b. Lafayette, Ind., 20th cent.
    teacher. songs, violin.   IA p38, 51*

SCHUMANN, Clara (Mrs. Robert). nee Wieck. b. Sept. 13,
    1819, Leipzig. d. May 20, 1896, Frankfurt-am-Main.
    songs, piano.   AD   BC   BR   BS   BT p32   EA*
    EG p90-110, 169, 234, 238* +pict (under W and S)
    EH p294   EK March 1938 p138 +pict   FH   GB
    GF*   GH p6   HC p18-20, 32-3* +pict   HH   HL
    HM   ID   LF   MG   MX*   MY   QA   RH* +biblio
    RM p47   SF p48-9*   SG p261-4, xi, xiv-xv, xviii,
    xxiv, 67, 130   SV   WA

SCHUMANN, Meta. b. 1887, St. Paul, Minn. soprano,
    teacher, accompanist. songs.   BE p23*   EK March
    1938 p138 +pict   ID

SCHUYLER, Georgina. fl. 19th cent., America. songs.
    EA*

SCHUYLER, Phillipa Duke. b. Aug. 2, 1931/2, New York
    City. d. May 9, 1967, DaNang Bay, Vietnam. pi-
    anist, writer. piano, orchestra.   AN*   AJ p508*
    BT p34, 36*   ID   RJ*   WE p82-7, 99, 120-1*
    +biblio +recordings

SCHWARTZ, Julie. b. April 17, 1947, Washington, D.C.
    teacher. chamber.   AJ*

SCHWARZ, Friederike. b. 1910, Prague. (German-Bo-
    hemian.) pianist. chamber, piano, songs.   HL

SCHWERDTFEGER, E. Anne. formerly Sister Ernest.
    b. Feb. 1, 1930, Galveston, Tex. teacher, head

music dept. choral, piano, orchestra. AJ* SN

SCHWERTZELL, Wilhelmine von. fl. 19th cent., Germany. songs. EA

SCOTT, Beatrice MacGowan see MacGOWAN-SCOTT, Beatrice

SCOTT, Clara H. b. 1841, America. d. 1897. songs. EA

SCOTT, Lady John Douglas. née Alicia Anne Spottiswoode. b. 1810, Spottiswoode, Berwickshire, Scotland. d. March 12, 1900, Spottiswoode, Berwickshire, Scotland. songs. EA* EG p136* (Lady Jane Scott) FQ p101, 336* +biblio HD p74 HL LF*

SCOTT-HUNTER, Hortense. fl. 20th cent., America. 2 operas, incidental. AJ*

SCOVILLE, Margaret. b. May 3, 1944, Pasadena, Cal. chamber, electronic. AJ*

SEALE, Ruth (Mrs.). b. Alabama, 20th cent. choral, songs. PC* +pict

SEARCH, Sara Opal. fl. 20th cent., America. 1 symphony. SN

SEARS, Helen. fl. 20th cent., America. songs, piano. SN

SEARS, Ilene Hanson. b. Aug. 31, 1938, Crookston, Minn. teacher, pianist. 2 chamber, 1 choral. AJ

SEAVER, Blanche Ebert. b. Sept. 15, 1891, Chicago. songs, orchestra. AJ AN* EG p265 SN

SEAY, Virginia. b. Aug. 8, 1922, Palo Alto, Cal. musicologist. piano, songs, chamber, choral. ID

SEEGER, Ruth see CRAWFORD-SEEGER, Ruth

SEIPT, Sophie. b. Cologne, Germany, 19th cent. cello. EA* EG p172-3

SELMER, Kathryn Lande. b. Nov. 6, 1930, Staten Island,

N. Y. singer. songs, operas. AJ p508*

SELTZNER, Jennie. b. Jan. 19, 1895, Bristol Township,
Wis. teacher. chamber, piano. WI p69*

SEMEGEN, Daria. b. Jan. 27, 1946, Bamberg, Germany.
U. S. citizen 1957. electronic center technician, lec-
turer. chamber, orchestra, instrumental. AJ* NA
SN

SENEKE, Teresa. b. 1848, Italy. d. 1875, Rome. 1
opera, songs, piano. EA* EG p215*

SESSI-NATORP, Marianne. b. 1776, Rome. d. March 10, 1847,
Vienna. soprano, court musician. songs. FG HL

SEUEL-HOLST, Marie see HOLST, Marie Seuel

SEVERY, Violet Cavell. b. May 26, 1912, Pasadena, Cal.
teacher. songs, instrumentals. AJ*

SEWALL, Maud Gilchrist. fl. 20th cent., America. choral.
SN

SHATIN, Judith. b. Nov. 21, 1949, Boston. teacher.
chamber. AJ*

SHAW, Alice Marion. b. Rockland, Me., 20th cent. teacher, accompanist. songs, choral, piano, organ, violin,
flute, cello. LF SN

SHAW, Carrie Burpee. b. 1850, Maine. d. 1946, ?
choral, songs. SN

SHELDON, Lillian Traitt. b. Sept. 10, 1865, Gouveneur,
N. Y. d. Jan. 10, 1925, Gouveneur, N. Y. organist.
choral, songs. EK May 1938 p280 ID LF

SHELLEY, Margaret Vance. fl. 20th cent., America.
choral. SN

SHEPARD, Jean Ellen. b. Nov. 1, 1949, Durham, N. C.
chamber. AJ*

SHERMAN, Elna. fl. 20th cent., America. chamber.
AJ* SN

SHERRINGTON, Grace. b. 1842, Preston, England. d. ?
teacher. songs. EA

SHERRINGTON, Helena L. Mrs. Nicolas Jacques Lemmens.
b. Oct. 4, 1934, Preston, England. d. May 9, 1906,
Brussels. soprano, teacher. songs. EA HL
(under L)

SHIELDS, Alice. b. 1943, America. electronic. AJ*

SHREVE, Susan E. b. Nov. 24, 1952, Detroit. instrumental. AJ

SICK, Anna Laura. b. 1803, Germany. d. ? pianist.
piano, songs. EA

SIDDALL, Louise. b. ?, Winston-Salem, N.C. d. Dec. 8,
1935, Sumter, S.C. teacher. organ, choral. EK
May 1938 p280 ID

SIEGFRIED, Lillie Mahon. b. Buffalo, 20th cent. songs,
operetta. EG p206

SILBERTA, Rhea. b. April 19, 1900, Pocahontas, Va.
d. Dec. 6, 1959, New York, N.Y. singer, educator,
vocal coach, pianist. piano, songs, orchestra. AJ*
AN EK June 1938 p388 ID SN

SILSBEE, Ann L. b. July 21, 1930, Cambridge, Mass.
teacher, lecturer. chamber. AJ*

SILVER, Sheila J. b. Oct. 3, 1946, Seattle. chamber.
AJ*

SILVERBURG, Rose (Mrs. Joseph S.). fl. 20th cent.,
Louisiana. organist. songs. PC*

SILVERMAN, Faye-Ellen. b. Oct. 2, 1947, New York City.
teacher, assistant editor. songs, 1 opera. AJ*
CK 1974*

SIMMONS, Kate. fl. 19th cent., America. "dances."
EA*

SIMONS, Nettie. b. 1913, New York City. producer,
vocal coach. chamber, piano, choral, opera, songs,
orchestra, theater. AJ* AO p111* CK 1975*

SN

SIRMEN [Syrmen], Maddalena di. née Lombardini. b. 1735, Venice. d. ca. 1800, Venice. singer, violinist. chamber, orchestra. EA* EG p214 HL ID SL*

SKAGGS, Hazel Ghazarian. b. Aug. 26, 1924, Boston. author, teacher. instrumentals. AN* SN

SKELTON, Nellie Bangs (Mrs.). b. Aug. 15, 1859, Lacon, Ill. pianist. piano, songs. BE p37 EA MI p713 ("Skklton")

SKILLINGS, Cora see BRIGGS, Cora Skillings

SKINNER, Fanny Lovering (Mrs.). fl. 19th cent., America. teacher, singer. songs. BE p37* EA*

SKINNER, Florence Marian. Mrs. Stuart Stresa. fl. 19th cent., England. (2) operas. EA* EG p142 HL

SKJEVELAND, Helge. b. 1950, Provo, Utah. 1 orchestra. AJ*

SLEETH, Natalie. b. Oct. 29, 1930, Evanston, Ill. organist, secretary. choral. AJ*

SMART, Harriet Anne. Mrs. William Callow. b. Oct. 20, 1817, London. d. June 30, 1883, London. songs, choral. EA p129 HL

SMILEY, Pril. b. March 19, 1943, Lake Mohonk, N.Y. teacher, electronic music consultant. electronic, incidental. AJ*

SMITH, Alice Mary. Mrs. Frederick Meadows White. b. May 19, 1839, London. d. Dec. 4, 1884, London. chamber, orchestra, choral, songs. EA* EG p137-8, 234* GF* HL ID LF

SMITH, Anita. b. Dec. 19, 1922, New York City. author. piano, songs. AJ* AN*

SMITH, Eleanor. b. 1858, America. d. 1942. songs, choral. BE p37* EA* EA p208* ID

SMITH, Eleanor Louise. b. 1873, St. Louis, Mo. d. ? pianist, organist. songs. LF

SMITH, Ella May. b. Feb. 20, 1860, Uhrichsville, Ohio. d. 1934, Oak Park, Ill. pianist, teacher, organist. songs. EK July 1938 p480 + pict ID

SMITH, Florence B. fl. 20th cent., America. songs. SN

SMITH, Mrs. Gerrit. fl. 19th cent., America. singer. piano, songs. BE p37* EA

SMITH, Gertrude. b. New York, 19th cent. songs. BE p37* EA

SMITH, Ida Polk. fl. 20th cent., America. piano. SN

SMITH, Julia Frances. b. Jan. 25, 1911, Denton, Tex. pianist, author, lecturer, head music dept. (adminis-trator). choral, piano, chamber, orchestra, 5 operas. AJ* AN* HD p76 HL ID SN

SMITH, Laura Alexanderine. fl. 19th cent., England. au-thor. songs. EA p131 HL

SMITH, Mary Barber. b. 1878, England. songs, organ. KA p252

SMITH, May Florence. fl. 19th cent., America. writer, musician. songs. EA

SMITH, Nettie Pierson. fl. 19th cent., America. songs. BE p37* EA*

SMITH, Rosalie Balmer. fl. 19th cent., America. musi-cian. violin. BE p37* EA*

SMITH, Ruby Mae. b. March 20, 1902, Joplin, Mo. au-thor, publisher, teacher, artist manager. songs. AN* SN

SMYTH, Dame Ethel Mary. b. April 23, 1858, Foots Gray, Kent, England. d. May 9, 1944, Woking, Surrey, England. author, journalist. songs, orchestra, piano, 2 operas, choral, incidental. BB* BC BT p32* DC EA* EG p140-1, 237* FA p238 GF HL

HN (b. Sidcup, Eng.)   ID   LF   MX*   PJ*   RM
p48, 51   SC   SP   YA p539-40*

SNEED, Anna.   Mrs. Cairn.   fl. 19th cent., America.
    songs.   EA*

SNODGRASS, Louise Harrison.   b. 1890, Cincinnati, Ohio.
    d. ?   pianist.   songs, instrumental.   BE p28*   EG
    p265   EK July 1938 p480 +pict   ID   SN

SNOW, Mary McCarty.   b. Aug. 26, 1928, Brownsville,
    Tex.   teacher.   electronic.   AJ*

SONNTAG, Henriette.   Mme. la Comtesse de Rossi.   fl.
    before 1800.   singer.   FG*

SOPHIE, Elisabeth.   b. Aug. 20, 1613, Güstrow, Germany.
    d. July 12, 1676, Lüchow, Germany.   HL

SOUERS, Mildred.   b. Feb. 26, 1894, Des Moines, Iowa.
    accompanist, lecture-recitalist, coach.   piano, choral,
    chamber, organ.   AJ*   AN*   SN

SOULAGE, Marcelle.   b. Dec. 12, 1894, Lima, Peru.
    French.   pianist.   chamber.   EK July 1938 p480
    HL   ID   RO

SOUTHAM, Ann.   b. Feb. 4, 1937, Winnipeg, Manitoba.
    teacher.   electronic, piano, chamber, orchestra.   HL
    MA* +biblio

SPECHT, Anita Socola (Mrs.).   fl. 20th cent., America.
    pianist.   1 piano.   PC* +pict

SPENCER, Fanny Morris.   b. Newburgh, N.Y., 19th cent.
    songs, choral.   BE p37*   EA   HT p441

SPENCER, Marguerita.   b. 1892, Glace Bay, Nova Scotia.
    pianist, organist, cellist.   piano, choral, songs.
    HL   KA*

SPENCER, Williametta.   b. Aug. 15, 1932, Marion, Ill.
    teacher.   choral.   AJ*   JH*

SPIEGEL, Laurie.   b. Sept. 20, 1945, Chicago.   guitarist,
    teacher.   electronic, multimedia, incidental.   AJ*

SPINDLE, Louise Cooper. b. Muskegan, Mich., 20th cent. piano, choral, songs, orchestra. AJ* AN SN

SPIZIZEN, Louise. b. Aug. 24, 1928, Lynn, Mass. music director, teacher. 2 choral, 1 ballet, 1 theater. AJ*

SPORLEDER, Charlotte. b. 1836, Cassel, Germany. piano. EA*

SPRADLING, Maurine. fl. 20th cent., America. songs. SN

SPRAGINS, Florence. fl. 20th cent., America. choral. SN

SPROTT, Nelle McMaster see McMASTER, Nelle

STAIR, Patty. Martha Greene. b. Nov. 12, 1869, Cleveland, Ohio. d. April 26, Cleveland. pianist, organist, teacher. songs, choral, 1 opera, organ. AL p155 BE p5* EA p133 EG p260 EK Sept 1938 p558 +pict GF HL HT p441 ID LF PL SN

STAIRS, Louise E. pseud. Sidney Forrest. b. 1892, Troupberg, N.Y. conductor, pianist, organist, teacher. piano, choral, songs. AJ BE p23* EK Aug 1938 p548 ID SN

STANLEY, Helen. Mrs. Denby Gatlin. b. April 6, 1930, Tampa, Fla. violist, music director, lecturer, pianist. chamber, electronic, piano, songs. AJ* SN

STECHER, Marianne. fl. 19th cent., Germany. organist. organ, piano. EA* EG p172

STEELE, Helen. b. June 21, 1904, Enfield, Conn. teacher, accompanist. songs. AJ p509*

STEINER, Emma. b. Baltimore, 20th cent. musician. 3 operas, songs. BE p37* EA* EG p205-6* ID

STEINER, Gitta. b. April 17, 1932, Prague, Czechoslovakia. U.S. citizen 1941. teacher. songs, choral, piano, chamber, percussion. AJ* SN

STEWART, Mdm. fl. 19th cent. 1 opera. EA*

STEWART, Annie M. fl. 19th cent., America. songs.
EA*

STEWART, F. M. fl. 19th cent., America. songs, piano.
EA

STEWART, Hascal Vaughan. b. Feb. 17, 1898, Darlington,
S. C. teacher. piano. AJ*

STILMAN-LASANSKY, Julia. b. Feb. 3, 1935, Buenos
Aires. American. choral. JA*

STIRLING, Elizabeth. Mrs. Frederick A. Bridge. b. Feb.
26, 1819, Greenwich, England. d. March 25, 1895,
London. organist. organ, songs, piano. EA*   EG
p133-4*   GF*   HL   ID

STITT, Margaret McClure. fl. 20th cent., America.
choral, songs, opera. SN

STOCKER, Clara. fl. 20th cent., America. piano. SN

STOCKER, Stella Prince. b. April 3, 1858, Jacksonville,
Ill. d. ? Indian music specialist, teacher. songs,
piano, 4 operas, incidental. BE p5-6*   EA*   EG
p209   GG p11   HL   MI p714 (not as composer)
PL

STOEPPELMANN, Janet. b. Dec. 5, 1948, St. Louis, Mo.
choral, multi-media. AJ*

STOLLEWERCK, Nina von. b. 1825, Vienna. d. ? songs,
choral, piano, orchestra. EA   EG p163   FG*

STORY, Pauline B. b. Cincinnati, 20th cent. pianist.
piano. EK Oct 1938 p630 + pict

STRATTON, Anne. Mrs. Thomas S. Holden. b. 1887,
Cleburne, Tex. songs. BE p23-4*

STREATCH, Alice. fl. 20th cent., America. choral,
songs. SN

STRICKLAND, Lily Teresa. Mrs. J. Courtney Anderson.
b. Jan. 25, 1887, Anderson, S. C. d. June 6, 1958,

Hendersonville, N. C.   author, organist, singer.   piano,
choral, songs, 3 operas, orchestra.   AJ*   AL p153*
AN*   BA   EG p266   EK Oct 1938 p630 +pict   FD
Sept 1933 p626* +pict   HL   HR* +pict   ID   LF
SN

STRONG, May A.   fl. 20th cent. , America.   singer, teacher.   songs.   EK Oct 1938 p630 +pict   ID

STROZZI, Barbara.   b. ca. 1620, Venice.   d. ?   singer.
3 operas, songs, choral.   BE p30   BK p30   EA*
EG p65   FG*   GH p5   HL

STUDER, Carmen Weingartner   see   WEINGARTNER-STUDER,
Carmen

STURKOW, Theodora Ryder   see   RYDER, Theodora Sturkow

SUCHY, Gregoria Karides.   b. Milwaukee, 20th cent.
teacher.   orchestra, piano, songs.   AJ*

SUESSE, Dana Nadine.   b. Dec. 3, 1911, Kansas City, Mo.
author, pianist, arranger.   orchestra, songs, piano.
AN*   HP p313*   ID   SN

SUMNER, Clare.   b. 1886, Birmingham, England.   pianist,
organist, teacher.   piano, choral, songs.   KA*

SUMNER, Sarah.   fl. 20th cent. , America.   songs.   AJ*

SUTRO, Florence Edith (Mrs. Theodore).   née Clinton.
b. May 1, 1865, London.   d. 1906, ?   pianist, author,
teacher, administrator.   songs, piano.   BE p37-8*
EA*   EG p209   GG p11   HL (not as composer)
LF   MI p714   TE

SWAIN, Freda.   b. Oct. 31, 1902, Portsmouth, England.
pianist.   chamber, songs, piano, saxophone.   HL
LH (b. Oct. 13, 1912)

SWEPTSTONE, Edith.   fl. 19th cent. , England.   teacher.
orchestra, chamber, choral, songs, piano, violin.
EA*   EG p139, 238*   HL

SWIFT, Gertrude H. (Mrs.).   fl. 19th cent. , America.
songs.   BE p38*   EA*

SWIFT, Kay. Mrs. Paul Warburg. b. April 15, 1905, New
     York City. songs, piano, theater.   AJ*   AN*   SN

SWISHER, Gloria Wilson. b. March 12, 1935, Seattle.
     teacher. orchestra, choral, 1 opera.   AJ*   SN

SYNGE, Mary Helena. b. Parsontown, Ireland, 19th cent.
     pianist. songs.   EA*   HL

SYRMEN, Maddalena di see SIRMEN, Maddalena di

TAILLEFERRE, Germaine. b. April 19, 1892, Parc-de-St.
     Maur, near Paris. pianist. orchestra, piano, cham-
     ber, songs, 1 opera, incidental.   BC   BQ p53*
     CE   EK Jan 1939 p2 +pict   FP p246, 352, 403*
     HC p27-8*   HL   ID   MX*   PM*   RH* +biblio
     RM p48   RO*

TAIT, Annie. b. ? d. Feb. 24, 1886, Eastbourne, Eng-
     land. pianist. piano, chamber, songs.   EA*   HL

TALMA, Louisa. b. Oct. 31, 1906, Archacon, France.
     teacher. piano, chamber, orchestra, choral, songs,
     1 opera.   AJ*   AL p155*   AN   BB   HD p77-8*
     HL   ID   JA*   PE p355*   PJ*   RM p48   SD p4
     SN   TC p175-6*

TAMBLYN, Bertha Louise. b. Oshawa, Ontario, 20th cent.
     piano, choral, songs.   HL   KA*

TAPPER, Bertha (Mrs. Thomas). née Feiring. b. Jan.
     25, 1859, Christiania, Norway (to America 1881).
     d. Sept. 2, 1915, New York City. pianist, teacher.
     piano, songs.   EK Jan 1939 p2 +pict   HL (not as
     composer)   ID   LF (not as composer)   PL

TARBOS, Frances. b. St. Paul, Minn., 20th cent. pianist.
     1 opera, songs.   ID

TARDIEU DE MALLEVILLE, Charlotte see MALLEVILLE,
     Charlotte Tardieu de

TARLOW, Karen Anne. b. Sept. 19, 1947, Boston. songs,
     chamber.   AJ*

TATE, Phyllis Margaret Duncan. Mrs. Alan Frank.
    b. April 6, 1911, London. saxophone, songs, orches-
    tra, 1 opera. BB   FJ p55   HL   LH*   PJ*

TATTON, Madeleine. fl. 20th cent. , America. chamber.
    SN

TAYLOR, Mrs. A. H.   fl. 19th cent. , America. songs.
    BE p38*   EA*

TAYLOR, Eleanor. fl. 20th cent. , America. choral, songs,
    organ, orchestra. SN

TAYLOR, Laura W. (Mrs. Tom) <u>see</u> BARKER, Laura

TAYLOR, Mary Lyon. b. Indianapolis, 20th cent. songs.
    IA p40*

TEMPLE, Hope. Mrs. Andre Messager. pseud. for
    Dotie Davies. b. 1859, Dublin. d. May 10, 1938,
    Folkestone, England. pianist. songs, 1 operetta.
    EA*   EG p152*   EK Feb 1939 p74 + pict   GF*   HL
    ID   LF*

TENNYSON, Lady. b. ? d. 1896, Aldworth, England.
    songs. EA*   EG p152

TERHUNE, Anice (Mrs. Albert Payson). née Potter.
    b. Oct. 27, 1873, Hamden, Mass. d. Nov. 9, 1964,
    Pompton Lakes, N.J. pianist. songs, 2 operas,
    piano. AJ*   HI   HL   ID

TERRIER-LAFFAILLE, Anne. b. July 22, 1904, Laval,
    France. chamber, orchestra, choral, songs. HL

TERRY, Frances. b. 1884, Windsor, Conn. pianist,
    teacher. piano. AJ   AL p153*   BE p31*   EK
    Feb 1939 p74 + pict   FD March 1937 p209* + pict
    ID   SN

THEIS SALM-DYCK, Constance Marie de (Princess).
    b. Nov. 7, 1767, Nantes. d. April 13, 1845, Paris.
    songs. FG

THOMAS, Adelaide Louisa. b. Clapham, London, 19th
    cent. pianist, administrator. "church music. "   EA
    HL

THOMAS, Helen. b. East Liverpool, O. , 20th cent. songs, 1 opera, piano. AJ* AN SN (Helen Thompson Thomas)

THOMAS, Joyce Carol. b. May 25, 1938, Ponca City, Okla. writer. MK

THOMAS, Mary Virginia (Mrs. Michael Daraban). b. Elkins, W. Va. , fl. 20th cent. author, pianist, organist. songs. AJ SN

THOME, Diane. b. Jan. 25, 1942, New York City. pianist, lecturer. electronic. AJ* WN

THOMPSON, Alexandra. fl. 19th cent. , England. songs. EA* HL (Thomson)

THOMPSON, Leland. fl. 20th cent. , America. piano, songs. SN

THORN, Edgar see MERRICK, Mrs. C.

THORNE, Beatrice. b. April 14, 1878, London. pianist. piano. HL

THURBER, Nettie C. fl. 19th cent. , America. songs. EA

THYS, Pauline (Thys-Sebault). b. 1836, Paris. d. ? writer. songs, 6 operas. EA* (Labault Pauline Thys) EG p188* HL

TIBALDI, Rosa (Mrs. Giuseppe Luigi). née Tartaglini. b. ? d. Nov. 17, 1775, Bologna. singer. HL

TIERNEY, Kathleen. fl. 20th cent. , Canada. violinist. songs. AL p163

TILLETT, Jeanette. fl. 20th cent. , America. piano, choral. SN

TODD, Esther Cox. fl. 20th cent. , America. songs, piano, violin. SN

TODD, M. Flora. fl. 20th cent. , America. choral. SN

TONEL, Leonie. fl. 19th cent. , France. piano. EA*

TORRY, Jane Sloman. fl. 19th cent., America. piano, songs. BE p38* EA*

TOWER, Joan. b. Sept. 6, 1938, New Rochelle, N.Y. lecturer, pianist. chamber, orchestra, percussion, instrumental. AJ JA* SN

TOWNSEND, Marie. fl. 19th cent., ? opera, songs. EA* (also known as Mansfield Townsend)

TRAIN, Adeline. fl. 19th cent., America. songs. BE p38* EA* EG p209

TRAVENET, Mme. B. de. fl. 18th cent., France. poet. songs. EA* EG p193

TREMBLAY, Amedee. b. April 14, 1876, Montreal. d. 1949. choral, songs, piano. HL

TRETBAR, Helen. b. Buffalo, N.Y., 19th cent. songs. BE p38 EA* EG p209, 240 MI p715 (not as composer)

TREWS, Susan (Mrs. Charles A.). fl. 19th cent., England. pianist. 1 chamber. HL

TRIMBLE, Joan. b. June 18, 1915, Ulster, Ireland. pianist. piano, chamber. FJ p55 HL

TRINITAS, Sister M. b. Union City, Ind., 20th cent. teacher. 1 song, 1 choral. IA p29*

TRIPP, Ruth. fl. 20th cent., America. operas, choral, songs. SN

TROENDLE, Theodora. b. Chicago, 20th cent. violinist. piano. EK April 1939 p219 + pict ID

TROUP, Emily Josephine. fl. 19th cent., England. songs, piano, chamber. EA EG p144 HL

TROWBRIDGE, Leslie. fl. 19th cent., England. soprano. songs. HL

TSCHETSCHULIN, Agnes. fl. 19th cent. songs, violin. EA*

TSCHIERSCHKY, Wilhelmine. fl. 19th cent. , Germany.
     songs.   EA

TUCKER, Mary Jo. fl. 20th cent. , America. choral.
     SN

TUCKER, Tui St. George. fl. 20th cent. , America. 1
     chamber.   AJ*

TUNISON, Louise. fl. 19th cent. , America. songs.   EA*
     EG p209

TURGEON, Frances. fl. 20th cent. , America. piano,
     songs, chamber.   SN

TURNER MALEY, Florence see MALEY, Florence

TURNER, Mildred Cozzens (Mrs. Huntington M.). b. Feb.
     23, 1897, Pueblo, Colo. songs.   AJ*   AN   SN
     ("Turned")

TURNER, Myra Brooks. fl. 20th cent. , America. choral,
     songs, musicals.   AJ   SN

TURRELL, Margaret B. Hoberg. b. Terre Haute, Ind. ,
     fl. 20th cent. pianist, organist. harp, songs.   IA p42*

TWOMBLY, Mary Lynn. b. Jan. 8, 1935, New York, N. Y.
     conductor. 2 operas, orchestra, incidental.   AJ*

TYRELL, Agnes. b. Sept. 20, 1848, Brunn, Austria.
     d. April 18, 1883, Brno, Moravia. pianist. orches-
     tra, piano, 1 opera.   EA*   EG p164   HL

TYSON, Mildred Lund. Mrs. Harold Canfield. b. March
     10, 1900, Moline, Ill. teacher, organist, choir di-
     rector. songs, choral.   AJ*   AN*   SN

UCCELLI, Carolina. née Pazzini. b. 1810, Florence.
     d. 1855, Florence. 2 operas.   EA*   EG p215*
     FG

UGALDE, Delphine. Mme. Valcollier. b. 1829, France.
     d. 1910. 1 opera.   GF*   HL

ULEHLA, Ludmila. b. May 20, 1923, New York, N.Y.
 teacher. songs, piano, chamber, orchestra. AJ*
 GH p7   SN

VALENTINE, Ann. fl. 18th cent. , England. musician.
 chamber, piano. EA*   EG p133*   HL

VAN DER LUND, Agnes see LUND, Agnes van der

VANDERPOEL, Kate. fl. 19th cent. , America. songs.
 BE*   EA*

VAN DE VATE, Nancy Hayes. pseud. Helen Huntley.
 b. Dec. 30, 1930, Plainfield, N.J. teacher, lecturer.
 songs, piano, chamber, orchestra, 1 opera, choral.
 AJ*   CK 1975* + address   JA*   SD   SN   SR*

VANDEVERE, J. Lilien. b. Canton, Pa. , 20th cent.
 teacher. piano.   EK June 1939 p358 + pict   ID

VAN DE WIELE, Aimée see WIELE, Aimée van de

VANIER, Jeannine. b. Aug. 21, 1929, Laval, Quebec.
 chamber, piano. HL

VAN KATWIJK, Viola Edna Beck see KATWIJK, Viola
 Edna Beck van

VANNAH, Kate. writer under name Kate van Twinkle.
 b. 1855, Gardiner, Me. d. 1933. pianist, organist,
 poet, writer. songs, piano, orchestra, 1 opera.
 BE p10*   EA*   EG p251-2   EK June 1939 p358
 + pict   GG p10   ID   SN

VAN VLIET, Pearl H. see VLIET, Pearl H. van

VAN ZANTEN, Cornelia see ZANTEN, Cornelia van

VASHAW, Cecile. fl. 20th cent. , America. band.   SN

VATE, Nancy Hayes Van de see VAN DE VATE, Nancy
 Hayes

VAURABOURG, Andree. Mrs. Arthur Honegger. b. Sept.

8, 1894, Toulouse, France. pianist. songs. HL

VELTHEIM, Charlotte. b. March 30, 1803, Breslau, Germany. d. April 27, 1873, ? singer, pianist. songs, piano. EA

VENTH, Lydia Kunz (Mrs.). fl. 19th cent., America. pianist. piano. BE p38* EA*

VERGER, Virginie Morel du. b. 1799, Metz, France. d. 1870, Verger Castle. pianist, chamber, piano. EA* EG p191-2

VERRILL, Louise Shurtleff. b. 1870, Brown, Me. d. 1948. piano, songs. PL SN

VESPERMANN-GUDRES, Marie. Mrs. Arndts. b. April 5, 1823, Munich. d. May 23, 1889, Munich. piano. EA

VEZZANA, Lucrezia Orsina. b. 1593, Bologna, Italy. d. ? motets. EA (under both O. Vizzani and O. Vezzana) EG p64, 65 (under both O. Vizzani and L. Vezzana) FG (under Lucrece O. Vezzana and O. Vezzana) SN (Vizani)

VIARDOT, Louise Pauline Marie. Mme. Heritte. b. Dec. 14, 1841, Paris. d. Jan. 17, 1918, Heidelberg. teacher, contralto. chamber, choral, songs, piano, 2 operas. EA* (under H) EG p185* HC p23* HL (Viardot, L. P. M. Heritte de la Tour) ID LF RH

VIARDOT-GARCIA, Pauline Michelle Ferdinande. b. Aug. 29, 1821, Paris. d. 1910. singer. songs, piano, 3 operas, chamber. BC (not as composer) EA* EG p183-4* EJ Dec 1910 p801-2 + pict FB p173-5 FI + biblio GF* HC p20-3, 33-4* + pict RH* + biblio SF p57

VIGNY, Louise von. fl. 19th cent., Germany. songs. EA* EG p172

VILLARD, Nina de. fl. 19th cent., ? piano. EA*

VILLENEUVE, Marie-Louise Diane. Rev. Soeur Marie-Héloise, S.S.A. b. Aug. 15, 1889, St. Anne des

Plaines, Quebec, Can. pianist, organist, choral conductor, teacher. piano, songs. HL KA*

VINETTE, Alice. Rev. Soeur Marie-Jocelyne. b. April 24,
1894, Saint-Urbain, Prov. Quebec. pianist, organist.
songs. HL KA*

VIRGIL, Antha Minerva. b. ?, Elmira, N.Y. d. 1945,
New York City. pianist, teacher. "technical works. "
EG p268 EK July 1939 p478 ID (d. 1939!) LF

VIZZANI, Orsina see VEZZANA, Lucrezia Orsina

VLIET, Pearl H. van. b. Cedar Rapids, Iowa, 20th cent.
pianist. songs, chamber. WI p74*

VOLKART, Hazel. fl. 20th cent. , America. songs, chamber, orchestra, piano. SN

VON CERRINI DE MONTE-VARCHI, Anna see CERRINI
DE MONTE-VARCHI, Anna von

VON DECKER, Pauline see DECKER, Pauline von

VON HAMMER, Marie see HAMMER, Marie von

VON HOFF, Elizabeth see HOFF, Elizabeth von

VON KALKHÖF, Laura see KALKHÖF, Laura von

VON KLENZE, Irene see KLENZE, Irene von

VON LASZLO, Anna see LASZLO, Anna von

VON MIER, Anna see MIER, Anna von

VON PARADIS, Maria Theresa see PARADIS, Maria
Theresa von

VON SABININ, Martha see SABININ, Martha von

VON SCHÄTZELL, Pauline see DECKER, Pauline von

VON SCHAUROTH, Delphine see SCHAUROTH, Delphine
von

VON SCHRÖTER, Corona Elizabeth Wilhelmina see

SCHRÖTER, Corona Elizabeth Wilhelmina von

VON SCHWERTZELL, Wilhelmine see SCHWERTZELL,
Wilhelmine von

VON STOLLEWERCK, Nina see STOLLEWERCK, Nina von

VON VIGNY, Louise see VIGNY, Louise von

VON WALDBURG-WURZACH, Julie see WALDBURG-
WURZACH, Julie von

VON ZIERITZ, Grete see ZIERITZ, Grete von

VOSS, Marie Wilson. fl. 20th cent., Louisiana. teacher.
songs. PC*

VREE, Marion F. fl. 20th cent., America. teacher.
choral. AJ SN

WAINWRIGHT, Harriet. Mrs. Colonel Stewart. fl. 19th
cent., England. writer. songs, choral. EA* HL

WAINWRIGHT, Mary Lee. b. April 24, 1913, Ruby, S. C.
author. songs. AN* SN

WAKEFIELD, Augusta Mary. b. Aug. 19, 1853, Sedgwick,
England. d. Sept. 16, 1910, Grange-over-Sands,
Lancs, England. editor, contralto, writer. songs,
choral. EA* HL

WALDBURG-WURZACH, Julie von. b. 1841, Vienna. d. ?
songs, piano. EA

WALKER, Ida. fl. 19th cent., America. songs, piano.
BE p38* EA*

WALLACE, Kathryn F. b. Oct. 21, 1917, Shawnee, Okla.
choral. AJ* SN

WALLACE, Mildred White. b. Aug. 25, 1887, Columbiana,
Ala. author, singer, publisher. songs. AN* SN

WALPURGIS, Maria Antonia (Electress of Saxony). (pseud.

E[rmelinda] T[alea] P[astorella] A[rcada]). b. 1724,
Munich (July 18). d. April 23, 1780, Dresden. writer,
artist. 2 operas. DD EA* (d.1782; under Maria)
EG p155* (under Maria Antonia) EK Jan 1936 p2 +pict
(under Maria) HL RB (under M) RH* +biblio

WALTER, Ida. fl. 19th cent., England. songs, 1 opera.
EA* EG p142* HL

WARD, Clementine. fl. 19th cent., England. organist,
singer. piano. HL

WARD, Diane. Corajane Diane Bunce. b. Jan. 10, 1919,
Jackson, Mich. singer, actress, writer, teacher.
2 operas, 1 choral. AJ p510* AN

WARD, Kate Lucy. b. 1833, Wilts, England. d. ? songs.
EA* EG p152

WARE, Harriet. Mrs. Hugo Montgomery Krumbhaar.
b. Aug. 26, 1877, Waupun, Wis. d. Feb. 9, 1962,
New York City. pianist. songs, piano, choral, 1
opera. AJ* AN* BB BE p18 EG p253-4
EH p397 EK Sept 1939 p554 HI HJ p421-2, 360-
1* HL (b. 1884) HT p569-70 ID JD LF PL
SN WI p75-6*

WARE, Helen. b. Sept. 9, 1887, Woodbury, N.J. violinist.
violin, songs, chamber. EK Sept 1939 p554 +pict
HL ID LF

WARNE, Katharine Mulky. b. Oct. 23, 1923, Oklahoma
City, Okla. teacher. chamber, songs, piano. AJ*

WARNER, Grace see GULESIAN, Grace

WARNER, Sarah Ann. b. Oct. 16, 1898, Idaho Falls,
Idaho. author, pianist, publisher. songs. AN*
SN

WARNER, Sylvia Townsend. b. Dec. 6, 1893, London.
novelist, writer, editor. songs. HL

WARREN, Elinor Remick. b. Feb. 23, 1906. pianist.
songs, choral, orchestra. AJ* BE·p33* EK
Sept 1939 p554 +pict HL ID MH* +pict SN

WARTEL, Atale (Alda) Therese Annette. b. July 2, 1814,
    Paris. d. Nov. 6, 1865, Paris. pianist, writer.
    piano. EA   FG (pianist only) HL (born Adrien)

WASSALS, Grace. (Grace Chadbourne.) fl. 20th cent. ,
    America. songs. EG p263

WATERHOUSE, Frances Emery. b. 1902, America.
    d. 1966. songs. SN

WATERMAN, Constance Dorothy. b. London, 20th cent.
    pianist, accompanist. songs. HL KA*

WATSON, Regina (Mrs.). b. 1854, Germany. d. ? songs,
    piano. GF*

WEAVER, Mary. b. Jan. 16, 1903, Kansas City, Mo.
    pianist, teacher. songs, choral. AJ* SN

WEBB, Alliene Brandon. b. Jan. 2, 1910, Palestine, Tex.
    d. Nov. 16, 1965, Dallas. choir director, singer.
    piano, choral, songs. AJ* SN

WEIGL, Valley (Mrs. Karl). b. Sept. 11, 1889, Vienna.
    U. S. citizen 1944. lecturer, music therapist. choral,
    chamber, songs. AJ* (Vally) HL SN

WEINGARTNER-STUDER, Carmen. (Mrs. Felix.) b. 1907,
    Winterthur, Switzerland. conductor, lecturer, musi-
    cian. songs. EK Nov 1938 p702 HL ID (under
    S) SK*

WEIR, Mary Brinckley (Mrs.). b. 1783, ? d. Nov. 12,
    1840, New York. 1 song. WJ*

WELDON, Georgina. nee Treherne. b. May 24, 1837,
    London. d. Jan. 11, 1914, Brighton, England. so-
    prano, choir conductor. songs. EA p144 HL

WENDELBURG, Norma. fl. 20th cent. , America. choral,
    chamber, orchestra, "church music. " SN

WENSLEY, Frances Foster. fl. 19th cent. , England.
    pianist. songs. EA* HL

WERTHEIM, Rosy. b. Feb. 19, 1888, Amsterdam.
    d. May 27, 1949, Laren, Netherlands. choral, songs.

HL

[WESENDONK, Mathilde; given incorrectly in ID as composer]

WEST, Lottie. b. Nov. 5, 1865, South Hackney, England. contralto, pianist, teacher. songs. HL

WESTBROOK, Helen Searles. b. Oct. 15, 1898, Southbridge, Mass. d. ca. 1965, Chicago. organist, music director, recording artist. organ, songs, piano. AJ AN* SN (Searlees)

WESTENHOLZ, Elenore-Sophie-Marie. fl. 18th cent. , ? piano. FG

WESTON, Mildred. b. Gallitzen, Pa. , 20th cent. teacher. piano. EK Nov 1939 p690 + pict ID

WESTROP, Kate. fl. 19th cent. , England. organist, pianist. organ, songs. EA EG p144 HL

WEYBRIGHT, June. fl. 20th cent. , America. chamber, piano. SN

WHITE, Claude Porter. fl. 20th cent. , America. piano, harp, choral, chamber, orchestra, songs, 1 opera. SN

WHITE, Elsie Fellows. b. 1873, Skowhegan, Me. d. 1933, ? violinist. songs, violin. AJ BE p18 EG p252-3 ID SN

WHITE, Emma C. fl. 19th cent. , America. songs, piano. EA

WHITE, Mary Louisa. b. Sept. 2, 1866, Sheffield, England. d. Jan. 1935, London. teacher. piano, songs, 2 operas. HL

WHITE, Maude Valerie. b. June 23, 1855, Dieppe, France. d. Nov. 2, 1937, London. songs, chamber, piano. BC EA* EG p150-51, 237, 238* EK Nov 1939 p690 + pict GF* HL ID LF YA p539

WHITE, Ruth Eden. b. Dec. 25, 1928, Florence, S. C. organist. choral. AJ*

WHITE, Ruth S.   b. Sept. 1, 1925, Pittsburgh.   school
supervisor.   electronic, incidental, multi-media.
AJ*

WHITECOTTON, Shirley.   b. Sept. 23, 1935, Aurora, Ill.
teacher.   choral.   AJ*

WHITELEY, Bessie W.   b. 1871, St. Louis.   d. ?   opera.
JD*

WICHERN, Caroline.   fl. 19th cent. , Germany.   songs.
EA*

WICKDAHL, Lillian S.   Lynn Sandell.   b. Seattle, 20th
cent.   author, publisher.   songs, instrumentals.
AN*   SN

WICKERHAUSER, Natalie.   fl. 19th cent. , Germany.   piano,
songs.   EA*

WICKHAM, Florence.   Mrs. E. Lueder.   b. 1880, Beaver,
Pa.   d. Oct. 20, 1962, New York, N. Y.   contralto.
choral, songs, 1 opera.   AJ*   HL   ID   SN (b.
1882)

WIECK, Clara Josephine see SCHUMANN, Clara

WIECK, Marie.   b. Jan. 17, 1832, Leipzig.   d. Nov. 2,
1916, Dresden.   teacher, pianist.   piano, songs.
EA* (b. 1835)   EG p171, 91   GF   HL (not as composer)

WIELE, Aimée van de.   b. March 8, 1907, Brussels.
harpsichordist.   harpsichord.   HL

WIENIOWSKI, Irene Regine (Lady Dean Paul).   pseud. Poldowski.   b. May 16, 1880, Brussels.   d. Jan. 28,
1932, London.   piano, songs, chamber, opera.   GH
p6   HC p25, 35*   HL (under P)

WIERUSZOWSKI, Lili.   b. Dec. 10, 1899, Köln am Rhein.
organist, choral conductor.   choral, organ, instrumental.   HL   SK

WIGGINS, Mary.   b. Feb. 10, 1904, Indiana, Pa.   teacher,
organist.   piano, organ, violin, bassoon, choral,
songs.   AJ*   SN

WIGHAM, Margaret.   fl. 20th cent. , America.   piano.   AJ
    SN

WILHELMINE, Markgrafin von Bayreuth.   b. 1709, ?
    d. 1758, ? 1 orchestra.   MX*

WILLIAMS, Frances.   b. Caernarvonshire, England (Wales),
    20th cent. editor. choral, songs.   AJ   SN

WILLIAMS, Grace.   b. Feb. 19, 1906, Barry, Glamorgan-
    shire, Wales, England. choral, incidental.   HL
    PJ*

WILLIAMS, Jean E.   fl. 20th cent. , America. songs,
    choral, piano, organ, orchestra.   AJ   SN

WILLIAMS, Joan Franks.   fl. 20th cent. , America. cham-
    ber, instrumental, songs, electronic.   SN

WILLIAMS, Margaret.   b. Tennessee, 19th cent. 1 opera,
    1 orchestra.   BE p38   EG p205

WILLIAMS, Mary Lou (Mrs.).   Mary Elfrida Scruggs.
    Burley is mother's maiden name; Winn is stepfather's
    name. b. May 8, 1910, Pittsburgh. arranger, pianist.
    songs, choral.   AJ*   AN*   CC p346* (b. 1914)   ID
    MK   PG +pict   SS p390, 394, 395, 485*   WE p99-
    100, 123-4* +biblio   WF* +pict

WILLIAMSON, Esther.   b. 1915, America.   1 piano.   FP
    p296, 298, 353*   SN

WILLMAN, Regina Hansen.   b. Oct. 5, 1914, Burns, Wy.
    d. Oct. 28, 1965, Portland, Ore. chamber, choral.
    AJ*

WILLS, Harriet Burdett.   fl. 19th cent. , America. songs.
    EA*

WILSON, Addie Anderson.   b. Lawrenceville, Ala. , 19th
    cent. organist, carillon player. songs, piano.   BE
    p8*

WILSON, Mrs. Cornwall Baron.   b. 1797?, England.
    d. 1846, London. poet. songs.   EA   HL

WILSON, Dorothy.   fl. 20th cent. , America. piano,

chamber.   SN

WILSON, Karen.   b. Jan. 9, 1942, Cincinnati.   teacher.
1 piano.   AJ

WINDSOR, Helen J.   fl. 20th cent. , America.   1 opera.
SN

WING, Helen.   fl. 20th cent. , America.   pianist, violinist.
EK Oct 1940 p714   ID

WINKEL, Therese Emile Henrietta aus dem.   b. Dec. 20,
1784, Weissenfels, Germany.   d. ? harpist, teacher.
chamber.   EA   EG p173   FG

WIRE, Edith.   fl. 20th cent. , America.   piano.   SN

WISE, Jessie Moore.   b. 1883, Bloomington, Ill.   d. 1949.
author.   songs.   EG p262-3*

WISENEDER, Caroline.   b. 1807, Brunswick, Germany.
d. 1868, Brunswick, Germany.   teacher.   songs, 2
operas.   EA   EG p167   GF*

WISHART, Betty Rose.   b. Sept. 22, 1947, Lumberton,
N. C.   teacher, pianist.   chamber, piano.   AJ*   CK*
(1974)

WITKIN, Beatrice.   fl. 20th cent. , America.   electronic,
chamber, instrumental.   AJ*   SN

WITNI, Monica.   fl. 20th cent. , America.   operas, chamber, orchestra.   SN

WOLLNER, Gertrude Price (Mrs.).   b. May 15, 1900, New
York City.   author, teacher, lecturer.   chamber, incidental.   AJ*

WONG, Betty Anne.   Siu Junn.   b. Sept. 6, 1938, San
Francisco.   teacher, pianist.   electronic.   AJ*

WONG, Hsiung-Zee.   b. Oct. 24, 1947, Hong Kong.   U. S.
in 1966.   designer, artist, illustrator.   chamber,
electronic.   AJ*

WOOD, Mrs. George.   fl. 19th cent. , America.   songs.
EA*

WOOD, Julie McIver. fl. 20th cent., America. choral, songs. SN

WOOD, Mary Knight. Mrs. Alfred B. Mason. b. April 7, 1857, Easthampton, Mass. d. Dec. 20, 1944, Florence. pianist. songs, chamber. AL p154* (May) BC BE p6* EA* EG p206-7* EK Feb 1940 p138 +pict GF HL HT p440 HV HX p774, 778* ID LF PL TE* p120, 121

WOOD-HILL, Mabel. b. March 12, 1870, Brooklyn. d. March 1, 1954, Stamford, Conn. teacher. songs, orchestra, choral, chamber. AJ* AL p153* BE p16* EG p264 (under H) EK July 1934 p392 +pict (under H) GG p11 HL ID SN

WOODS, Eliza. fl. 19th cent., America. songs. BE p38 EG p205 GG p10

WOOLF, Sophia Julia. b. 1831, London. d. Nov. 20, 1893, West Hampstead, England. pianist. piano, songs, 1 opera. EA* EG p136* HL

WOOLSEY, Mary Hale. b. March 21, 1899, Spanish Fork, Utah. d. 1969. songs, operas. AJ* SN

WORGAN, Marie. fl. 18th cent., England. songs. EA HL

WORRELL, Lola Carrier. fl. 20th cent., America. songs. AL p154-5 BE p10-1* HT p570 LF

WORTH, Amy. b. Jan. 18, 1888, St. Joseph, Mo. d. 1967. choral director, pianist, organist. songs, piano, choral. AJ* AN* EG p263 EK Feb 1940 p138 +pict ID SN

WRIGHT, Ellen. née Riley. b. London, 19th cent. songs. EA* HL

WRIGHT, Nannie Louise. b. 1879, Fayette, Mo. d. ? pianist, teacher. piano. BE p18-9* EG p270 EK Feb 1940 p138 FD April 1933 p284* +pict LF

WRONIKOWSKI, Florence F. b. June 3, 1916, Milwaukee. piano, songs. WI p78*

WUIET, Caroline. née Auffdiener. b. 1766, Rambouillet.
    d. 1835, Paris. songs, piano, chamber, 1 opera.
    EA   FG*

WUNSCH, Ilse Gerda. b. Dec. 14, 1911, Berlin. organist,
    pianist, choral director, teacher. songs. AJ*

WURM, Marie J. A. b. May 18, 1860, Southampton, Eng-
    land. d. Jan. 21, 1938, Munich. pianist, teacher,
    conductor, writer. piano, chamber, 1 opera.   EA*
    EG p140*   EK April 1940 p282   GF*   HL   ID   LF

WURMBRAND, Stephanie Vrabely (Countess).   fl. 19th cent.,
    Germany. piano.   EA*   EG p169

WURZACH, Julie von Waldburg see WALDBURG-WURZACH,
    Julie von

WYETH, Ann. Mrs. John W. McCoy II. b. March 15,
    1915, Chadds Ford, Pa. piano, songs, orchestra.
    AJ*   SN

WYLIE, Ruth Shaw. b. June 24, 1916, Cincinnati. teach-
    er. piano, chamber, choral, orchestra.   AJ*   JA*
    MP*   SN

YAZBECK, Louise. b. Shreveport, La., 20th cent. teach-
    er. piano, songs.   PC*

YOUNG, Mrs. Bicknell see MAZZUCATO, Eliza

YOUNG, Harriet Maitland. fl. 19th cent., England.   2
    operas, songs.   EA*   EG p141-2*   HL

YOUNG, Jane Corner. b. 1916, Athens, Ohio. teacher,
    head music dept., state hospital. 1 violin, 1 piano.
    AJ*

YOUNG, Pearl Reimann. fl. 20th cent., America. songs.
    SN

YOUNG, Polly [or Mary]. Mrs. Francois Hippolyte Barthel-
    emon. b. 1749, London. d. Sept. 20, 1799, London.
    singer, harpsichordist. songs.   HL (not as composer;

GJ indicates as composer however)

YOUNG, Rolande Maxwell. b. Sept. 13, 1929, Washington, D. C. pianist. songs. AJ*

YOUSE, Glad Robinson. b. Oct. 22, 1898, Miami, Okla. songs, choral. AJ SN

ZAIMONT, Judith Lang. b. Nov. 8, 1945, Memphis, Tenn. pianist, teacher, lecturer. choral, chamber, piano, songs. AJ* SN

ZANTEN, Cornelia van. b. Aug. 2, 1855, Dordrecht, Netherlands. d. Jan. 10, 1846, The Hague. soprano, teacher. songs. HL

ZAUBITER, Ida. fl. 19th cent., Germany. zither player. zither. EA EG p173

ZECKWER, Camille. fl. 20th cent., America. piano. SN

ZEISSLER, Mrs. Bloomfield see BLOOMFIELD, Fanny

ZENTNER, Clary. fl. 19th cent., Italy. piano. EA* EG p216

ZEVE, Julia (Mrs. Louis). fl. 20th cent., Louisiana. songs. PC*

ZIERITZ, Grete von. b. March 10, 1899, Vienna. teacher, pianist. songs, orchestra, piano, chamber. FL p623 GI* HL MH* +pict MW PJ* RH* +biblio

ZIFFER, Fran. fl. 20th cent., America. incidental. SN

ZIFFRIN, Marilyn J. b. Aug. 7, 1926, Moline, Ill. teacher. piano, organ, choral, opera, chamber, percussion, songs, orchestra. AJ* JA* SN

ZIMMERMANN, Agnes Marie Jacobina. .b. July 5, 1847, Cologne, Prussia. d. Nov. 14, 1925, London. pianist, editor. piano, songs, chamber. BB (b. 1845)

EA*   EG p145, 237   GF   HL   ID   SF p64*

ZUMSTEEG, Emilie. b. Dec. 9, 1796, Stuttgart. d. Aug.
    1, 1857, Stuttgart. teacher, singer, pianist. piano,
    songs.   EA*   EG p159-60   FG   GF*   HL   ID

ZUZAK, Doris. fl. 20th cent. , Louisiana. piano.   PC*

ZWEIG, Esther. b. July 29, 1906, New York, N.Y.
    teacher, ensemble director. 2 songs, 1 choral.   AJ*

ZWILICH, Ellen Taaffe. b. April 30, 1939, Miami, Fla.
    chamber, songs.   AJ*

SUPPLEMENTARY LIST
OF COMPOSERS
(See comments on page vii)

Abel, Adelina L.
Abel, Marion
Aborn, Lora
Ackerman, Jeanna
Adams, Amy
Adams, Gertrude E.
Adamske, Sylvia F.
Adamson, Gladys
Adelung, Olga
Adlerflug, Olga von
Agazzari, A.
Agnesi, Elisa d'
Air, Kathleen
Akerhjelm, Agnes
Akers, Sally F.
Albanie, Clementine
Albareda, Marcia
Albrecht, Lillie
Alpy, Mlle. Bonne d'
Ancele, Sister Mary
Anderson, Florence
Andreas, Eulalie
Andrews, Mrs. George H.
Androzzo, Alma B.
Angelina
Armansperg, Marie d'
Armstrong, Mrs. Robert
Ashmore, Miss
Asmussen, Emma
Atkinson, Mrs. S. Phyllis
Aubigney, Nina d'
Auenbrugger, Mary Anne
Augusta, Princess of England

Aurelia, Schwester
Austin, Dorothea
Austin, Grace Leadenham
Aylwin, Josephine Crew

Bagliani, Carmela Abate
Bailey, Marie Louise
Bainbridge, Katherine
Ballard, Carrie
Bannister, Miss
Barival, Marquise de Presle
Bartlett, Caroline Clarke
Bartlett, Gertrude
Batcheller, Maude
Bauer, Caroline
Bayer, Caroline
Bazin, Mlle.
Beach, Bonnie
Beardsmore, Mrs.
Beatrix, Comtesse de Die
Becker, Angela
Bellman, Helen M.
Ben, Anna
Benedict, Ida
Bennett, Claudia
Berge, Irenee
Berky, Georgia Guiney
Berlot, Elisa
Bernard, Caroline
Berry, Adaline H.
Besthoff, Mabel
Bestor, Dorothea Nolte

Bibern, Maria Anna Magda-
lena
Bircsak, Thusnelda
Bish, Diane
Blanch de Castile, Queen of
France
Blondel, Mlle.
Bloom, Shirley
Boesing, Martha
Bohannan, Mrs. Ord
Boleyn, Anne
Bolton, Fannie E.
Bonaparte, Hortense
Bonar, Jane
Bond, Victoria
Bondurant, Dorothy
Bonewitz-Volkmann, Mme.
de
Bonnay, Mlle.
Boundy, Kate
Bovia, Laura
Boyd, Jeanne
Boyle, Mrs. C. A.
Brahe, May H.
Bratschi, Adele
Braun, Edith Evans
Bremont, Countess de
Brine, Mary D.
Brinsmead, Rosa
Brown, Clemmon May
Brown, Gertrude M.
Brown, Mrs. Henry Temple
Burbage, Alice Edith
Burt, Clara Phillips
Byles, Blanche Douglas
Byrne, Flora

Camp, Mabel Johnston
Campana, Francesca
Campbell, Caroline
Campbell, Olive D.
Cannon, Tracy Y.
Carodoni-Allan, Maria
Carruthers, Julia
Carver, Miss
Cecile, Jean

Chanbrier, Emm.
Chandler, Mary
Charlotte, Princess of Meck-
lenburg-Strelitz
Charriere, Sophie de
Chauncey, Ruth Glassburner
Chavannes, Mme.
Chevalier de Montreal, Julia
Christensen, Betty
Clark, Caroline
Clark, Ella D.
Clarke, Irma A.
Clarke, Phyllis Chapman
Clarkson, Jane
Clery, Mme.
Cobena, Pepita
Coleman, Mrs. Satis N.
Collier, Susannah
Collver, Harriet Russell
Combie, Ida Mae
Comfort, Annabel
Conant, Grace Wilbut
Contamine, Mlle.
Cook, Catherine
Cooper, Alinda B.
Copeland, Bernice Rose
Corelli, Marie
Coryell, Marion
Coudin, Mrs. V. G.
Courmont, Countess von
Cowan, Marie
Cowling, Elizabeth
Cox, Jean
Crament, Maude
Crane, Alice
Crane, Charlotte M.
Crane, Helen C.
Crawford, Caroline H.
Crawford, Jane Romney
Crisp, Barbara
Crumb, Berenice
Curtis, Helen
Cuthbert, Elizabeth Howard

Dal Carretto, Cristina
Dale, Mrs. Henry

Dalton, Edith
Dana, Mary S. B. (Mrs.
    Shindler)
Daniel, Kathryn
Danielson, Janet
Danziger, Laura
Dare, Marie
Darion, Mlle.
Daschkow, Princess de
Dauvergne de Beauvis, Mlle.
David, Elizabeth H.
Davis, Mary
Davisson, Genevieve
Deacon, Miss E. L.
Demilliere, Marthesie
DeRoo, Cornelia
Deshayes, Marie (Mme. de
    la Popliniere)
Dessarz-Khom, Louise
Devisme, Jeanne Hippolyte
Dietz, Mme. de
Dieude, Mme.
Dishrow, Mrs. William H.
Dolby, Madame
Dorothea of Anhalt, Princess
Douglas, Sallie Hume
Dress, Lillian Nelding
Duchamp, Marie Catherine
    Cesarine
Duff, G. S.
Dufresnoy, Mme.
Dulcken, Louise
Dunlap, Gern G.
Dupre, Mme.
Durand de Fortmague,
    Baronesse
Dyer, Susan

Eagles, Moneta
Ebeling, Margaret Snow
Edwards, Rose
Efrein, Laurie
Eisenstein, Judith Kaplan
Ellis, Vivian
Erskine, Augusta Kennedy
    (Lady)

Essex, Margaret
Estelle, St. Rita

Faucette, Nanka
Fauche, Mary
Fehring, Margaret Kramer
Fellman, Hazel
Ferdin, Michelle
Ferrand-Teulet, Denise
Ferris, Joan
Fields, Dorothy
Fitzgerald, Lady Edward
Fleet, Esther E.
Flotow, Martha von
Folts, Martha
Forrest, Margaret
Founk, Pauline
Fourier, Sister Mary
Fowler, Miss
Fox, Pauline S.
Franz, Marie Hinrichs
Frazer, Mrs. Allan H.
Freake, Lady
Freeman, Elizabeth W.
Frick, Bertha R.
Fulton, Florence Mary

Gade, Margaret
Gagnon, Blance
Garnett, Louise Ayres
Garrigus, Malvina
Gatehouse, Lady
Gattie, Mrs. John Byng
Geddes, Kate Grahan
Genty, Mlle.
Gerbini, Luigia
Gibbings, Miss
Gibson, Florence
Gilbert, Gladys
Gilbert, Marie
Giles, Caroline J.
Gillett, Minnie E.
Gillis, Emma H.
Glasscock, Miss
Gleason, Mary W.

Glick, Henrietta
Gore, Blanche
Gottschalk, Clara
Gougelet, Mme.
Gould, Mina
Gould, Janette
Graefin, Sophia Regina
Gray, Judith
Grazie, Giselda delle
Gregory, Elsa
Gresham, Ann
Gröbenschütz, Amalie
Guerini, Rose

Habert, Fanny
Haden, Mrs.
Hagley, Sarah
Haines-Kuester, Edith
Hall, Edythe Pruyn
Hall, Frances
Haman, Elizabeth
Hambrock, Mathilde
Hammond, Elizabeth Esther
Hankwitz, Anita
Hansen, Lillie A.
Hardin[g], Elizabeth
Hardy, Mrs. Charles S.
Hargreaves, Emma
Hatch, Mabel Lee
Hauteterre, Mlle. de
Havergal, Frances Ridley
Hedge, Edna Zema
Heim-Brehm, Mathilde
Heinefetter, Sabine
Helbig, Ilse
Herault, Palmyre
Hervey, Eleonora Louise
Hinckesman, Maria
Hinsdale, Isabelle
Hodges, Ann Mary
Hoffman, Miss J.
Holberg, Margaret
Hübner, Caroline
Hudson, Mrs. John
Hunt, Gertrude
Hunter, Henrietta Elizabeth

Hutton, Laura Josephine

Irvine, Jessie Seymour
Ives, Emma

James, Heidi
Jankowski, Loretta
Jervis, Mary Ann
Johnson, Clair W.
Johnson, Harriett
Jones, Mrs. Floyd F.
Jung, Helge

Kelly, Edith
Kennedy, Amanda
Klage, Marie
Knebel-Doberitz, Mme.
Knerr, Katrina
Koch, Minna
Kotschoubey, Princess L.
Krauth, Harriet Reynolds
     (Mrs. Adolph Spaeth)
Kreutzer, Hilde
Krone, Beatrice

Lachaume, Aimee
Lackner, Mrs. de
Lamballe, Mary Theresa
     Louisa la Princesse de
Larkin, Etta
Latz, Inge
Leaycroft, Agnes
Lechtin, Ruth
Lee, Harriet
LeFanu, Nicola
Lehmbruch, Amalie
Lejet, Edith
Le Jeune, Mlle.
Lemert, Gladys Fulbright
Lennox, Lady William
Leonard, Antonia Sitcher de
     Mendi
Leupold, Therese

Levi, Mme.
Lewis, Louise Hills
Licht, Martha B.
Liju, Annette de
Lively, Katherine Allen
Locke, Flora Elbertine
Lodbell, Edith
Löwenstein, Sallie
Lorenziti, Josephine
Lottin, Theodora
Love, Loretta
Lubi, Mariane

McCoy, Nadine
McCoy, Rose
MacDonald, Charlotte
Macintosh, Mary
McKinley, Mabel
MacKown, Marjorie T.
MacLean, Eleanor
MacMillan, Margaret
Maier, Catherine
Mainwaring, Miss
Manning, Emma
Martin, Elizabeth B.
Martin, Josephine
Martinez, Isidor
Mary Bernice, Sister
Mathews, Sarah R.
Mattingly, Jane
Maxim, Florence
Maynard, Catherine
Maynard, Emma
Meacham, Margaret
Medeck, Mme.
Meeks, Anna Connable
Megarey, Anne
Melling, Ellen Knowles
Mellish, Miss
Menetou, Mlle. de
Menke, Emma
Mercie-Porte, Mlle.
Mercken, Sophie
Merelle, Mlle.
Merley, Judith
Metzger-Vespermann, Clara

Meyer, Emilie
Meyers, Blanche B.
Mezangere, Marquise de
Michon, Mlle.
Middleton, Jean B.
Miles, Mrs. Philip Napier
Miles, Renee
Miller, Alma C.
Minke, Emma L.
Mitford, Eliza
Moline, Lily Wadhams
Molza, Tarquinia
Moneymaker, Georgia
Monnot, Marguerite
Moody, May Whittle
Moore, Mrs. A. W.
Morey, Florence
Morris, Mary S.
Morrow, Jean
Mosel, Catherine de
Mueller, Lenora A.
Mulock, Miss
Munn, Mrs. S. E.
Munt, Mrs. Isabella
Musigny, Mme. de

Nafziger, Olive
Natalie
Nelson, Mae Louise
Nevin, Alice
Nitske, Betty F.
Norris, Dorothy
Novello, Mary Sabilla
Novich, Clara Kors
Nye, Susanna Wetmore

O'Brien, Ellen Fanny
Ochse, Orpha Caroline
Olmstead, Bess Heath
Orleans, Duchess of
Orme, Mrs.
Owne, Mrs.

Paessler, Fraulein

Palico, Lucie
Parkhurst, Mrs. E. A.
Payne, Harriet
Pean de la Roche-Jagu, E.
  Francoise
Pelzer, Anne
Pennant, Adela Douglas
Pepe, Carmine
Peremann, Dora (Deborah)
Percy, Mrs. Berty
Perkins, Emily Swan
Perwich, Susanna
Piaget, Ada May
Pichaud, Marie-Claire
Pilleverse, Suzanne
Polmartin, Mme.
Provost, Yvonne
Ptaszynska, Marta
Puchtler-Wilhelm, Maria
Pyne, Louise (not the prima
  donna)

Rainforth, Elizabeth
Randecki, Olga von
Rawls, Katheryn H.
Rea, Florence P.
Read, Sarah Ferris
Reid, Edith Lobdell
Rendle, Lily
Rhys-Williams, Elspeth
Rinehart, Marilyn
Roberts, Madeline
Rocherolle, Eugenie
Rohnstock, Sofie
Roma, Elise P.
Root, Grace W.
Rose of Jesus, Sister
Rounsefell, Carrie E.
Ruff, Edna
Runkle, Helen M.

Sainte Cecile des Anges,
  Soeur
St. Michel, Mme.
Salisbury, Cora Folsom

Sanford, Lucille Mandsley
Sanks, Mary C.
Saudners, Florence Ward
Schmidt, Maria Susanne
Schulz, Louise
Schwartz, Helen
Screinzer, Fräulein
Sernien, Maddalena
Sessi-Freyse, Emma
Seydel, Irma
Shapley, Dinah
Sheldon, Mrs. G. M.
Shields, Elizabeth McE.
Shurtleff, Lynn R.
Slade, Mary E.
Smart, Marion
Smith, Miss
Smith, Augustine H.
Smith, Eva Munson
Smith, Lucia May
Spalding, Eva
Spratt, Ann Baird
Stevenson, Mrs. O. W.
Stillings, Kemp
Stock, Sarah Geraldine
Stoltz, Rosine
Stone, Louise Phebe
Stopel, Helene
Storey, Marian
Straunch, Bertha
Stressa, Signora F. M.
Strohman, Dorothy
Stutsman, Grace May
Summers, Myrna

Taggart, Genevieve
Tanner, Mrs. F. G.
Tarbé des Sablons, Mme.
Tarvin, Ann
Taylor, Dorothy J.
Taylor, Priscilla
Templar, Joan
Teresine, Sister Mary
Têtedoux, Emile
Tetewsky, Mrs. Hyman
Thibault, Angelique

Thicknesse, Miss
Thompson, Kathryn
Tiddeman, Maria
Tindel, Adela
Tollefsen, Augusta
Tourjee, Lizzie Esterbrook
Troschke et Rosenwerth,
    Wilhelmine (Baronesse)
Troubetzkoi, Princess Lisé
Turner, Carolyn Ayres

Varroc, Mme. E. P. de
Velkiers, Esther Elizabeth
Vokhine, Marie
Voorhees, Mary Helen

Walker, Caroline
Ward, Beverly A.
Warnots, Elly
Watters, Lorrain E.
Webster, Mary Phillips
Welchman, Miss M. E.
Werner, Hildegard
Wesley, Alice Putman
White, Mrs. John
Whitman, Mary L.
Wildshut, Clara
Wilkins, Margaret Lucy
Willman-Huber, Mme.
Willson, Mrs. Hill
Wilson, Emily D.
Wilson, Lelia Waterhouse
Woodhull, Mary G.
Woodstock, Mattie
Worth, Adelaide
Wuras, Clara

Yelverton, Mrs. F.
Young, Mrs. Corrine

Zimmerman, Phyllis
Zittelman, Helene

SUPPLEMENTARY BIBLIOGRAPHY

ASCAP Symphonic Catalog, 2nd ed. New York, 1966. 576p.

Albrecht, Otto E. A Census of Autograph Music Manuscripts of European Composers in American Libraries. Philadelphia: University of Pennsylvania Press, 1953. 331p.

Barbacci, R. "La inferioridad de la mujer y su reflejo en la actividad musical." Revista Musical Peruana, September 1939, p. 105.

Bauer, Marion. Twentieth-Century Music. New York: G. P. Putnam's Son, 1934. 349p.

_____ and Peyser, Ethel. How Music Grew. New York: G. P. Putnam's Sons, 1939. 647p.

_____ and _____. Music Through the Ages. New York: G. P. Putnam's Sons, 1967. 748p.

Becker, Carl F. Systematisch-chronologische Darstellung der musikalischen Literatur. Leipzig: Robert Friese, 1836. 605p.

Bernhardt, Karl Fritz. "Zur musikschopferischen Emanizipation der Frau." Gesellschaft für Musikforschung, Kongress-Bericht. Kassel: 1956, p. 55-58.

Bielefelder Katalog. Bielefelder: Bielefelder Verlanganstalt, 1952-

Broadcast Music Inc. Symphonic Catalogue. New York: Broadcast Music, 1963. (Not paginated.)

Brower, Edith. "Is the Musical Idea Masculine?" Atlantic

Monthly, March 1894, pp. 332-39.

Clarke, Helen A.   "The Nature of Music and Its Relation to
the Question of Women in Music. "   Music 7 (1892/
1896):453.

Diehl, Katharine.   Hymns and Tunes: An Index.   New York:
Scarecrow Press, 1966.   1242p.

Drinker, Sophie Lewis.   Die Frau in die Musik.   Zurich:
n. p. , 1910.

_____.   Music and Women: The Story of Women in
Their Relation to Music.   New York: Coward-McCann,
1948.   323p.

_____.   "The Participation of Women in Music. "   Na-
tional Federation of Music Clubs Official Bulletin 14
(December 1934):11-13.

Ebel, Otto.   Les Femmes Compositeurs de musique.
Paris: n. p. , 1910.

Elson, Louis.   The National Music of America and Its
Sources.   Boston: L. C. Page & Co. , 1924.   367p.

_____.   Woman in Music.   New York: University So-
ciety, 1918.   99p.

Finck, Henry T.   "Women in Music Today. "   Nation 106
(June 1, 1918):664.

Fisher, Fred.   "Why Beethoven Was a Man. "   Music & Man
1 (1975):331-40.

Galloway, Tod B.   "Noted Women in Musical History. "
Etude, November 1929, pp. 809-10.

Galt, Martha Carolina.   Know Your American Music; A
Handbook.   Augusta, Me. :   Kennebec Journal Print
Shop, 1943.   86p.

Gaul, Harvey B.   "Women in Music. "   Musician 21 (March
1916):143.

Gilman, Lawrence.   Phases of Modern Music.   New York:
Harper & Brothers, 1904.   165p.   "Women and

modern music": pp. 93-101.

Greene, R. L. "Male Oppression of Women Composers. "
Saturday Review, January 8, 1972, p. 6.

Haddon, C. "Women and Music. " Musical Courier 47
(1903):34.

Historical Records Survey, District of Columbia. Bio-bibli-
ographical Index of Musicians in the United States of
America Since Colonial Times. 2nd ed. Michigan:
Scholarly Press, 1972. 439p.

Howard, John Tasker. Our American Music. New York:
Thomas Y. Crowell, 1931. 713p.

Kagen, Sergius. Music For the Voice; A Descriptive List
of Concert and Teaching Material. Rev. ed. Bloomington, Ind. : Indiana University Press, 1968. 780p.

King, Mrs. A. T. "Women as Composers. " Musical
Courier 79 (1919):8-9.

Krebs, T. L. "Women as Musicians. " Sewanee Review 2
(1893):76-87.

Kruhm, August. "Musikalisch-schöpferische Frauen. "
Neue Musikzeitschrift, July 1948, pp. 211-12.

Ladd, George Trumball. "Why Women Cannot Compose
Music. " Yale Review 6 (July 1917):789-806.

Lerma, Dominique-René de. A Name List of Black Composers. Minneapolis: AAMOA Press, 1974.

_____ . Women Composers: A Highly Provisional and
Initial Draft of Names and Sources. Bloomington:
Indiana University Music Library, 1975. 78p.

Locke, Arthur Ware, and Fassett, Charles K. Selected
List of Choruses for Women's Voices, 3rd ed.
Northfield, Mass. : Smith College, 1964. 253p.

Maier, G. "Great Woman Composer? When?" Etude,
May 1954, p. 21+.

Miller, Philip. "Over the Distaff Side Mostly--Miriam

Gideon and Four Other Americans. " American Record Guide 39 (November 1972):742-3.

Möller, Heinrich. "Can Women Compose?" Musical Observer 15, no. 5 (1917):9-10; no. 6, pp. 11-12.

Neuls-Bates, Carol, ed. The Status of Women in College Music: Preliminary Studies. New York: College Music Society report no. 1, 1976. 34p.

Oyler, William, et al. "Letters: Composing Women. " High Fidelity/Musical America, May 1973, p. 8.

Pert, Yvonne. "Women in Music; An English Writer's Opinion of Some Present Day Composers. " Musician, October 1924, p. 26.

"Programs of Works by Women Composers from Contemporary American Publishers. " Etude, November 1918, p. 690+.

Raabe, Peter. "Die Frau im musikalischen Leben. " Neue Zeitschrift für Musik 108 (August 1941):501-08.

Rezits, Joseph and Deatman, Gerald. The Pianist's Resource Guide: Piano Music in Print and Literature on the Pianistic Art. Park Ridge, Ill.: Kjos Pallma Music Corp., 1974. 993p.

Ritter, Francis Malone (Raymond). Woman as a Musician. New York: E. Schuberth & Co., 1876. 15p.

Samaroff Stokowski, Olga. "Women in Music." National Federation of Music Clubs Book of Proceedings 2 (1937):31-8.

Slonimsky, Nicolas. "Musical Oddities: Feminism in Musical Composition. " Etude, March 1955, p. 5.

Smith, E. M., comp. Woman in Sacred Song; A Library of Hymns, Religious Poems, and Sacred Music by Woman. Boston: D. Lothrop & Co., 1885.

Sonneck, Oscar George Theodore. A Bibliography of Early Secular American Music. Washington, D.C.: Library of Congress, Music Division, 1945. 617p.

Stieger, Franz. "Opernkomponistinnen. " Die Musik 13
     (1914):270-2.

Stratton, Stephen S.   "Women in Relation to Musical Art. "
     Musical Association, Proceedings, Session 9, 1883,
     pp. 115-46.

Swinburne, J. "Women and Music. " Musical Association,
     Proceedings.   (Leeds) 46 (1921):21-34.

United States.   Library of Congress.   Library of Congress
     Catalog, Music and Phonorecords, A Cumulative List
     of Works Represented by Library of Congress Printed
     Cards.   Washington, D. C. : The Library, 1954- .

_____. _____. Music Branch, Information Center
     Service.   Catalog of Published Concert Music by
     American Composers.   Washington, D. C. : U. S. Gov-
     ernment Printing Office, 1964.   175p.

Upton, George Putnam.   Woman in Music, 6th ed.   Chicago:
     A. C. McClurg & Co. , 1899.   221p.

Van de Vate, Nancy. "The American Woman Composer:
     Some Sour Notes. " High Fidelity/Musical America,
     June 1975, MA 18-19.

_____. "Every Good Boy (Composer) Does Fine. "
     Symphonic News 24 (December 1973-January 1974):11-
     12.

"Women Composers Listed in the Schwann-I Catalogue,
     March 1975. " High Fidelity/Musical America, June
     1975, MA-20.

Wurm, Marie. "Quellenlexikon der Tonsetzerinnen und
     Musikschriftstellerinnern seit dem 12.   Jahrhundert,
     deren-Werke-im-Druck-erschienen sind. " Unpublished,
     1905; Rev. 1914.

_____. "Woman's Struggle for Recognition in Music. "
     Etude, November 1936, p. 687+.